Penguin Boo g

DIFFEREN

After graduating in law from the University of Western
Australia in 1969, Jocelynne A. Scutt undertook
postgraduate studies in law at the University of Sydney,
Southern Methodist University and the University of
Michigan in the United States, and Cambridge University
in England. She spent twelve months at the Max-Planck-
Institut in Freiburg im Breisgau, West Germany before
taking up a position with the Australian Law Reform
Commission.

Subsequently Jocelynne Scutt has worked with the
Australian Institute of Criminology, as associate to a High
Court judge, and as director of research with the Legal and
Constitutional Committee of the Parliament of Victoria.
She spent some time at the Sydney Bar in 1981-2, and
before returning to private practice in Melbourne was
deputy chairperson of the Law Reform Commission,
Victoria.

Other books by the same author

Violence in the Family (editor, 1980)
Rape Law Reform (editor, 1980)
Restoring Victims of Crime (1980)
Women and Crime (editor with S.K. Mukherjee, 1981)
Even in the Best of Homes (1983)
For Richer, For Poorer (with Di Graham, 1984)
Growing Up Feminist (1985)
Poor Nation of the Pacific—Australia's Future? (editor, 1985)

DIFFERENT LIVES

edited by Jocelynne A. Scutt

Penguin Books

Penguin Books Australia Ltd,
487 Maroondah Highway, P.O. Box 257
Ringwood, Victoria 3134, Australia
Penguin Books Ltd,
Harmondsworth, Middlesex, England
Penguin Books,
40 West 23rd Street, New York, N.Y. 10010, U.S.A.
Penguin Books Canada Ltd,
2801 John Street, Markham, Ontario, Canada L3R 1B4
Penguin Books (N.Z.) Limited,
182-190 Wairau Road, Auckland 10, New Zealand

First published by Penguin Books Australia, 1987

Typeset in Plantin by Midland Typesetters
Made and Printed in Australia by the Australian Print Group, Maryborough, Vic.

CIP

Scutt, Jocelynne A., 1947- .
Different lives.

ISBN 0 14 006899 6.

1. Women – Australia – Social conditions –
Case studies. 2. Women's rights –
Australia – Case studies. 3. Feminism –
Australia – Case studies. I. Title.

305.4'2'0926

In memory of Maud Helen McIlroy Needham and
Frances Elizabeth Davies Scutt

Contents

Acknowledgements

In compiling and writing *Different Lives* I have been sustained by the changing, frustrating, painful and glorious women's movement. It is impossible to name all who have been supportive, stimulating and provocative. Those who must be named, however, include Carla Taines – for her editing skills, interest and ideas; Robin Joyce – for her strong support, caring and critical eye; Felicity Beth – for support and caring from further away; Carmel Niland – for providing a 'room of my own' in the early stages; Meryl Potter – for indexing; Elaine Thibou – for proof-reading; Di Graham, Jennifer Aldred, Kerry Heubel, Lesley Norris, Yvonne Carnahan, Beth Wilson, Pauline Martin, Margaret McHutchison and Robin Jackson for many reasons; Faith Bandler, Irene Greenwood, Joan Huggett, Pat Giles, Julia Ryan and Joan Ross for their insights into the 1970s women's movement. Bob McMullan, Fleur Joyce and Kate McMullan have been important too. And thanks go also to my publisher Brian Johns.

Photographs of the following people are reprinted with permission from the copyright holder: Diane Bell (*Age*), Joan Russell (Adelaide *Advertiser*), Jocelynne Scutt (Australian Institute of Criminology).

Jocelynne A. Scutt
Melbourne 1986

Jocelynne A. Scutt

1 | _Noisy Women_

Women have been taught to be silent. Despite accepted wisdom, it is untrue that women talk more than men; the contrary is so. And when women have spoken, our words have been trivialised in a culture dominated by men, who listen mostly to themselves. Yet since the late 1960s and early 1970s in Australia, women have ceased to pretend to be silent with each other. Women have refused to relegate our conversations with each other to the realm of the unimportant. We have grasped the significance of what we have to say, the value of what we have to say to one another, and we have recognised the importance of women's voices of the past. More often, in present years, our voices have broken through the barriers set up by a world that subscribes to machismo. And as a result, we have begun to recapture the talk of our foremothers.

The late 1960s saw a greater acceptance of women's right to speak out. There was a recognition that women collectively refused to accept the silence. The days when Dr Johnson could liken a woman speaking from a platform to a dog walking on its hind legs, or women could be derided and spat upon for claiming the right to speak publicly on topical issues, were well and truly routed. Women around the country were invigorated by the sheer volume of noise created by a revitalised women's rights movement. The years since then have wrought changes in individual women's lives, and those changes add up to a collective experience demanding its rightful place in the records.

It would be wrong to assert that the changes taking place have occurred only in the lives of those women who identify with feminism, or describe themselves as feminists or women's liberationists. 'Ordinary' women, and 'ordinary' women's lives, have changed since the early 1970s. It would be wrong to assume that changes in women's lives have been wrought directly as an exclusive result of the resurgence of women's liberation. But though not necessarily direct, the impact of activists' demands and the response of governments to restated goals of child-care, women's health services, support for victims of violence, equal opportunity in education and employment, the right to

1

abortion, free access to birth control, has played a crucial role in the reorientation of women's lives.

With the advent of the Whitlam Labor government in 1972, many women who would otherwise have had tertiary education denied to them, found themselves able to attend university. The abolition of university fees meant that women, long since married, or women who had begun university and stopped on marriage, or who had gone to university and taken an Arts degree as an 'easy option', were presented with openings not previously existing for them. In the late 1960s and early 1970s women who had never been politically active, or who had operated in male-dominated groups not recognising that 'comradeship' can extend from woman to woman, took up political cudgels. Some gained their blooding in areas directly related to their own needs, such as child-care, fighting for the establishment of centres at universities. Later, their political activism took them to demand that like facilities be established in less privileged areas, among less privileged women. Others called on male politicians, forcing them to take 'women's issues' seriously by measuring the man's performance and attitudes against lists of women's demands. Some joined traditional political parties, their aim later crystallising into struggles within those parties for greater female representation at all levels, executive and political, and the incorporation of feminist principles into party platforms. Women already in political parties acted concertedly to change the masculine orientation of Liberal, Labor and Country Party philosophies and practice. Black women, white women, women descended from convicts and free settlers, those recently arrived in Australia, all were confronted with new ideas, new perspectives. Consciousness-raising became the *raison d'être* for some women's groups; other meetings of women took a directly political approach, lobbying for anti-discrimination legislation, equal opportunity laws, affirmative action, rape law reform; some women organised to secure government grants (and later, for on-going funding) for women's health centres, rape crisis centres, women's refuges and shelters.

Women living 'ordinary' lives listened and watched the marches that had always taken place on International Women's Day, 8 March, grow and swell, the ranks filled with radicals dressed in jeans or long flowing skirts mingling with their stocking-legged, high-heeled sisters. Gradually, these 'ordinary' women came out of their homes (their husband's houses, the law named them) and joined in. The lie of 'bra burning' was imported from the United States by journalists looking for a 'good story' – or perhaps threatened by the thought that these women might so easily be their own mothers, girlfriends, wives, mistresses; no doubt *were* their mothers, girlfriends, wives, mistresses. As time went on and the marches and demonstrations grew noisier, bigger, stronger, coverage grew shriller and the efforts of news media to make the women appear ridiculous intensified. Still, women's demands did not cease or lessen. The women's movement was here to stay.

Each of the women in this book, whether 33, 64, 18 or 40 in the late 1960s and early 1970s has been profoundly affected by the passage of those years. Most have learned to speak and to listen to other women, and thereby to gather strength to change vital areas of their own lives. Some are striving to talk and to listen. Some have simply acknowledged the value of other women's talk, where in the past they were afraid to recognise the importance of women's words in their lives. Some lives have changed direction; some have come to encompass new perspectives on living; some have stayed roughly on the same path taken before women's liberation, but have developed new insights, new consciousness.

Different Lives is about individual lives and the changes fifteen years or more of the new women's movement have brought about. Each woman is different. Some came into the women's movement through consciousness-raising groups; some because of their disenchantment with male-dominated political parties; some through joining women's organisations. Some rejected women's organisations as not for them, as being too formal, too restrictive, finding their own way into sisterhood and collective action.

Each woman is unique. But universal themes dominate the late 1960s and 1970s each traversed. In their own words, these women relate their growing awareness of the politics of oppression and their efforts, together with other women, to transcend and change that oppression in their own lives, and in the lives of other women.

Lilla Watson, Pat Eatock, Franca Arena, Patricia Boero and Elizabeth Williams are part of minorities within the 51 per cent 'minority'. Growing up in a foreign culture, or between two cultures, each is representative of a minority group: black Australians, being Aboriginal or Pacific Islander by parentage and identification; arriving in young adult years from Europe and Latin America. Yet within their own group, these women were apart: they recognised the differences they had with the men of their own culture and experienced conflicts in determining what they should do to alleviate the pain they saw in themselves and in their sisters and their menfolk. Within the larger group 'women', they were sometimes alienated by their racial, ethnic and cultural backgrounds, those factors linking them to their male compatriots. Confronted with a society which dichotomises reality, they often felt they were faced with a need to choose: their blackness or ethnicity over their womanness, or their unity with women over their unity with men in their minority group, themselves facing discrimination and oppression. Some, more than others, turned to the women's movement; some saw their destiny as linked with their brothers and sisters, away from the white culture whether it be male or female; some worked to combine their feelings of outrage and sorrow at cultural oppression, to work within the black rights or ethnic movements, and within the women's movement. Each suffered both from men in their own group and in the culturally dominant group, and from white Anglo-Australian women. But each agrees that the women's movement has affected her life.

When the new women's liberation movement rocketed onto the scene in the late 1960s and early 1970s, it caught some women quite unawares. Elizabeth Ward, Vera Levin and others had always felt moderately secure in their being. They had lived lives as wives and mothers, not noticing that they were treated differently from their men (or not acknowledging any differential treatment). They had accepted that women married, cared for the kids, made the beds and did the cooking while their husbands hit the breadwinner trail. Even where engaging in paid employment, they saw their jobs as secondary to the careers of their husbands. Then, suddenly, in 1969, or 1970, or 1972, whenever, they saw the world through new eyes. In the world of 1972, it was no longer necessary or correct for men alone to be breadwinners, women to sit at home and wait, or rush out from work at lunchtime to do the family shopping. Elizabeth Ward and Marjorie Luck, living in Canberra and Hobart, rebelled against the lesson of their former lives, finding new selves in women-only weekends. Liza Newby and Vera Levin, separated by the Nullabor Plain and twenty years, found their old worlds were no longer enough; they went to university looking for something more – and found it. Elisabeth Kirkby and Elsa Atkin came in, from the other world of middle-class suburbia (and, for Elisabeth Kirkby, an almost achieved rural retirement), and got political. Elisabeth Kirkby joined the Australian Democrats and Elsa Atkin worked hard to have a woman elected to the local council.

For other women, the change was not so much an opening up of a new world, a new way of looking at their own existence, but a growing recognition of earlier misgivings about the social order. 'Something's out of kilter', each had thought as a child, a young woman, a woman in her child-bearing years. The coming of women's liberation lifted the veil; the mystery was solved. Betty McLellan knew 'something was wrong' when her young fiancé made it clear to her that her career was to be his wife rather than, as she had imagined, being a preacher in her own right. Myfanwy Gollan and Di Bell in their early years had support from their families for egalitarian ideas: Di Bell studied physics; Myfanwy Gollan went to university – it was natural to do so. Joan Russell and Diana Warnock thought some rules of the world odd. But they married as a matter of course. For each of these women, some ideas and desires gained support; women's intellectual abilities were recognised and each felt 'right' in developing them, at least for a time. But other 'unconventional' ideas – such as not marrying – could not be accepted.

There were women, too, who knew the wrongness of the world from birth, and who were never deflected from that recognition. Di Graham and Suzanne Dixon married, bore children and lived outwardly conventional lives. But inwardly, and in some of their activities, they registered each day the injustice of a world where women's achievements were relegated to the ranks of second best or ignored. Sue Bellamy grew up with a tradition of protest against the 'natural' order, inherited from her mother and grandmother. Carol Ambrus lived a life of protest from her youth, determined to fight against the rules which she saw as operating unfavourably toward women. Each of these women fought throughout the years of barrenness between the so-called waves of feminism. They were part of the flow between the crests of the waves, so that the women's movement never died, not after the 1890s, not after the years before and between the wars, not in the time leading up to the 1970s, which has been depicted as a period when women all went home to cook and breed. At that time, women continued to espouse women's liberationist ideals. It was just that their voices were not heard, or their voices were drowned out in the push to deny women rights as individuals, as people who could work collectively, and as a group with aspirations different from those set down by the dominant ideology.

The 1970s, and women's significant role in those years, cannot be understood without acknowledgement of the first consolidated infiltration of women into the interstices of government, by those designated 'women's advisers' (and later, by the women's movement itself, capped with the wry title 'femocrats'). In the past, there had been isolated instances of women being named advisers to government. During the

second world war women were advisers to the Minister for Recon-
struction, and before that time. Jessie Street, worker for women's rights,
the labour movement, Aboriginal land rights and constitutional recognition of Aboriginals as equal to all other Australians, was one such
appointment. She played a role, on Australia's behalf, in the United
Nations area too. Yet the 1970s were different.

One of the first acts of the incoming Labor government in 1972 was
to advertise the position of women's adviser to the Prime Minister.
Elizabeth Reid was selected, after the media had promoted the uniqueness of the proposed appointment, at least one newspaper running a
series of articles on various applicants for the job. Elizabeth Reid was
not, in fact, the first 'femocrat'. She was not promoted from within
the public service, but was a political appointment from outside, with
broad-ranging responsibilities, answerable to the Prime Minister. To
her fell the task of channelling women's demands, women's needs,
through to the top, and getting the information out from government
to women.

Elizabeth Reid led an important march of women into the
bureaucracy, whatever her own or others' views on the rights or wrongs
of women becoming engaged in the bureaucratic process. Some fifteen
years on, it falls to her (for the first time since leaving the job – and
expatriating to the United States, Iran, and more recently Zaire) to
set the scene in *Different Lives*. It falls appropriately to her to deline-
ate the parameters in her terms of women's liberation, the women's
movement, the feminist activism that developed during those early
years, and the outcome – so far.

Women in Australia have a right to express themselves in their own
terms. To make it real, women must be able to put that right into
effect. Women have a right to find an identity as women, and an identity as members of a culture which is Australian, in the widest sense.
Women have a right to be Australian, be they black, white, immigrants
of ancient or recent origin. That right is the essence of this book, in
the search by each woman for an identity. The identity of women is
linked with women's perceptions of themselves as members of families, of cultural groups; as persons performing particular roles, such
as mother, daughter, friend, wife, sister, spinster; as workers, careerists,
tradespeople, professionals; and as women, with a woman's culture and
a woman's history.

This book is a part of the history of individual women's lives. And
it is a part of the history of the lives of all women who have lived

through the 1960s, the 1970s and into the 1980s in an Australia that has had to come to terms with women's demands for a voice, for rights and for personhood.

2 | Elizabeth Reid

Elizabeth Reid was born at Taree, NSW in 1942. She has a post-graduate degree in philosophy in which she has a continuing interest. She attended her first women's liberation meeting in Canberra in 1970. In 1973 she was appointed adviser to the Prime Minister, the Hon. E. G. Whitlam, on matters relating to the welfare of women.

Since the end of 1975, Elizabeth Reid has lived outside Australia working initially in the area of women and development in the Asian and Pacific region and, since 1981, on food production, marketing and transportation in Central Africa. She has now returned to live in Canberra.

The Child of Our Movement:
A Movement of Women

The women's liberation movement in Australia in the late 1960s and early 1970s was very much a child of its times. The middle to late 1960s saw the emergence in Australian society of a number of quite radical social movements. The libertarian movement was at its peak. Student politics were revitalised, activated and internationalised in particular by their opposition to the White Australia Policy, conscription and the Sharpeville massacre with its apartheid setting. The anti-Vietnam war movement drew men and women, parents and children, politicians and university students as well as the older peace activists into forms of political activity well nigh forgotten on the Australian scene. It was a time of single-issue campaigns: immigration law reform; abortion law reform; homosexual law reform; and family planning. We were affected by, but not imitative of, the social movements burgeoning elsewhere: the black rights movement, the flower people, the women's liberation movements of the United States and Europe.

The roots of the women's liberation movement in Australia do not lie in any of these movements. They, themselves, were also children of the times. Rather, the movement began as a reaction to the increasing confinement, truncation and vulnerability of women in post-war Australia. What was left to each woman after society's procrustean guillotine had fallen was a headless and immobilised trunk, a trunk judged by conformity to the prevailing statistic, generally 36-24-36. A woman was a passive object to be tastelessly assessed. She was immobilised by Bowlby's theories of child-rearing. It was an imprisonment of timidity and guilt.

It is symptomatic of those times that what was created was a movement and not, as in earlier times, a women's group or organisation. The women's liberation movement saw itself as concerned with the restructuring of society and of personal relationships. It took a revolutionary stance and its concerns for reforms arose out of that stance. Its demands included the redistribution of access to wages and to services, not to wage earners, the concern of the trade union movement, nor to households, but to individuals; legal and social acceptance of a woman's ultimate right of control over her body; the dismantling of the dichotomy between the personal and the political; and an end to the violence towards women which so tragically characterised and continues to characterise our society.

My overwhelming impression more than a decade later is that this child, the women's liberation movement, has, in those intervening years, matured, borne fruit and died. What lives on is the child of that movement and those times, what might be called a movement of women.

This movement of women is not peculiar to Australia, it is a global phenomenon. Almost nowhere in the world now are women passively accepting rape or other forms of violence, the demeaning alcoholism of the men of their families or communities, the wanton destruction generated by ethnic, national or international strife or conflict, or the seemingly irreversible descent into poverty presently being experienced by an increasing number of women.

In Australia, this movement of women is characterised by a widespread refusal among women to accept denigrating attitudes or behaviour, a belief that their lives can be changed, much greater knowledge of how to bring about those changes, and a range of support systems, personal, economic and social, which offer help to women in that process of change. This movement of women has not led to a revitalising of the traditional women's organisations nor to the establishment of a nationally unified women's liberation movement; rather it has led to a fragmentation and diversification of effort. The Women's Electoral Lobby and the women's services movement have grown out of it but form only a small part of it. The movement of women has strengthened each woman individually and given her the knowledge that elsewhere, in her suburb, in her office, in her school or laboratory, there is a background of support. Women now support women.

It is because this movement of women exists that governments subsequent to the Whitlam government have been unable to dismantle the reforms for women started in that era. The movement of women can and does, from time to time, mobilise itself around issues, although activism is not its main *raison d'être*. The perception of women as wielding power as voters has its roots in it. The plethora of women in the arts, as writers, sculptors, weavers, painters, film makers, actors, comedians, poets, stage designers, is a part of it. The ABC's 'Playschool' has been transmogrified by it. The women appointed to boards and councils and recruited into the public sector have played a part in it.

Because there is now a movement of women in Australia, there are certain things that women need no longer tolerate, there have been changes that women will not allow to slip backwards and women's expectations of themselves and of others are maturing. Women now have hope and the determination and knowledge to do something about it. This movement of women is low key. It is not a highly visible phenomenon. Few, other than women, even remark it. But it is there, and it is the yeast of our society.

The direction taken by the early women's liberation movement in Australia was influenced, in most states, by the predominance of historians among its members: Ann Curthoys, Kay Daniels, Jill Matthews, Sue Bellamy, Edna Ryan, to mention but a few. Most came from or were influenced by the tradition of social history. Their concern was not so much the re-writing of history to include women, nor even the writing of the history of the subjugation of women – the history, that is, of women as victims and their responses to it. Rather, their concern was the re-writing of the history of our society, a history which was to read differently because of the inclusion of women within it.

Their concerns, and the concerns of the movement, were the analysis of the concept of patriarchy and the description of how it and the associated concept of sexism had functioned within Australian society; of the way society had constructed the notion of womanliness, of femininity; of the ways in which women had been divided and the issues which had brought them together; and, of the different experiences of women from different classes and backgrounds as well as of their common experiences. We were particularly concerned with an analysis of women in the context of social structures and processes. The movement in France, the United States or England had different interests and approaches, different analytical tools reflecting the different disciplines which predominated in their early days.

This emphasis was not universal throughout Australia. It was less true of the women's movement in Western Australia, which seemed more like a broad-based coalition of individual women caught up in the changes occurring around them and of women who had long associations with a range of the older women's groups and organisations. The women's movement in Western Australia had its historical parallels, perhaps, in organisations such as the Union of Australian Women or in the Modern Women's Club established in Perth in 1938 by Katharine Susannah Prichard and others. This older movement seems to have remained stronger and lasted longer than others in Australia.

The historical approach, that of looking backwards to understand the present, and the associated stance of observing rather than changing, were to influence the ability of the women's movement to respond to the opportunities created by the Whitlam government. The keen analytical powers of the early members of the women's movement had been used to understand the past and this understanding had, on the whole, taken place in an academic context. There was little experience in the women's movement in policy analysis or programme formulation and implementation.

When, in December 1972, the advertisement appeared for an adviser to the Prime Minister in matters relating to the welfare of women, there were two reactions within the women's movement, often within individual members of it. Most of us in the movement had been associated with single-issue reform groups: abortion, homosexuality, equal pay. We had chained ourselves to the bars of pubs. When the position was advertised, I and many others felt it was a challenge needing a response. For the first time in our history we were being offered the opportunity to attempt to implement what for years we had been writing, yelling, marching and working towards. Not to respond would have felt as if our bluff had been called.

The other reaction was equally appropriate. It was a re-examination of the traditional debate of reform versus revolution. It was clear to us all that our society was in need of radical restructuring if we, as women, were to be able to live equitably and humanely within it. We were very clear that our agitation was not aimed to get women a bigger or better share of the existing pie. The ingredients of the pie had to be changed. Neither the Labor Party, nor the anarchists, were our natural allies. In broad terms our goals were clear, but we had no programme and thus we were uncertain whether such a position in the politic-governmental structure would further or harm our goals.

On the other hand, however, it was equally clear to us that there was a desperate need for many of the reforms that it might be possible to bring about through legislative and associated changes at the national level, changes which could immeasurably improve the lives of women: equal pay, retraining, child-care, part-time employment, control over our health. The question was one of cost. Power corrupts and politics necessitates compromise. We rejected both. After the position had been advertised and before I was appointed to it, the Sydney *Mejane* collective, and Sue Bellamy in particular, had expressed deep reservations about the establishment of the position and of the type of reformism necessarily associated with it. These women were concerned about the lack of awareness within the women's movement of the potential impact on the movement of such changes.

History has proven this concern to be justified. The invitation to storm the political arena came at too early a stage of our formation. We had not formulated the details of our programme and had certainly not come to grips with the question of acceptable and appropriate means of achieving it. We were on our way. These issues were constantly debated by the Hobart women's liberation group in the pages of its newsletter *Liberaction.* The national conference at Mount Beauty in January 1973 was an important milestone in the growing-up of the movement. There we had attempted to clarify the meaning for us of notions of sisterhood, of claims that the personal is political and of debates between reform and revolution. It was the beginning of the formulation of an ideology of praxis. But we were still toddlers when the Whitlam government confronted us with its challenge.

Those early years had, however, brought about dramatic changes in the personal lives of all those involved in the movement. Consciousness-raising groups had not yet been begun. Instead, we explored the issues of concern to us, analysed social structures and processes binding us, in a seemingly objective fashion. The pronoun 'I' was relatively rare. But in fact, the public dilemmas and problems that we were discussing overlapped with our own personal dilemmas and problems and the discussions deeply affected the ways each of us lived. We explored the shape of a feminist utopia and reluctantly pushed and twisted that dream until it became relevant to our lives. We changed our lives so that they more closely fitted the dream. But above all, we came to accept our daily lives as a continuing series of compromises. We had not begun to understand, much less to accept, that compromise exists in all spheres, that some things are worth doing even if imperfectly because the result is needed. This again was to affect our ability to cope in the political arena.

As we struggled with our lives and our ideology, a much more pragmatic part of the women's movement sprang into existence: the Women's Electoral Lobby (WEL). This organisation was modelled to a great extent on the National Organization of Women, then recently formed in the United States, and better fitted the tradition of women's organisations passed on to us by our foremothers. Its first action was rare in Australian history. It interviewed every candidate in the 1972 federal election and, using an extended questionnaire, recorded their stance on issues of basic concern to women: abortion, child-care, equal pay and so on. To my knowledge the only precedent for this was the work of the Women's Political Association in 1914 when women voters were asked to judge each candidate for the electorate of Kooyong on a number of issues relevant to women.

The excitement generated among women by this bold action and the pleasure we took in WEL's skilful use of the media to publicise the results gave the women's movement a new impetus at the end of 1972. Few candidates did well. Pat Eatock was a notable exception. Since then, politicians have rarely answered similar questions so naively, so arrogantly, with such blatant sexism. This was WEL's birthing and initiation all in one.

After the election, WEL, too, had to ask itself serious questions regarding its future. Similar movements in the United States had focussed on all or some of these activities: submission writing, lobbying, monitoring government legislation and budgets, and educating their members through their increased knowledge of governmental programs and procedures. They chose a two-way flow from women to government and from government to women. The Women's Electoral Lobby was to give prime importance to the writing of submissions and to lobbying, to the flow from women to government.

Peter Wilenski, appointed principal private secretary to Whitlam after the Labor government came to power, had previously spent time studying at Harvard where he came into contact with the newly emerging women's liberation movement in the United States. His previous concern and activism around issues such as abortion law reform and family planning were expanded into an understanding of the radical demands of the women's movement. It was he who, understanding that the changes already occurring in women's lives would soon be making demands on the governmental arena, suggested that someone should be brought onto Whitlam's staff who could take up these demands and show their political and governmental relevance. There were almost 450 applicants for the job, a dozen or so men and many women associated with either WEL or the Women's Liberation Movement. The challenge of the job was clear to the movement.

Unlike all other areas with which the Whitlam government concerned itself, there was no Labor Party platform or policy relating to women. Within the broad ambit of areas of concern to women, the 1972 policy speech touched on only three: equal pay for work of equal value, the lifting of the sales tax on contraceptives, and access to pre-school education for all children under five in Australia. The first two were initiated within days of the election. The third was changed into a comprehensive programme of diversified and integrated services for children, in particular child-care, in Whitlam's policy speech for the May 1974 election.

The significance of the lifting of the sales tax on all contraceptives and the addition of the pill to the National Health Scheme list should not be overlooked. It was the first acknowledgement in Australian politics of women's right to control their bodies. Since the first world war, successive governments had abrogated this right in order to enforce policies of rapid population growth, policies culminating in 1943 with the introduction of the child endowment payment. The symbolism of these decisions to women was immense.

The first thirteen months following my appointment were spent travelling around Australia listening to women talk about their problems, about the changes they wanted. The women who spoke out came from all backgrounds: migrant, Aboriginal, rural, elderly, suburban, working, single, wealthy, married. We talked in factories, in housing estates, on farms, in schools, at women's meetings, in dairies, in gaols, in universities – in short, wherever women were. I was deluged with letters invariably beginning: 'Thank god that at last there is someone to whom I can talk, someone who might listen and understand.' In a short time I was receiving more letters than anyone in government other than the Prime Minister.

These letters were important not only because of the range of problems covered in them and the depths of despair and frustration they expressed, but also because they could be used to start the long overdue process of changing the bureaucracy. Where these letters dealt with matters falling under the jurisdiction of a particular department, they were sent to that department to draft a reply for my signature. Almost without exception the letter drafted was identical to the letters sent out for decades to these same women: unhelpful, uncaring, insensitive. They were returned with a note indicating what was wrong or offensive about the draft and with a suggested outline for a more appropriate response. The bureaucracy took a long time to understand, not only that the Whitlam government was serious about the changes it wished to introduce for women, but that the most fundamental reform required was an alteration in its own attitudes and practices. One of the most important changes necessary to be brought about was the institutionalisation of women's concerns. My position was clearly transient, dependent totally on political goodwill and understanding. Women's problems were not transient and lasting machinery had to be established within the bureaucracy to deal with them. These letters forced the beginning of this process.

As I listened to and reflected on what women were saying, I revised and refined the theoretical framework I had brought to the job. I believed there were basic preconditions that had to be fulfilled in order for women to lead a decent life. Child-care, adequate health services, equitable workforce conditions, equitable educational opportunities, an assured minimal income and protection from violence, all these were necessary to bring women to the threshold of financial and emotional independence, to the possibility of sufficient peace of mind to look at and reflect upon their lives, their values and their wishes for the future. None of these changes was revolutionary – the personal relationships that women were in and the society in which they lived would not have been radically restructured in the ways demanded by the women's liberation movement even if these changes had been achieved.

The most difficult challenge was to identify the required revolutionary changes, the changes over and above those which could bring women to the threshold of choice, those that would lead to the structural changes rather than merely reinforcing and bolstering the present structure. For a time after my appointment, while lots of women would have helped with the analysis, most were either geographically separated or felt themselves distanced from the job. In Canberra, Helen Shephard and others worked with me on the development of our long-term goals and the identification of appropriate means to achieve them. We began to work on a number of charts: one to categorise and classify reforms, another to list long-term aims, and another to formulate the steps which might get us there. The task we set ourselves was well nigh impossible. We faltered and ultimately foundered as we realised that to determine the realm of the possible required a very detailed knowledge of political and governmental machinery, knowledge that most outsiders neither have nor want to have.

Meanwhile, the women's movement was raising its own questions about its ability to respond to the problems of women in our society; indeed, whether it should. The analysis of the situation of women had shown areas of desperate need to which no governments had responded. There was widespread frustration and anguish within the movement in the face of this want. The question was: should the women's movement itself do something to alleviate it, or was its role rather that of an educator, a wielder of whatever sledge hammer was required to get governments to respond? The debate centred on the establishment of women's refuges. Some felt that the need was too urgent to wait for the debate, and so the movement itself became a provider of services for women. Refuges and health centres for women were established. Ultimately the demand placed on women's time and energies by the provision of these services stifled the debate.

By the time Labor had won a second election in May 1974, the outline of a programme for women had been formulated. Then began a period of intense activity, getting agreement in principle to the required changes, drawing up the policy or programme and monitoring its implementation. The workload was immense and the overwhelming necessity for a section in the Department of Prime Minister and Cabinet to back up my job was finally recognised. Two activists from the women's movement were appointed to it: Sara Dowse and Lyndall Ryan, the former as section head. With this expanded capacity, we were able to divide responsibilities and to function more efficiently. The needs were so great and so pressing, however, that one effect of these changes was to increase the number of people whose private lives were compromised by the long hours and exhausting nature of the work we did.

We were still predominantly concerned with the threshold reforms, yet we were very aware that these reforms could well have little long-term effect unless the basic attitudes of our society with respect to women were changed. The advent of International Women's Year was to provide an opportunity to tackle these attitudes. It was proposed to the Prime Minister that Australia should give proper recognition to the year, that the government should set aside a significant amount of money during the year and that these activities should have a threefold aim: attitudinal change, the lessening of discrimination and suffering, and the encouraging of women's creativity.

A National Advisory Committee for International Women's Year was appointed in July 1974 with its members chosen, not because of their affiliation with any particular group, but because in their own lives they had experienced the different aspects of the lives of women in Australia. Among them was personal experience in living as an Aboriginal woman, as a migrant woman, as the wife of a man in public office, as a radical feminist activist, in the trade union movement, as a self-employed woman, of working as a cleaner in a hospital, as a social worker, of using the media to communicate to women, and many others. A secretariat was established within the Department of the Special Minister of State. During the life of the National Advisory Committee, $3 million were set aside for activities celebrating the year.

The approach taken to International Women's Year was drawn from the ideology of the women's liberation movement. It was an explicit recognition of sexism as the primary cause of women's oppression in society. The means taken to challenge this sexism were drawn from the governmental arena: the funding of community submissions. The awareness within the women's movement that 1975 had been declared

International Women's Year was widespread and the early requests
for funding of projects received by the National Advisory Committee
came overwhelmingly from the movement. International Women's Year
funding was to prove a watershed for the women's movement in a number of ways.

The first indication of this occurred after the Darwin cyclone at
Christmas 1974. Word reached the National Advisory Committee that
the women of Darwin needed help and when committee members asked
how they could be of help, they were requested to provide skin cream,
sunburn lotion, sanitary pads and tampons, combs and lipstick. The
latter seemed to outrage some of the prominent leaders of the Sydney
movement. A public meeting was called at Balmain Town Hall to criti-
cise this funding. Shirley Castley, a member of the National Advisory
Committee and long active in the women's liberation movement, was
brave enough to attend. No matter what ideological position one took
on the use of make-up, or more generally on women as sex objects,
in these circumstances we felt we should respond to an expressed need.
It was a point of difference between us, exacerbated by the opposi-
tional style adopted by the Sydney movement. Few other funding
decisions were as contentious. What remains contentious to this day
is what the impact of the decision to fund itself has been on the women's
movement.

Whatever the impact on the women's movement itself, the impact
in the community in general was significant. The year built on initiatives of the women and men in our community who were already
concerned with the problems facing women. To a large extent it was
these people who were funded during the year. Their activities
expanded the feminist consciousness within the community and
challenged attitudes in all spheres of women's lives. The report of the
National Advisory Committee for the year discusses in detail the pro-
gram for the year, the projects funded and the reaction of the Australian
media to the year.

The coincidence of this attack on sexism and its concomitant releas-
ing of women's potential and creativity, along with the other reforms
introduced by the Whitlam government, led to what might be called
a revolution of rising expectations, the basis of the movement of women
and the beginning of women's consciousness of, and pride in, themselves as women.

The empowerment of this revolution of increasing expectations came
about most significantly through the Women and Politics Conference

held in Canberra in September 1975 and funded as part of the International Women's Year programme. This conference was open to all women and women's groups, to all political parties, trade unions and other relevant organisations. It was widely advertised, and to ensure equitable geographic and class access, travel and accommodation were subsidised. Individuals attending did not pay in excess of the return air fare from Melbourne to Canberra, no matter from where they came. Women from minority groups who nevertheless could still not afford to attend were subsidised. The aim of the conference was to provide as many women as possible from all backgrounds with the opportunity to discuss the actual and possible roles of women in politics, not only as voters and as members of political parties, but in all spheres of political activity: trade unions, the bureaucracy, lobby groups, social movements.

Almost 800 women attended the conference. The programme was designed to reflect diversity, to capture all interests. Initial mistrust, wariness and dissension were inevitable in such an undertaking and they surfaced immediately. The conference was opened by the Prime Minister with a reception in Kings Hall at Parliament House on Sunday evening. Aboriginal women demonstrated outside, criticising inadequate representation of their concerns in the programme. Labor women stood behind the Prime Minister during his opening speech with placards denouncing the decisions recently taken by him on East Timor. His speech was interrupted when the Aboriginal women proceeded into the hall chanting and singing. Women from the women's movement wearing men's suits mingled in the audience with farm women, factory workers, church women. The invitations sent out by the Department of Prime Minister and Cabinet for the reception had stated that the appropriate dress was lounge suits. A more insensitive gaffe for such a conference is hard to imagine. The statue of George V in King's Hall was draped with a placard reading 'Women and Revolution, Not Women and Bureaucracy', and 'lesbians are lovely' and similar slogans were written in lipstick on the mirrors in the men's toilets. The press, accustomed to sensationalising every possible aspect of my work, and my beliefs, had a heyday. Pictures appeared on the front pages of all the papers showing the draped statues, the women in suits, the demonstrators. Articles highlighted the dissension and reported the slogans as best they could find the wit to do so.

Monday was little different. *Monday Conference* was televised live that evening from the conference. We waited with trepidation to see in what ways the women would express the as-yet unresolved discord.

We should have had more faith. The differences and contentions were aired, but in a way that implicitly recognised the importance to them of the conference.

The rest of the week was dramatically different. By the end of the conference the disagreements had been talked through, changes made and the lives of every one of those almost 800 women had been altered. The trivialisation of the conference by the media was, for many women attending, their first experience, not just of the inherent sexism of the press, but of the damaging way in which this distorted the reality that they had experienced. This was a uniting force during the conference, and the unity was reinforced by the growing realisation that the concerns of the conference were their concerns and that the skills and knowledge they were learning would be of inestimable value to them.

But the damage to my job had been done and was irrevocable. By mid-week during the conference, Whitlam's political advisers had deluged him with a barrage of newspaper clippings and their own prejudices and convinced him that his commitment to women's issues was electorally disadvantageous, if not disastrous. They argued that he should distance himself from me and back-pedal on his public commitment to women. Eventually he concurred.

After the conference, I became aware that this had happened. My first concern was how I could make clear to the women of Australia that there was no longer any political commitment to their issues without detracting from the record up until then of the Whitlam government. I had often publicly stated that I would continue in the position of adviser only for as long as I felt that the government had a genuine commitment to women. For two and a half years, there had been a commitment, not based on any deep understanding of the position of women in our society, based rather on basic principles of participatory democratic socialism: the principle of equity and a commitment to the redistribution not only of income but of access to services and to benefits. As this commitment waned and political expediency waxed, I resigned.

In the years since then, the momentum generated in those days carried women forward. To a great extent, action became centred on the self rather than on others, except within the women's peace movement. Women more and more took control of their lives, demanded the services they needed, expressed their priorities electorally as well as through lobby groups and meetings, and insisted on respect and the right to independence. All sorts of women. In small ways. A movement of women.

Part One

Minorities within a Minority

3 | Pat Eatock

Pat Eatock was born in December 1937. In 1978 she graduated BA from the Australian National University, majoring in history and philosophy, with sub-majors in history and sociology, including specific units on urban Aborigines and women's studies. She has published articles and papers on Aboriginal attitudes to abortion and contraception; racism and sexism; and campaigning for political office.

Pat Eatock spent the first years of the 1980s living on the land in Pillar Valley in New South Wales, then returned to Sydney to complete her MA in history at Macquarie University. She currently lives in Woolloomooloo.

There's a Snake in My Caravan

There's a snake in my caravan and I don't know what to do. A nasty dull-black sinuous thing that has made its home in the back of a large electric fridge that's in storage, with other furniture, in the caravan annex. It has bitten my dog (which barely survived) and forced me to install my latest batch of hijacked hitch-hikers in the front bedroom of the little old farmhouse where I live. If I could pluck up the courage to go after it with the '12 bore', the only result would be a dead caravan. The snake would then settle down to a snug winter and a productive spring in its comfortable, new, all mod. cons. accommodation. I can envisage the scene sixty years from now: my daughter, Amanda, then seventy-five, leaning on her walking stick while gesturing expansively at a tangled heap of aluminium and steel, a tatter of canvas still fluttering defiantly through the bracken and weeds, as she explains to *her* hijacked hitch-hikers that 'there's a snake in the caravan, so you'll have to stay up at the house'.

With just a cursory glance and a swish of its tail, that snake has reduced me to utter powerlessness. Inadequate, ineffectual, I fall into the pit of what must be the ultimate of peculiarly female 'downness': I am no longer in control of my life. My caravan, the private space in which I write, is denied me. Yet this feeling of powerlessness is all too familiar. In 1971 I was a suburban housewife, the mother of five children. The youngest, then seven years old, was severely retarded and epileptic. Then I became pregnant again.

In those days, one could get a legal abortion only on grounds that the pregnancy presented a danger to the physical or mental health of the mother. Unaware that I would have qualified for a termination on medical grounds, and having lived the previous seven years on the brink of a total breakdown, I signed myself into a mental institution. I did not have an abortion. I was told that I was 'too sane'. I had not come in dripping blood. They suggested I 'have her adopted'. This decision, made by *others*, was the beginning of my conscious desire for *real* control of my life.

I had been married for fifteen years. The fifth child was placed in an institution for the intellectually handicapped just one month before the youngest was born. Married life was soured even before the handicapped child, whose illness created a social and economic barrier to our ending the marriage. The marriage disintegrated with frighteningly violent scenes.

Being of mixed racial origins, my identity resolved and focussed on my Aboriginality more and more throughout the years. Childhood and marriage (to a first cousin on the Aboriginal side of the family) led to an incredibly isolated existence providing no real protection against continuing racist barbs. However, during 1971 I was increasingly active in the Aboriginal land rights movement, visiting a number of Aboriginal reserves throughout New South Wales. At easter, 1972, I attended the National Land Rights Conference in Alice Springs.

The land rights movement would not have survived had it not been for the role of Aboriginal women. The Gary Foleys, Paul Coes, Mick Millers and others fought long and hard throughout the 1970s, and into the 1980s. But the strength of nameless hundreds of women, tempered by years of direct conflict with bureaucracies (police, welfare agencies, schools) in defence of their children, played an important role in the development of Aboriginal organisations and the general demand for land rights. Yet while the land rights issue has passed from the hands of the young male militants of the late 1960s and early 1970s to the National Aboriginal Conference (predominantly mature males), Aboriginal women have consistently demanded that the needs of women be taken into account in land rights legislation. So far little has been achieved.

In April 1972, I took the baby and left my home in Sydney's outer western suburbs, arriving in Canberra, the first 'refugee from suburbia' that the Canberra Women's Liberation group had to deal with. Nine months later my eldest daughter joined me, and in December 1973 the remaining children came to Canberra for the christmas holidays, and stayed.

I participated in the activities which saw the brutal but triumphant demise of the Aboriginal Embassy in Canberra in August 1972, and stood as an independent 'black liberation' candidate in the 1972 federal elections in the ACT. In 1973 I became the first non-matriculated mature-age student at the Australian National University.

As a child I had been fascinated by the distant white gleam of buildings at the University of Queensland at St Lucia. I gradually realised that working-class kids don't go to university. At least not unless you were a 'real brain'. High school didn't enter my thinking because, in my day, you didn't enter high school until you were thirteen or fourteen. I left school at fourteen, beginning a 'career' in factory process work. Years later I realised how lucky I was to be in school at all. Until 1948 (the year I was ten), any principal could refuse to accept any Aboriginal child into his school.

When a friend first suggested I go to university, I laughed. I laughed again when Liz Reid suggested it in 1972. After dropping out for a year in 1975, I completed my degree in 1977 at the age of forty. Six years after arriving in Canberra, I worked for more than two and a half years as a project officer in the Department of Social Security's 'Aboriginal Unit'. The frustrations of working in the bureaucracy, together with health and other problems, led to my resignation in January 1981. For the next two years I lived in 'rural retreat' near Grafton.

To grasp the real impact of women's liberation on my life requires an awareness of the tremendous dynamism of the women's movement in 1972 and my relationship with the Bremer Street Women's House. Early in 1972 Bobby Sykes and I were invited to speak to a group of Canberra women about land rights, the Aboriginal Embassy, and other issues of concern to Aboriginal women. It was the day Canberra Women's Liberation took formal possession of the Bremer Street house. This was my introduction to Women's Liberation. One week later I arrived in Canberra, penniless, with a five-month-old-baby – to stay. After three weeks, still penniless, Amanda and I moved into the Bremer Street meeting room, having passed from hand to hand among some of the 'sisters' in a vain attempt to find a less inconvenient niche for us.

The atmosphere at Bremer Street in 1972 was electric. Hardly an evening passed without some sort of meeting, with twenty to sixty women. Consciousness-raising was a twice-weekly event. General meetings, action groups, and the embryonic Women's Electoral Lobby had a weekly time and space. Days were filled with the comings and goings of newsletter production, the preparation of leaflets, classes in screen printing, the establishment of the feminist library, or just dropping in.

I was an active participant. Not only by choice, but also because baby Amanda and I couldn't go to bed until the meetings ended. We stayed for about six weeks. Then, when I lost my recently acquired public service job as a temporary clerical assistant because of my activities in the Aboriginal Embassy, I also lost my accommodation in a government hostel. Amanda and I returned to Bremer Street.

If nothing else, I can claim to have done much to assist the establishment of a women's refuge in Canberra. The physical presence of the 'Green Valley housewife', her baby, the nappies and disorder, and the endless recitations of my latest trauma as I fought for recognition of entitlements as a *deserting* wife with the ACT welfare authorities, were concrete evidence of the urgent need for a 'real' women's refuge. (In 1972 only 'deserted' wives were entitled to welfare.)

These periods of residence in Bremer Street also had a great impact on me. I managed to rate a 100 per cent score on the Women's Electoral Lobby survey of candidates in their attitudes to issues relating to women in the 1972 federal election. Yet, as early as 1973, I began using my university studies as an excuse to withdraw from feminist activity. Or, more accurately, the women's movement withdrew from me.

1972 had been an extremely traumatic year. Separated from my children, I was often in despair. When meetings closed, usually in the early hours of the morning, I was left alone to cry myself to sleep: no future, no place to go. Too 'working-class' proud to ask for charity, I fed the baby sugar-water while humorously describing my latest battle with welfare. During the first nine weeks I received only two $10 food vouchers. Few women at the meetings noticed. I understand, but still resent, the pressures put on me to 'move on'. Three or four weeks is insufficient time for a woman in crisis to get back on her feet.

The advent of the Women's Electoral Lobby (WEL) caused the numbers of women at the house to grow rapidly. Consciousness-raising sessions were divided in two. The activity-oriented, newer, WEL women did not always succeed in grasping the 'personal is political' ambit of feminist theory. The potential growth of consciousness-raising 'rap' groups bogged down for lack of leadership and inspiration. And hard-core feminists were avoiding discussion about the role and validity of the position of adviser to the Prime Minister on women's issues; the appointment of Elizabeth Reid to that position; and the relationship of the Canberra women's movement to both the position and its incumbent.

The last 'rap' I attended was on 'my mother and me'. Many women sat silent, making no contribution. I suspect that the articulate, competent, well-educated Canberra women felt more threatened by the processes of consciousness-raising than I. I could only benefit (in the long term) by discarding the 'shit' elements of my socialised role as a woman, housewife and mother. By society's chauvinistic criteria, my 'inadequacies' and 'unworthiness' had constantly been confirmed to me. Through consciousness-raising, I came to realise a new and autonomous self.

Yet consciousness-raising was difficult. It was like peeling an onion to its core. Fear and despair come as layer after layer of 'garbage' is torn away. Perhaps at the end there will be nothing left at all of the 'identity' that is *you*. Then, miraculously, there *is* a small piece, perhaps merely the size of a pea, but it is there, and it's you, and you build on it. Then, a few months (or years) later, you start the whole process again. This time, you're a walnut, or perhaps even larger.

The Elizabeth Reid situation did not improve my relationship with the Canberra women's movement. I was closely identified with Liz who had been a tremendous support to me in 1972, not only as campaign manager, but by sharing her home with the baby and me for many weeks prior to the election, and in raising funds for my campaign. Labor Party feminists were attempting to block Bremer Street involvement in my election campaign, using their influence to prevent any direct or specific endorsement of me from the Women's Electoral Lobby. Other 'sisters' stood back and observed my campaign, amazed at my impertinance and gall.

In 1975 I was selected together with nine other women of all backgrounds to attend the International Women's Year Conference in Mexico City. Even my few remaining feminist friends were disturbed that this may have been an example of 'special patronage'. Well, whether by intention or not, the Canberra women's movement actively destroyed any validity that my experiences in Mexico may have had, by the simple expedient of not listening when I returned. Two attempts were made to organise meetings on my behalf to discuss the conference, one at the Women's House, one with the ANU Radical Feminist Group. Neither attempt even went so far as a date for discussion. The message was loud and clear: the women's movement of Canberra just did not want to know what had happened in Mexico.

The information they rejected, the great news from Mexico in 1975, was that Australian feminist theory was leading the world. Liz Reid, Laurie Bebbington (the radical lesbian activist from the Australian Union of Students), Pat Giles (trade unionist and now ALP senator from Western Australia) and other Australian women caught and held the centre stage of world interest as their theory of feminism related to practice in their fields. At the same conference, American feminists were booed from the stage when, with chauvinistic arrogance, they attempted to align the weight of the international conference on one side or the other of their internal schisms and disputes.

The Canberra women's movement was predominantly middle class, educated and articulate, with an intimate knowledge of the public service structure and the complexity of its mechanisms. They participated in legislative reforms by submissions on family law reform, anti-discrimination legislation and others, and giving evidence at enquiries such as the enquiry into poverty by Henderson and the Australian Council of Social Service. However as time passed, many chose action in fields like child-care, the women's refuge, abortion counselling and the rape crisis centre. Others took a more 'revolutionary' stance or withdrew under the guise of having to 'sort out your own problems before you can solve the problems of society'.

The political assessment of the 'correct direction' for the women's movement unfortunately led many Canberra women into 'concrete' activity or to a 'self'-centred encounter group/meditation direction, and away from the 'reformist' submissions and other legislative processes where their unique talents could be fully utilised. Those women who did persist from within the bureaucracy were seen to be vaguely 'invalid'. They were either not *real* feminists, or not really 'Canberra'.

I see the grand finale for the women's movement as being the Women and Politics Conference in 1975. I was an official rapporteur on the 'campaigning' session of the conference, but throughout that week I was under constant attack from my Aboriginal sisters. Tolerance – if not complete forgiveness – was extended to me for my political consciousness of my working-classness and femaleness, as well as my Aboriginality. But then a sister started a rumour that I was not Aboriginal at all. This charge was not made easier by originating from a sister-by-blood (my biological sister) in a futile attempt to retain her Queensland country town eminence as a member of the Junior Chamber of Commerce and president of the local Parents and Citizens Association. (Years later my mother accused me of 'destroying' my sister's life by 'coming out' as an Aborigine: my sister was forced to retreat into the anonymity of Brisbane's suburbia!) Fortunately, all but a few die-hards accepted the truth when confronted with it.

Personal traumas aside, the Women and Politics Conference was a triumph of feminist sisterhood. Over 800 women of almost all political persuasions found that their female identity gave them more in common than the arbitrary divisions of party politics and ideologies. That this groundwork was not followed up was *the* tragedy of the more recent years of feminism, even surpassing the competiton for, and distrust of, the funding hand-outs of 1975–7.

Feminism has had a major impact on the lives of my children. My eldest daughter became involved in the establishment of the rape crisis centre. She was pack-raped at fifteen, and through the writing of other women on their experiences of rape, she had taught herself to read at the age of seventeen, thus overcoming a long-standing learning difficulty. Through the rape crisis centre, she attended a counselling course and made herself available to assist other victims. Unfortunately, she was never called upon to counsel others, presumably because she was less articulate, less educated, and therefore less valued by other rape crisis activists.

My sons, now in their twenties, were also exposed to large doses of feminist ideology at a time when the vast majority of young working-class women with whom they might expect to associate appear to live, still, in the 1950s and 1960s. The impact of women's liberation on their lives has not made easier their relationships with other young working-class unemployed of either sex.

Feminism seems to have made little impact on the consciousness of working-class suburbia, although the benefits have a daily effect on many aspects of their lives. The exception appears to be homosexuality. My second daughter has found exceptionally aware young working-class male companions with older brothers or sisters who are practising homosexuals. This consciousness of a feminist perspective within a limited number of working-class youth reflects the success of the gay movement in promulgating its ideology, even in working-class suburbia. The women's movement (as I experienced it in Canberra) cannot claim similar success.

However, despite this breakthrough, the sexuality of both my older daughters is often almost as restricted as is my own. I live a celibate life, mainly because the few men I meet are so incredibly YUCK! I had the occasional 'one-night stand' in the first few years, but don't relish changing my lifestyle and adjusting to the complications of an intimate relationship: 'A lover is like a child.' One has to put in a lot of work straightening out their headspace and moulding them into a state of political, social, non-sexist and (in my case) non-metaphysical consciousness that in some way approximates one's own. The emotional energy expended does not seem worth the paltry rewards. Perhaps I've been a mother too often and too long.

At this stage of my life I cannot see myself joining a political party, although intellectually I value the formal co-ordination of efforts directed to reform – that is, re/form – society. I do, however, watch the political scene at both the global and national levels with avid interest. Conversations with strangers invariably centre on socio-economic, feminist and Aboriginal issues; hence my addiction to hijacking hitch-hikers. (The latest were from Prince Rupert, Canada. He a left-wing trade unionist working for a right-wing trade union with unemployed youth. She a feminist whose theory was weak. If feminism sickened elsewhere at the same time ours did, perhaps Australian feminist theory still leads the world!) Philosophically, I'm a dialectical materialist. Emotionally, I'm an anarchist and a cynic. Physically, I'm lazy. I disapprove of (other) armchair revolutionaries for their failure to *act*.

And of the alternative 'drop-out' society (environmentalists notwithstanding) who are tucked away at Nimbin (or elsewhere) on their own few acres with their covert incipient conservative capitalism intact: Cardwell in Queensland was the Nimbin of the late 1920s and early 1930s, and look at *it*! Yet I'm sufficiently hypocritical to live on a farm without electricity or running water and surrounded by chooks and ducks and geese. At least I have a landlord to help keep me 'honest'. He has been trying to evict me ever since he 'discovered' my Aboriginality.

I also resent the 'spiritual revolution' of the 1970s, which continues to divert energies from a more positive reaction to the mercenary rat race of consumer capitalism. By the simple expediency of mislabelling it 'materialism' and juxtapositioning an appropriately metaphysical 'revolution', a truly revolutionary force has been successfully misdirected. That the 'spiritual revolution' was necessarily a part of the peace movement of the 1960s is debatable. Although I participated in the campaign against the Vietnam war from the early years, for me the 1960s remain 'the Valium years' when, despite its apparent affluence, suburbia was a vast, dull-witted and boring expanse of alienated 'factory fodder' hitting up on the booze, while their equally alienated 'maintainers of labour' popped a few more Valium. My experience of the 'spiritual revolution' came in 1973 and 1976 when encounter groups, behavioural psychology, zen buddhism and meditation made serial inroads into Canberra society.

So where do I go from here? Despite having written the foregoing on my experiences of women's liberation and feminism in Canberra, I confess to being greatly in their debt. I would have survived without them. I would have broken out of my marriage somehow. But I certainly would never have gone to university, and I would have been socially, emotionally and psychologically 'other' than I am today. I value the few steadfast friendships, the two or three sisters, I retain.

Despite many snakes – in differing forms, but invariably male – the changes in my life have, for the most part, resulted from my own decisions. Or, at least, the limitations on my freedom of choice have been more covert, more indirect, than in earlier days. The women's movement has done more for me than simply encouraging me to redirect my guilt from my poor housekeeping skills to my inability to deal with a snake. By the way, if *you* have a snake in your caravan and you don't know what to do, try Ratsac in milk! A woman told me . . .

4 | Franca Arena

Born in Genoa, Italy, on 23 August 1937, Franca Arena was educated at schools in Genoa and spent one year studying English at Syskon College in London before emigrating to Australia. She serves and has served on many boards, committees and councils, including the National Population Council and various government and community organisations. From 1980 to 1984 she was a commissioner on the Education Commission of New South Wales.

In 1981 Franca Arena was elected to the New South Wales Legislative Council as a member of the Australian Labor Party (ALP), and serves on various caucus committees. She has also been member and deputy chairperson of the New South Wales Women's Advisory Council. In 1980 she received the Order of Australia for services to the ethnic communities.

No More Crumbs

I was born in Genova, on the Italian Riviera, in 1937. The history of my home town goes back to ancient time, Genova being an ally of Rome in the first Punic war in 218 BC. In the centuries that followed Genoa, as it is known in English, became an independent republic which in its hey-day was one of the great powers of the Mediterranean. Genoa has been called since time immemorial 'La Superba' (the proud one) and its people have been known for their honesty, tenacity, hardiness and pride. Genoa was the birthplace of the great navigator Christopher Columbus, the great musical genius, Nicolo Paganini, and the great patriot and philosopher Guiseppe Mazzini; Sandro Pertini, Italy's most loved and respected president, was born not far from Genoa. I have always been proud of my place of birth, and this pride and love deepened every time, in Australia, I was made to feel I came from some inferior place and inferior race.

I was born into a middle-class family. My father was a good man whose difficult life had shaped his character; he was hard, severe and strict with my sister and myself. I lost my mother when I was nine. I cannot remember many happy times during my childhood or my youth. At twenty-one I applied for an assisted passage to Australia. On payment of £10, I left Italy on my own, for a country where I knew no one. On leaving Genoa, some friends gave me a gold pendant with the famous lighthouse (La Lanterna) of Genoa and a scroll which said: 'As this lighthouse has guided our navigators through the centuries, may it guide you through the unknown oceans of your life.' It is to this very day one of my most precious possessions.

Before having a family I had worked for seven years at the Italian-language newspaper *La Fiamma*. I produced and announced Italian-language programmes for them on radio stations 2SM, 2KY and 2CH. In 1966, with the birth of my twins, I became a full-time mother and housewife. They were difficult years – economically it was not easy to live on one salary. We had many debts, and the children were very demanding. With no family, I had no help except my husband's. I experienced all the housewife blues! To keep my mind alert, in 1968

I started WEA classes at night. Then as the children began kindergarten a few days a week, I worked for *La Fiamma* again. It was only part-time and often for no pay. I loved it nonetheless. Little by little I was starting to become a human being again, not only a mother and a wife, roles which have always been important to me, but separated me for a while from the rest of humanity.

I joined the Australia-China Society. In those days the society organised trips to China, as it does now. The difference is that when I took mine, in September 1972, Australia did not recognise the People's Republic even though both Nixon and Whitlam had visited there. *La Fiamma* agreed to publish a series of articles I would send back. The first two were on the front page under the heading 'The first Latin Australian to visit China'; I was delighted. I wrote nine in all. It was a scoop for me and for *La Fiamma*.

My work in radio in the first part of the 1960s, articles for *La Fiamma* on China, and a series exposing a racket rife in the Italian community in Sydney which sent people to Manila to be cured by 'holy men', made me a well-known figure in the Italian community. In the late 1960s I had begun work in voluntary organisations, but many of them, run by conservative, wealthy Italian-Australians, found me too political and vocal for their liking. Italian women, especially in Australia, were divided strongly on class lines. The great majority of Italian immigrants were working class and busy trying to overcome the 'survival stage' to establish some economic base for themselves and their families. Well-to-do Italians were often snobbish, conservative and old-fashioned.

In Australia I felt little in common with the established leaders of the Italian voluntary organisations, and I looked to other groups through which to express my broadened interests. Through people I met while attending the Mosman Debating Society, I joined the ALP early in 1973.

My position as a woman living between two societies was difficult: in the Italian community I was ill at ease, as there were many conservatives among my middle-class friends; in the wider Australian community I still felt a stranger and at times not accepted. Immigrants had had years of facing a policy of assimilation, being 'factory fodder' expected to leave all decisions to those 'born to rule', the very people who seemed to think Australia was not an independent nation but an appendage to Mother England. For years we saw the spectacle of an Australian prime minister making annual visits to England to watch the wretched cricket, which was alien to so many of us. Very few courtesy visits were made to the Mediterranean countries from where so many of our immigrants came. But in 1972 a Prime Minister was elected, whose electorate of Werriwa was based on working-class areas with a high component of people coming here in the post-war migration. With Gough Whitlam a majority of migrants felt they could identify. His was a government wanting to discard vestiges of British colonialism, even to such small but significant changes as Australianising our letter boxes by boldly replacing Elizabeth Regina II with Australia Post.

Women also felt a new era of reform had begun. In those days I developed strong feminist views. I attended meetings of the Women's Electoral Lobby and other women's groups. But slowly I concluded I was most needed to fly the feminist flag in the ethnic communities, where male chauvinism was worse than in the Australian community at large. I have always been a feminist without knowing, because my feelings for equality and justice have always been strong. The feminist movement helped me to articulate my feelings and communicate them more sharply. Though my loyalty was strong to the feminist movement, I felt more needed in the developing ethnic consciousness movement. In the ethnic communities my identity became a dual one, of being a migrant woman: my feminist consciousness was something which informed and strengthened my work as a migrant woman, and helped to harden my advocacy of ethnic rights.

In 1973 I was appointed to a Federal Task Force on Immigration and went to Canberra, first as an interpreter for a meeting between Al Grassby, Minister for Immigration and Ethnic Affairs; Bill Hayden, Minister for Social Security; and Italy's Under-Secretary of Social Security; and then to my first big federal conference of the Task Force.

The few years of the Whitlam government were exciting. I learnt then how important it is to be well organised, to start the day early, to have some time up your sleeve for an emergency. I had, and still have, the support of my husband, who saw me take more and more responsibility and never questioned. Rather, he helped me through. I learnt to rise early, cook dinner often at breakfast time, do the housework whenever I had time, to make the most of every minute of my day, organising my life so I could be home most of the time when the children came home from school – because I could never free myself entirely of a feeling of guilt if I was not; my sons have always been the greatest joy of my life.

In the meantime, two important projects got underway. Many of us felt that as Australians of non-English-speaking backgrounds, we had many problems in common and that only by having a strong and united voice could we do something about them. Education was an issue uniting us all. Until the federal Labor government came to office, the conditions of the inner-city schools, where so many of our children went, were appalling. I had first-hand experience when I became a Board member of Stanmore's Inner City Education Centre in 1972 and got to know lots of dedicated teachers and parents. Thus began my involvement with education.

The second project began when Bill Jegorow, known affectionately as the Czar because of his Russian origin and stubborn determination, called meetings of people of different ethnic communities under the umbrella of Sydney's Inner Western Suburbs Regional Council. We met for many months, creating the nucleus of the Ethnic Communities Council of NSW. This council was officially formed at Sydney Town Hall on 27 July 1975; on that date we 'came of age': we ethnic communities became visible in the Australian community. At the inaugural meeting we had Gough Whitlam, Malcolm Fraser (then Leader of the Opposition) and an array of politicians, including Neville Wran and Al Grassby. More than 1000 people attended. When Whitlam arrived he was given a tumultuous welcome. But then a well-organised Central European group in the middle of the hall started singing 'Fraser, Fraser'; Fraser was nervous but elated. During the meeting while Whitlam spoke, Fraser pulled apart half a dozen or so camellias from the table decoration in front of him.

One of the few women speakers at the meeting, I pointed out that migrant women 'have for too long been the Cinderellas of the migrant programme. The system was not geared to include migrant women . . . many live in a silent lonely world, often unable to communicate with their children who develop hostile attitudes towards them.' The plight of my sisters in immigrant communities had come to me through my work for *La Fiamma* and radio. Women (especially Italian) wrote to me with their problems. With Radio 2EA I was inundated with letters from women of other ethnic communities too.

Ethnic Radio 2EA began on the initiative of Al Grassby. A group of ethnic activists started meeting at his place to lay the foundations of the station in mid-1974. The station was launched in June 1975. I was volunteer producer and announcer of the Italian-language programmes. We broadcast in seven languages. (Today, 2EA broadcasts in fifty-two languages in Sydney and 3EA in forty-seven in Melbourne.)

We were all thrilled to take part in the exciting project. But I look back in anger sometimes at our struggle to set up a station with no equipment and hardly any facilities. The underlying philosophy seemed to be that we had to prove ourselves to be 'good little ethnics', deserving a radio station of our own – and that after surveys showing that in Sydney and Melbourne 2 million people could not be contacted because of language difficulties. We had guidelines saying 'No controversy – no politics – no sectarianism'. I certainly agreed with the last, but for the rest . . . Perhaps, looking back at 1975 and the continuous attacks on the Labor government, it can be understood that the government did not want to be accused of setting up a propaganda station. It was difficult, demanding work. I had to buy my tape recorder, tapes, everything necessary to produce a good programme promoting responses from the community.

We were swamped with letters, most from migrant women or their children who wrote: 'Mother loves the programme, she loves to understand what is happening in the community, she feels so cut off by her lack of English', or 'My parents' language is spoken on the radio!' All this reinforced my feeling that there was a lot of work to do in ethnic communities. Dorothy Buckland and I set up a Migrant Women's Association in 1973 and invited Liz Reid, advisor to the Prime Minister on women's affairs, to address us. She seemed to us uninterested. In those early days of the women's movement, there was little time for minority groups.

I had difficulty keeping up with work coming from the many voluntary organisations to which I belonged. Not only was I not receiving any pay, but my running around was costing me money! I was grateful to my husband for the help he gave. But it meant we could hardly afford any holidays; an overseas trip I yearned to take to see my family in Genoa, and also to refresh my mind, seemed an impossibility for many years. Things started improving when the then Attorney-General, Senator Murphy, appointed me one of the first civil marriage celebrants. In 1974 I celebrated marriages all over Sydney. I met wonderful people of all social classes, making many friends. I celebrated hundreds of marriages and the fee I received helped subsidise my community activities. The advantage was that marriages were celebrated mostly on a Saturday, giving me the week free (it did, however, mean a six-day week). The point remains that so many of the feminist and ethnic activists come from the middle-class because working-class people do not have the resources (financial or time) to be heavily involved in public affairs.

With the constitutional coup of 1975, many things changed. If the
events of 1975 came as a shock to many people in this nation, they
were a rude awakening for a lot in the ethnic communities. Most of
us came from countries where politics had often been a dirty game,
where bitterness and vindictiveness were part of political life. For those
who thought politics in Australia was different, 1975 showed it was
not. The bitterness, divisiveness, even hatred, aroused in the Australian
community at large were reflected in the ethnic communities. I felt
the divisions in the councils, committees and organisations where I
served.

I worked desperately in the big election campaign, sure the ALP
would win. I went to Canberra to the Vigil by Candlelight on the Wednesday night before the election and remember talking to Bob Hawke
who said to me: 'It will be close, but we will win.' I still wonder whether
he believed it or if he was trying to cheer me up.

Because of my many activities, I took part in television, radio and
newspaper interviews. ABC *Four Corners* did a profile of me. I received
an incredible amount of mail and invitations to address various groups.
Accepting them all, I spoke to Lions clubs, Rotary clubs, women's
organisations, schools, universities and community organisations.
Mainly they wanted to hear about migrant groups, ethnic radio and
related issues. I felt it was important work, spreading the word to my
fellow Australians about the kind of multi-cultural and multi-racial Australia so many of us wanted. I gave a lot of time to the republican
movement, to which I have always had a strong commitment. (I therefore felt amused when, in late 1976, I was offered an OBE for my
services to the ethnic communities, which I naturally refused.)

At the NSW Ethnic Communities Council my activities, considered
too political, were not appreciated. My efforts to move a motion to
save Medibank and other Labor government reforms were ammunition for those wanting to oust me from the council. At the 1976 annual
election, the men, Liberal and Labor, who dominated the council, ran
tickets together, excluding me and other women who had been active
and vocal. It was a bitter disappointment and a great political lesson.
Two years later I was back on the council, both as a vice-president
and convenor of the women's committee, but the betrayal of my friends
was something I have long forgiven but not forgotten. I went back
because I have always believed in the council's concept and ideals,
because ethnic groups need a forum to discuss their problems, to help
and support each other, to struggle and debate amongst ourselves for

a more just society. But the way my fellow Labor Party members betrayed me taught me well. As a woman, fired by great ideals, I had felt there were groupings in society from which one could always expect loyalty. But I learnt then that Labor solidarity and ethnic friendship could all go out of the window very easily in the face of personal political ambitions. I have become a more cautious person since then.

Winning a Churchill Fellowship, I left Sydney early in 1977 to travel for nearly five months to Italy, England, the United States and Canada, studying the integration of minority ethnic groups into the host society with particular reference to the role played by the media. It was a heavy workload, a time of loneliness, travelling to places where I knew no one, but a wonderful experience where I learnt a lot and met strong women active in the women's movement in other parts of the world.

In Italy I saw how much things had changed for my Italian sisters. In a country where the clergy has been said to have more power than capital, my Italian sisters had won *Il Diritto di Famiglia*, giving them equal rights and authority in the family and equal share in family properties, equal pay, and the divorce referendum which was fought tooth and nail by the church.

During the trip I was struck by the universality of human experience, the similar needs, thoughts and feelings experienced by all human beings in all cultures: desire for acceptance; need for love, pride and self-esteem; fear of hunger and pain. I attended meetings organised by minority ethnic groups. At times I pinched myself to realise I was indeed abroad. Discussions in Toronto or Boston could just as easily have taken place at the ethnic community councils in Sydney or Melbourne. It was comforting to know that in many places people like us were struggling to find answers, to reach solutions, to build a better and more just society. People were also interested to know what we were doing in Australia. In Canada I saw the Quebecois and English Canadians often referred to as 'the two solitudes'. I determined that in Australia we would not create a multitude of 'solitudes' but a cohesive, pluralistic society where there was an understanding and acceptance of such diversity – 'unity in diversity'.

It was a great trip. In London I was interviewed by the *Times* and the BBC on republican feelings in Australia since the 1975 coup. I told them there would be peaceful demonstrations during the Queen's visit in March 1977. This was reported by Australian newspapers. The Sydney *Sun* published letters to the editor under the heading 'Activist

Insulting Australia'—accompanied by my photograph. My husband
and family, who received some nasty calls, took the matter to the Australian Press Council; the complaint was upheld.

Before leaving Australia I had been appointed to the Women's Advisory Council to the NSW Premier. I served for two years as a member
and one as deputy chairperson. I loved the work. It gave me a much
closer affiliation with all types of women's organisations, from left to
right. It was the first such council in Australia.We were fifteen women
of diverse cultural, political and social backgrounds, from both urban
and rural areas, working together on problems concerning migrant
women, Aboriginal women, single mothers; prostitution, child-care,
child welfare legislation. Through an extensive country visit programme
I discovered rural Australia. I also visited women's prisons, making
friends with some of the women. We organised important meetings
for the International Year of the Child and also the NSW response
to the United Nations Mid-Decade for Women: a big Sydney convention in December 1979, with nearly 1000 women at Sydney Town
Hall. I spoke that day, saying: 'There is a realisation that to treat women
as lesser beings is to diminish us as a society. Quite simply, we cannot
afford to waste a huge proportion of Australia's most valuable resources:
its people.' I recalled John Stuart Mill's words: 'the improvement of
women's social position goes hand in hand with general social improvement, so that the elevation or debasement of women is the surest and
most correct measure of the civilisation of a people or an age'. As a
delegate from that convention I went to Canberra for the 1980 Mid-
Decade Conference.

On the Women's Advisory Council I made firm friends, met wonderful women, capable women, women who were always there to give
support and strength, firmly committed to the cause of equality. We
won many fights together. Some are now in politics, others in important government jobs. I tried to bring migrant women into the women's
movement and to get the women's movement to understand the
problems of migrant women. Together we bridged many gaps. I always
felt sisterhood was wonderful, though I accepted at times we had to
travel in different directions and at different paces.

To involve migrant women we had often to emphasise children to
overcome the suspicions of husbands. The Ethnic Communities Council Women's Committee organised an International Year of the Child
essay competition entitled 'I am an Australian too, the joy and anguish
of living between two cultures'. Over 400 essays were received and
twenty-three published in a booklet widely distributed to schools,

teachers and educationalists. It is a vivid statement of what our society has done to the children of migrants, how our school system fails, how divisive it can be not to be accepted, and how hurtful name-calling can be. Children, through those essays, told us what a traumatic and scarring experience migration can be.

From about 1975 I felt a sense of political impotence, because in the final analysis it seemed ethnics and women never got to actually *make* the important decisions. Little by little I developed a desire to run for public office. In October 1977, with Evasio Costanzo and other friends I formed the Italian Friends of Labor, the first political organisation in the Italian community in Australia since the war. We were active during and between elections. In 1979 I decided to run for Senate pre-selection in the Labor Party. I knew that the factions in the party would not back me because they had their own candidates. But I decided to stand as I was strongly supported by many in the ethnic groups. I also wanted to make it more difficult for the party to say: 'Women don't stand – migrants don't stand.' I knew I had no chance, but worked very hard at it. 420 delegates voted. I wrote to them all twice. I rang the great majority. Some women delegates said: 'I would like to vote for a woman, I think you are a good candidate, but I always vote with my faction.' Friends in the media and in other areas helped me in the campaign. I received great support from the Italian-language and Australian media. All in vain! Out of 420 votes I got 14. Another important political lesson. Indeed one often learns more from political defeats than from victories. Somebody from the party had said to me prior to the pre-selection: 'Franca, in this game there are two types of people, the sprinters and the stayers. Which are you?' I decided to become a stayer who can also sprint. In 1981 I was elected to the New South Wales' Legislative Council.

It has been put to me several times that by appointing me to various committees I became a sort of 'token ethnic woman'. Maybe so. I have never minded. I have always taken seriously my work on various bodies and felt it important to be a voice in whatever group I found myself. I am well aware that rights are not won on paper, but by those who make their voices heard.

The racists, the bigots, the male chauvinists are still with us, but since the 1970s we have made great steps forward. The difficulties, the problems, the failures and the achievements of the 1970s have been a lesson to us all. The sprinters may have left, but the stayers remain fighting for a better deal and for justice. Too many people in our society still suffer the pain of exclusion – people with much to contribute, but not being given the old Australian 'fair go'. Women, Aborigines, Australians of non-English-speaking backgrounds, do not want any more crumbs from the table: they want their equal share of duties, resources and decision-making.

I am fond of an old Fabian dictum: 'For the right moment you must wait: but when the time comes you must strike or your waiting will be in vain and fruitless.' I have always felt the right moment was now and the responsibility ours.

5 | Lilla Watson

Lilla Watson was born in Queensland and has lived in various country towns, and in Brisbane, ever since. In 1979 she was appointed as tutor in the Department of Social Work, University of Queensland, the first Aboriginal to be employed by that university. She has conducted research and field work in relation to the problems faced by Aboriginals in Queensland, and in 1980 was invited to attend the Australia's Future Conference hosted in Melbourne by Australian Frontiers.

Sister, Black Is the Colour of My Soul

I was born in spring in 1940, given my mother's name 'Lilla'. My grandmother died before we met, but I know her through my mother. As a small child I grew up secure in my family; I knew my father, I knew my mother, I knew my sisters and brothers. It wasn't until I began school that I was brought to a rude awakening. There was a black world and a white world. In the black world I was safe; in the white world I was unsafe.

It was obvious to me from my first school days that white people were unpredictable. This understanding of unpredictability came when my big sister took me to school for the first time and introduced me to her girlfriend's little sister (who was starting school that day too). I thought I had made a friend for life. However that was not to be. Most white kids I met at school did not or would not play with me. Sometimes (rarely) they did. This is where the unpredictability came in. I was never sure when or if they would play with me. Eventually I worked out that they only ever spoke or played with me if there were no other (white) kids around.

Once, my middle brother was invited by a white boy in his class to a birthday party. When he came home and told us, we were excited for him. It was the very first time any of us had been invited to a birthday party. Mum washed his best shirt, pressed his best serge (short) pants, and sent him off all shining clean. Years later my brother told us that when he turned up at the party he wasn't allowed in the door: the child's mother had come to the door, and seeing who it was, demanded 'What do you want?' When he said he had come for the birthday party she sent her child out to say to my brother, 'Sorry but you can't come to my party because you're black.' That same brother was made to stand up in front of his class and empty his pockets whenever any money or a rubber or pencil was reported missing.

When
I think
of
my childhood
it's
like
a bad dream
filled with nightmares
but
I never screamed
it's frozen inside
locked up
in me
hidden
deep down
where
white folks
can't see . . .

I actually went to school wanting to learn, wanting to get to know other kids and to be part of everything at school.

I did most of my growing up in a small country town. One vivid memory is of going to school one morning when the whole school was buzzing with talk about how a family had been forced to move from their house into a disused dairy shed. The white children said it was dreadful that the family had to live in such terrible conditions. I couldn't understand why they thought a disused dairy was a terrible place. We lived in a bag hut with a dirt floor and scraps of iron, bark from trees straightened out by my dad for a roof. The dairy was a well-constructed building with good solid walls and concrete floor. No one had offered us a dairy to live in.

I
can remember
when I
went to school
how
I'd approach
the gate
to my awaited fate
how my head
felt tight

like being squeezed
in a vice
with hate
and always, always
I was late
dragging my feet
in the dust
head bowed low
trying to think
of some excuse
to allow me
to go home
to try
and escape
the misery
and hate
How I hated
this thing
'schooling'
they said
'education's the thing'
I'd sit at my desk
and not learn a thing
and wish to hell
it had never
begun

In my first year of primary school, I remember walking home one day with a group of white children ahead of me. They were calling a well-known Aboriginal couple awful names, throwing stones at them as they sat in the gutter in the street. I was shocked that children could be so disrespectful of grown-ups. As I walked past the couple sitting at the kerbside, their backs were towards me, so they could not see me. I walked about 50 yards down the road when I had a strong compulsion to go back, to acknowledge them.

My parents had taught us to respect elders. I could not ignore the Aboriginal couple in the gutter. So I returned, walked out onto the road, and stood in front of them: 'Hello Mrs *Fuller*! Hello Mr *Fuller*!' They looked at me smiling. The man said: 'Hello, little girl. You run along home now before it gets too late.'

I remember mum taking my two older sisters down to the local dances. She and I would stand on the verandah, looking through the door-

way at my sisters dancing inside. They never danced with men; only
with each other; except there was one fellow who they danced with
occasionally and he was considered an outcast because he had been
born out of wedlock. But he was the only man I ever saw them dance
with in that small country town, and of course they were the only
black people who ever went to those dances.

We lived in the bush during my middle primary school years. On
Sundays my dad taught us to box. We drew a square in the dirt with
a stick. That was the boxing ring. Those nearest each other in weight
would be opponents. It did not matter that the boys boxed with the
girls. Even weight was fairly unimportant; the serious matter was
that we learned how to fight and how to defend ourselves.

My dad was a learned man. He taught us much, never differentiat-
ing between males or females in our family. When a job required
doing, whoever was there did it regardless of whether they were female
or male: tractor driving, truck driving, droving cattle, sewing bags
of wheat, ring-barking trees, cotton picking, and on, and on.

My mum was an educated person in our terms. She had gone to
third grade in primary school, but there wasn't a word she couldn't
spell, not always correctly, but she never failed to spell a word. She
knew the meaning of so many words. She was my dictionary in my
growing years. Mum encouraged us to read as widely as possible and
never once attempted to censor our reading. Our white counterparts
at school were never, never allowed to read the newspaper the *Truth*.
Of course it was old hat to us, the sex scandals, the murders, robbery
with violence and so on. Our mum let us read it all. We were made
to feel ashamed that our parents were so lax in allowing us to read
anything, so we were never game to tell the white kids at school that
we read that 'awful' paper.

My school days were the horror of my life. Big blanks hide memories
too painful to recall.

> I
> can remember
> when I
> went to school
> who had come
> from afar
> I can remember
> when I
> went to school

I used to race
to the cafe place
to be first
at the counter
to be served first
was the prize
in the end
I gave up
the chase
for no matter
how many times
I won
that race
I was always
served last
in that
cafe place

In the mid 1960s and early 1970s it seemed the world was in revolt—
the French student demonstrations in Paris, the American blacks in
revolt with Watts 'Burn, baby, burn', the anti-Vietnam war moratorium marches, demonstrations overseas and here in Australia. I was
part of it all. I wanted a change in my life too.

It took me half my lifetime to realise I was entitled to my mother's
mother's country, I was entitled to my mother's mother's language,
my mother's mother's history, and the laws that belong to that country. The greatest sadness in my life is the realisation that I will never
have any of those things. Those things are rightfully mine, I am entitled to them, but I will never have them. Both my father's father's
country and my mother's mother's country have some of the richest
coalfields in the world, and I know I will never have any title to that
land, I or my brothers or sisters will never own (in white terms of
reference) any of the land rightfully belonging to us.

If you are born black in this country, from the instant of birth you
are involved in the black struggle whether you wish to acknowledge
it or not. So I have been involved all my life in struggle. During the
1970s I became more involved, more active in the black movement.

Tribal council happened in Brisbane, on a national scale, in those days
of the early 1970s. Lots of anger, lots of energy, lots of movement.
I went to countless meetings, all the conferences, all the protest
marches. Aboriginal people knew (know) what's wrong with the world,

and I was going to help change it overnight. I even thought I could do it by myself, and tried very hard, but I didn't have enough strength, enough energy, enough time.

I can remember a group of us breaking into an office, regularly, to print our leaflets, notices, newsletters simply because we had no money and no other way to get our stuff printed. I was the 'cockatoo'; also I was the only one with a car.

I had to listen more, to other voices, other struggles. When the anti-Springbox protest took off in this country, I was right in there, shoulder to shoulder with the whites. This created a bigger struggle for me, because here were whites protesting about the oppression of black people in another country, yet not out in the streets protesting about the oppression of black people in their own country. Small groups gathered all over Brisbane discussing tactics to impede the games. I went to a small group meeting with my red-haired, blue-eyed friend who jumped up and said 'Let's throw broken bottles and bent nails on the field.' The horrified silence following this suggestion was broken by a shocked whisper, 'But that's violence!' I was stunned. Looking around at that roomful of white people I hated them all. How could they sit up there in their white skins and be shocked by the suggestion of use of violence, when it is they, white people, the colonisers who have brought violence into the lives of Aboriginal people in this country?

I didn't want to go on scrubbing floors, cooking, cleaning, and when Aboriginal study grants became available in the early 1970s, I went back to school to educate myself to play a better part for the black movement.

While I was studying for matriculation in 1972, the Aboriginal Embassy in Canberra was brought down by the McMahon Liberal government. The day it happened my sister, my brothers, my cousins and myself saw it on the 6 o'clock television news. We cried. By 7 o'clock we had collected enough petrol money to take us to Canberra. There were five – my brother Len, our cousin Tiga and his then wife Laurel, and a friend Donna, and myself. We stopped at Newcastle air-force base to speak with my brother Charlie, who was then a member of the force, to learn he had gone on a one-man strike in protest at the government's action. His superior officers didn't know how to handle the situation, so when he said he was leaving the base to carry his protest to Canberra, I think they were glad to see him go. The Embassy was part of our history. Today I am pleased and humble to have been a part of it.

Women's liberation voices got louder, they were heard more clearly, their messages straighter. I listened, got it straight in my head but not my heart; there was something wrong. A good woman wrote a book about women in Australia. I thought it was great until I bought the book, and looked and looked for something on Aboriginal women, and found about two lines mentioning us. Then it began finally to dawn on me that when white women speak of women's liberation, they speak only of white women's liberation, and rightly so. But they don't make it clear. They talk and write as if they are speaking for all women. Maybe eventually we will reach that stage. We haven't got there yet. We shouldn't act as if we have.

I do not say the 1960s and 1970s increased activities of the women's liberation movement had no effect on me. They did. I had to look at the position of women in society – that is, the position of Aboriginal women and white women. Arguments between black women and white women about women's oppression did not always have a meeting place. At times a great deal of hostility was expressed by black women towards white women in the women's liberation movement. This told me just how much black women have been conditioned by white society. Colonialism in Australia was brought about by violence. It introduced into the minds of Aboriginal people the concept of the native. Before the colonisers, there were no natives; later Aboriginal people were defined only in relation to white people, Aboriginal women were defined as against white women – they were compared and contrasted with them, dividing them. Aboriginal society and its values were so foreign to white settlers that many myths and misconceptions developed. Through the writings of Aboriginal people themselves, a clearer picture will emerge to project Aboriginal women's order of priorities and values, which will play an important part in our own liberation, whether we be black or white.

'Women's liberation movements will split the black movement.' 'Black liberation before women's liberation.' These were faint echoes from black America finding voice here in the Aboriginal scene in the 1970s. Some black people agreed. I strongly disagreed.

There was and is no question that I support in strongest terms women's liberation, whether it be for black or white women. Simultaneously it must be recognised that these two groups – black women and white women – will take two very different roads. But that does not mean opportunities will not arise for us to walk down each other's road for a short time. And surely eventually there must be only one road for us all. Black women's liberation also must be part and parcel of the whole liberation movement of black people in this country, to sustain that movement, strengthen it, and hold it together.

No one group, no one experience, stands out of the 1970s into the 1980s. Rather it is a multitude of people and experiences. But the one people who have contributed most to my learning, my growth, to my understanding, are my own mob, the indigenous people of this my country.

6 | Patricia Boero

Born in Lima, Peru, in 1952, of Uruguayan/Cuban parents, from 1952 to 1972 Patricia Boero lived in Santo Domingo and in Montevideo; studied in Stockholm, Sweden, then completed secondary school in Montevideo, matriculating into the law faculty. Emigrating to Australia in 1973, she studied at the University of New South Wales as well as at its Institute of Languages. She graduated BA with first class honours and the University Medal in 1979.

Patricia Boero co-founded and edited *El Expreso*, an ethnic newspaper, and in 1977 directed an animated film on the origins of flags of the world. She was co-founder of La Mascara theatre group; has worked for Channel 0/28; is a member of the Council of Hawkesbury College, and has been a member of the New South Wales' Women's Advisory Council.

The Double Burden: A Woman and a Wog

1972: Aged 20, living with my parents in Montevideo, studying for matriculation into the law faculty. Uruguay undergoing great political turmoil. Elections (the last) held where the left coalition won a significant part of the vote, but the right-wing governing party got the majority. Civilians and para-military engage in armed confrontations. Academic year interrupted by strikes, demonstrations of solidarity with political prisoners, heated political debate, rumours of coup.

1982: having completed BA at University of New South Wales and held a number of jobs in the welfare and administrative fields, I begin work in television. Buying first house (ever) together with my de facto husband of five years, John. Combining part-time work and full-time study. Graduate law course.

In some ways, it felt like starting again: back to vocational training, after discovering that an Arts degree is too vague for many jobs I've wanted and missed out on. Buying a house seems a big commitment to actually staying in Australia, after years of considering it just another option. Almost each year of my residence in Australia I've had to ask myself the question and decide again what I want to do, where I want to live and whom I want to live with. It amazes me to think that I could buy several hectares of Uruguay in exchange for our few square metres in an inner-city suburb.

Buying a house also reflects my commitment to my relationship with John, a *compañero* in the true sense of the word, who shares my ideology and interests. We both feel strong ties with Latin America. I was able to travel back five times between 1972 and 1982, my own identity continuing to fluctuate between my growing Aussie-ness and my 'other half', still crying for Argentina, Uruguay, El Salvador. This doesn't mean I've been affluent here, but my economic policy has been to always leave enough saved in an emergency fund for a ticket back 'home', with my family. Even during my most frugal years as a student, I managed to set aside other consumer products and travel back. I do this partly to ease the guilt I still feel for having left, and to compensate for the pain and loss I've caused my family. But it's also pleasurable, uplifting, recharging all my energies to return 'home', too, to Australia to lead the life I've chosen.

For years I had argued against and resented the privileges that any society, and particularly the Latin-Hispanic one, gives to men. In my early memories I heard anecdotes of my parents' worry for only having daughters, and the prayers to produce a male heir. I always hated housework and resisted all attempts at indoctrination, but it was in the area of personal freedom that I felt most restricted. My sister and I had precise hours to be home at night, and strict rules for obtaining permission for any activity. Although the authoritarianism was amply compensated by the loving, almost excessive possessiveness of my parents and the strong support I received for my intellectual endeavours, I felt as if what mattered most was my hymen and not my brain. As a result of these restrictions, I developed into a compulsive liar and an accomplished actress, conducting my sexual life in the daytime under complicated alibis, returning home to play the 'good girl' at the dinner table. So, immigration to Australia was a fairly logical step to take, in view of the disastrous political and economic situation of the country, and it was also a way to achieve personal freedom that would have been impossible to obtain while depending on my father for economic survival. This is my briefest explanation to the question: 'Why did you migrate to Australia?' which I so often hear. The immigration was precipitated by my rash decision to marry an Australian resident I met in Uruguay.

My first months here, in 1973, seemed like hell. All the restrictions my father had imposed on me were now continued and worsened by my husband and his Catholic mother (both English). I realised to my surprise that people expected me to be a 'nice Catholic girl' with a solid training in household duties. Admittedly I had only known my husband for six months or so, under different circumstances. But now everything seemed more obvious and sinister, like a trap or a conspiracy to force me into submission. My reaction was violent, and that itself generated more violence. I ended up in Tasmania, and the expression 'just the two of us' took on a new terrifying meaning for me – I wondered how I would escape that situation. The first step had to be economic independence. Nothing is more humiliating and frightening than to realise you have no money of your own. That applies to any woman's liberation – the first step is economic independence; not in the sense that we have to save enough to actually pay for huge consumer commodities, but to have enough to survive on, and prove to men that they have no power over us. That is another reason why

giving women equal opportunity and access to employment is so
important.

In those circumstances, I came to appreciate the sense of security
that an extended family can provide. In early 1973 I had never heard
of a women's refuge, but was determined to leave and live on my own,
even if it meant in the poorest conditions. One of the greatest morale
boosts came from Germaine Greer and her book *The Female Eunuch*,
which I devoured during the peaceful hours at work. My first job,
after approaching the Tassie CES with my linguistic qualifications,
was as hat-check girl at Wrestpoint Casino. I had no time for self-pity
or anger about the kind of job I was given; I was grateful for any money
I could get. We lived with friends of my husband, and my hostess
Ruth, a beautiful woman I've always wanted to thank, sympathised
with me. She lent me feminist books, encouraging me to make it on
my own. She also provided concrete help – the circumstances of my
escape are so melodramatic, they are difficult to narrate. Let's just say
that after very angry scenes, Ruth called the police and I was escorted
to the airport.

In Sydney I remained paranoid about my husband reappearing, and
went through every possible precaution to avoid being tracked down.
Many women in refuges and hiding must have experienced that constant worry, looking over the shoulder, fear of ever being alone, giving
false names. I remember approaching the public solicitor in the city
to discover my rights to protection. I was horrified it took three years
to obtain a divorce and I could get no physical protection. (Those were
the olden days. The law is now much more realistic.) I felt betrayed
when my parents actually revealed a post office box number that I'd
given them, thinking they might help me reconcile with my husband.
I then completely broke with them. I kept to myself and my new-found
friends in Sydney. Now, as the years pass, all is healed, and my relations with my parents improved after they realised I was *not* going
to return to them and live under their wings as the 'disgraced divorcee'.

The Hobart CES experience was repeated in Sydney: as soon as I
arrived, I went looking for work. Then I was more fluent in the five
languages I had learnt; today I've been reduced to a mere bilinguist
through lack of practice. My skills did not impress the CES officer,
who directed me to a factory in Chatswood where I was put on a dirty
big bench to solder transformers – the 'training' lasted five minutes;
I sat next to a Chilean woman, Irma, who gave me the friendship and
solidarity I so badly needed. I thus became 'Maria en la Fattoria', an
ethnic version of Rosie the Rivetter.

I was frequently harassed by the foreman and other male workers. I was probably the youngest (and to all appearances single) woman on the factory floor. This meant a daily onslaught of innuendos and advances that infuriated me. Other young women seemed to be 'protected' by brothers or husbands who either worked there or were a deterrent for overt sexual harrassment. My first reaction was to counter attack and insult them back (something I'd do in Latin America if someone harrassed me in the street). That only brought hilarity and seemed to encourage the men even more. I was dubbed the 'women's libber' and they loudly speculated on whether I was wearing a bra or not. Most other women didn't support my sole stand against the men. They probably thought I must be a 'bad woman' for answering the men's remarks loudly and aggressively.

At home I cried with anger and frustration. But I was determined to become a self-made woman. I rejected my father's offer to return home conditional on my acceptance of his patriarchal authority. Had I known of a woman's group or refuge, perhaps those days would have been easier for me. I still felt luckier than the other women who had much more to lose and could not afford to put their job at risk by taking a more militant stand. Being fluent in English was important. But I too feared being sacked, and when it finally happened (a power strike coincided with the foreman's decision to get rid of the 'stirrers' first – most of us were casually employed and had no right to holiday or sick pay), I protested. They then threatened to 'dob me in' to the authorities. To their surprise I showed them my passport with resident's visa. I carried it everywhere, an old habit from the police-terror in Uruguay. I still lost my job and, as I collected my pay from the office, saw other migrant women queuing up to fill my vacancy. All were accompanied by men, and wore scarves over their hair, and aprons. The men did the negotiations. It was a heart-breaking and pathetic scene. I felt the impulse to run across to them and shout 'sisters, run away, you have nothing to lose but your chains'. But any notion of instant liberation seemed so distant, and their masters were so near to them. They looked terrified and maybe they were all illegal – the factory certainly had no union; it was like a medieval ghetto in the middle of Sydney's prosperous north shore suburbs.

Years later I still remember those women and ask myself how to reach their consciousness. They have been left so far behind by the confident, militant liberationists marching Sydney's streets each year, shouting slogans and reproaching their less articulate sisters for not coming out all the way. There is no quick or easy solution to this

problem. Access to education and increased migrant and female participation in trade unions seem to be the first steps towards protecting
their rights. Migrant women who march are usually concerned with
human rights in their own countries, or issues like the treatment of
female prisoners in the Villawood detention centre for illegal
immigrants. They protest against conditions as humiliating and oppressive as those underlying some of the other causes so strongly
campaigned for by liberationists born in Australia.

The reluctance of some of my migrant female friends to join the
feminist movement can sometimes be traced to that distrust (or mis-
conception?) of feminism as a 'divisive' and bourgeois invention that
puts women before the priorities of the Third World: the elimination
of poverty and racism, class struggle, human rights, the release of political prisoners, the defeat of fascism. These priorities may seem too
vague, distant or dramatic to a typical Australian feminist, but are
immediate and real to a Latin American. Although Australian women's
issues are of great importance to migrant women, they seem dispropor-
tionate to the suffering we know. Atrocities committed by our dictators,
the suffering of our compañeras – the Mothers of the Plaza de Mayo,
the prisoneras and campesinas – seem such urgent priorities, that an
issue like tax deductions for child-care pales by comparison (even
though the recognition of those concerns sometimes paralyses us in
despair – where do you start?).

It often angers me to hear well-intentioned left-wingers ask us about
'the situation with regard to abortion and homosexuality in your country'. Both Latin American women and men hearing this question cannot
immediately see these issues as urgent or isolated, when illiteracy or
infant mortality loom so large in the Third World. Many migrants
I've talked to might add that some of the current trendy gay cliques
can be right-wing or reactionary in their own right.

It is understandable that migrant women regard working in the larger
or mainstream organisations as more effective than joining the radical
fringe of the women's movement. The women's organisations I belong
to, like the Union of Australian Women and the Australian Federa-
tion of University Women, seem willing to listen to migrant women
and are beginning to make a conscious effort to incorporate us into
their ranks. Both groups have been accused of following too rigid political or class affiliations, but it's interesting to note that women's
organisations which are more middle-class or middle-of-the-road
oriented, like WEL or the women's advisory councils, have minimal
migrant participation.

There are also special interest groups formed by migrant women, like the Black Immigrant and Third World Women's Association, the Latin American Women's Group in the western suburbs of Sydney, or the committee which organised and follows-up the Migrant Women's Speak-Out Conference. Although for obvious reasons they too are led by women who are more articulate and educated, their work, focussed on local issues and needs, is as valid as that of mainstream groups. They are also an important starting point for raising consciousness and confidence in migrant women to participate more fully in broader areas. But there is a danger that our energies might be dispersed in too many different directions. This concern led me to consider joining larger organisations that would defend the rights of the working class. So in 1980 I joined the ALP.

I was lucky to have lived through the Whitlam years, thus knowing that an alternative to Fraserism was possible. Perhaps immigrants arriving much earlier or later would be more willing to accept the Liberals as the 'natural rulers' of this country. I was outraged at the 1975 coup, and disappointed that people did not take to the streets to protest – the least I expected was a general strike. After all, my own little country had braved a fifteen-day general strike after a much more threatening and bloodier coup in 1973. I was equally disappointed with each re-election of the Fraser government and this, plus encouragement from migrant friends who already belonged to the ALP, made me decide to join. The minority left-wing parties seemed too factionalised and weak. So I thought it may be more effective to have a say, however small, within a mass organisation. Of course the Labor Party has its own racists and right-wingers, but at least one sees the basic platform as more humane than the predatory free enterprise ideology that wants to institutionalise exploitation. (What is rather disconcerting is meeting progressive individuals within the Liberal Party who may be more sympathetic to migrants than our own true-blue-collar comrades!) Being in the same party as such intelligent and outspoken women as Senator Susan Ryan and Franca Arena, MLC, strengthens my commitment. It boosts my morale when I hear them speak, and I think women should more actively support them.

A common fallacy is to lump together all immigrant women, as if we were all clones. Even more sophisticated and sympathetic organisations claiming to be 'aware' and 'sensitive to' the diversity (so much 'nicer' than class distinctions) of migrant women, are still practising tokenism and burdening a single migrant woman with the responsibility of 'representing' the opinions and interests of all migrant women.

This is happening on committees, councils; in political parties, courses, programmes; especially where our time and skills can be used *free*. But we remain grossly underrepresented – or totally absent from senior levels, where decisions are being made, where our influence could increase and where it could be 'legitimised' by adequate remuneration and job security. Our minimal input into the policies of these venerable democratic institutions is limited and fragmented, falling on the already busy backs of a handful of 'migrant women activists' who have to put their own careers, families, or leisure aside, to dedicate themselves selflessly to the unpaid mission of sitting around tables waiting for the meeting to get to the bottom of the agenda, where lies the issue *we* are concerned about.

The pressures on us migrant women sometimes make us feel as if we are being forced into a 'mission' in life. A friend of mine doing a post-graduate degree complained the other day of her female supervisor encouraging her rather too forcibly to specialise in 'the psychology of migration'. I imagine other migrant women trapped in the same way, specialising in the sociology, history or economics of migration. That too is a limitation. Suppose we felt just as strongly about a career in fine arts, astronomy or hydraulic engineering? Are we to be confined to the narrow guidelines determined by the dominant culture, in order to relieve others of *their* responsibilities to 'specialise' in us as subject matter? The rise of a close network of Anglo-Australian 'sisters' in some white-collar occupations, and the proliferation of consultative committees could, paradoxically, be limiting our choices.

I hesitate after saying these things. Perhaps there will be a backlash, a reaction against us, thinking we are ungrateful for not accepting tokenism with gratitude, as a progressive step that will lead eventually to equal participation. I can identify with Aboriginal women, and feel we somehow share this dilemma: if we participate in the small way permitted, are we 'selling out'? Are we 'losing touch' with our communities? There will always be someone more militant, more outspoken, within our own groups, ready to point the accusation at us, the token participators. Do we have a right to speak for others who haven't actually voted us onto committees, but may have indirectly encouraged us to front up for them? Is the time spent on meetings, discussions, in lecture halls, street marches, better spent working directly in and with our 'communities'? How selective can we be about our own 'cultural heritage'? Can we actually rescue the values we want; or is there only a clear-cut choice between cultures, where we get the good and the bad in a 'package' deal?

Migrant girls and women are trapped in the worse aspects of the two cultures. At home they must be on the defensive, to prove they're not 'sluts', and at school or work or on the street they have to confront their peers' hostility for not being 'liberated' enough. But at least they can count on some of the benefits of an extended family network, like in Cuba where 'grannies' still seem to involve themselves actively with the young, not just as 'unpaid babysitters' but in the tasks of the whole neighbourhood; there, solidarity exists in all areas of life. For me, since childhood my 'role models' have been my revolutionary Cuban aunts. I finally met them in 1981, after years of correspondence, and confirmed my admiration for them. Yet there is another side. At times I fear that the price of company and solidarity in an extended family can be the lack of privacy, the gossip and interference in the lives of the young. The 'grannies' can reinforce the patriarchal values, smothering their male off-spring with domestic services which contribute to machismo, taking for granted the skills of cooking, serving; and 'competing' with the wife for domestic tasks. I experienced some of this schizophrenia in Stockholm, where I grew up and went to school, and I have been able to cope much better in Australia, where at least I could decide how to live my private life without the well-intentioned guardians policing all my actions. It's ironic that it was easier for me to become independent from my parents so many thousands of miles away. It would have been nearly impossible to do so in Montevideo, or any other Latin American city, because of a combination of tradition and economic obstacles.

As for Australian men, I have no complaints so far as personal experience goes. I lived with a man for several years, and he supported me through the traumas of factory jobs, encouraging me to study for my high school certificate and later through university. Tom had to bear the brunt of my 'growing pains' and my sometimes very selfish preoccupations with *my* rights to be free from housework, child-bearing, alienating work, and monogamous expectations. In later years I have come to realise how important his support was, and it would be unfair to attribute my success in academia and my active participation in politics and ethnic or women's affairs solely to the enlightened words of paperback feminist publications or sisterly solidarity.

But the women's movement helped immeasurably. It meant that universities, employers, institutions were more receptive to the needs of women and equal opportunity. My good fortune was to coincide with this public awakening and be able to take full advantage of the educational opportunities arising in the Whitlam years. So too did many older women returning to the workforce and studies, and I felt very close to them. My female teachers and tutors also gave me the support and trust that helped me overcome doubts about my career prospects.

People's assumptions that my successes in my studies were due to a migrant's 'ambition to progress' were odd. My story was actually more like 'from riches to rags', as I survived on TEAS and a little more than help from my friend. Some of the poorest but most rewarding years of our lives went by, enjoying the pleasures our bed, table and garden offered. I was no longer paranoid about participating in political activities, meetings, and rallies, wearing my ponchos and badges oblivious to the cameras of the ASIO men lining George Street as we marched by. Some of those marches were for International Women's Day. Tom and another male friend marched with me the first year, but later I marched alone, not because Tom felt any differently about the women's movement, but because, I think, he felt slightly uncomfortable in the same company as some of the more aggressive contingents. I think it a shame so few men march. When I visited Cuba, their celebration of women's day seemed to be more significant and joyful. *Every* woman was honoured that day, by *everyone*. Not just a 'separatists'' march, or a militant's conscious protest. Rather more like a national holiday set aside especially to honour all women. Every woman seemed to receive cards, or presents, or calls and visitors that day. The same thing happened on Mother's Day. I was staying at the flat of Angelica, an old, black, urban 'mamma' who that day received literally dozens of personal tributes from the people who loved her. They included men and women of all ages and backgrounds, some of whom she had helped to rear in the days before the revolution arrived with its welfare services for women, and its child-care facilities. Incidentally, her one and only biological son also turned up on that day but was treated no differently from the rest of us who were made to feel like her legitimate children too.

In my personal life I was probably less aware of the effects of feminism than in public. My rejection of marriage, and anything resembling domesticity, created some tensions. I became impatient with anyone who didn't fully agree. I postponed plans for motherhood, using contraceptives for years, resenting the risks I was taking to avoid pregnancy. (Contrary to myths of Latins' procreation rites, Uruguayan families are generally small; the country has one of the lowest birth rates in the world.) My then partner was going through his own traumas, having left a wife and two kids and suffering the worst consequences of her vendetta. She did not allow him to see his sons often and deliberately created distrust and distance between him and the children. I fully sympathised with *his* needs and *his* rights, and this really cut across any feeling of solidarity with her. Seeing him work his guts out, our frugal existence, I began to suspect an element of blackmail in the alimony payments and legal procedures. It took years for any 'friendly arrangement' to emerge, and I have always felt my share of the guilt associated with Tom's loss of his sons.

This may be an exceptional case. My present situation is far more civilised. My partner, John, has regular access to his daughters and we both participate in their upbringing. This is thanks to the co-operative attitude of their mother, of course. It has been an important lesson for me to see the two sides of the argument – the woman's, and the other, male, side. Again I see this issue in economic terms. It's really only the rich in this country who can afford divorce and multiple families. Usually the 'other woman' in a man's life has to arm herself with patience and understanding, postponing her own plans for maternity or career, helping to pay a higher proportion of household expenses to allow the first family to maintain its living standards. We stepmothers have also to keep a fine balance between loving his kids and wanting to be involved in their education, and still being regarded as a late-comer, an amateur by the 'real' or biological parents who claim, and have, ultimate say in questions relating to the children's education, ideology, time-tables, lifestyle. Sometimes I can't help feeling a little used, as a babysitter or financial contributor, and excluded when the joys and rewards of parenthood are dished out. But my feminism has helped me cope with this, because I am always aware of the 'legitimate' mothers' rights, and other women's plight in having to support their children single-handed. As I developed a feminist consciousness, I was a bit on guard, watching my 'maternal inclinations' with some mistrust and wondering whether they were the result of conditioning, brainwashing. I have seen many examples of people using children as blackmail, excuses or extensions of their egos, and I decided to have mine only after being absolutely sure. I have now reached the stage where I'm impatient to try it. I enjoy being with my step-daughters, and think this has also prepared me for maternity in a very realistic way.

Looking back, I don't think I would have got this far, this fast, alone. The women's movement certainly helped create a more favourable climate for my acceptance into the positions I have held in the workforce after university, and as an adviser. I sometimes think I am too actively sought out as the 'migrant women's spokesperson' or 'expert'. I am beginning to withdraw a little, feeling drained, regretting having postponed or repressed my own private needs and desires to pursue an active involvement in public concerns, and being considerate of the needs of the other women in my men's lives. I now feel ready for another season of studies and married life, without fear of becoming a stereotype of the bored and bourgeois housewife.

I changed jobs, resigning from a position involving direct one-to-one contact in community services to migrants, and administrative duties. I felt exploited and underpaid, not so differently from when I had had blue-collar jobs before university. Entering the media brought some strange reactions from other women, as if I 'betrayed' the cause by appearing on the TV screen. But it was a relief to have an exciting and satisfying part-time job after all those years of high pressure jobs in a semi-voluntary capacity.

My decision to study law in 1983, the thirty-first of my life, felt tentative. I was optimistic and enthusiastic but had doubts about my suitability. I was longing to understand fully our legal system, but the pomp and arrogance of it made me apprehensive. I wanted, in a very Aussie sense, to 'give it a go'. This did not mean turning away from the women's movements, but endeavouring to bring in other migrant women to participate in all Australian institutions, unions, political parties – even committees and sub-committees. We need many more trained specialists to assume the so-called leadership roles, and to break the barriers of ignorance and prejudice in the professions as well as on the factory floor. In the remaining years of the 1980s, I hope to continue my own modest contribution in the same direction. As our black comrades in Grenada say: 'Forward ever, backward never!'

7 | Elizabeth Williams

Elizabeth Williams was born in Cobram, Victoria, in November 1954. In 1980 she was appointed by the New South Wales Minister for Health to the Queanbeyan Hospital Board, and in 1982 was elected chairperson of the board. She is a health care worker who is currently director of family day care with the Queanbeyan City Council in New South Wales.

Aboriginal First, Woman Second

In 1972 I was eighteen years old, pregnant, and living in a housing commission flat in Sydney with my mother. Before becoming pregnant I worked as an office girl for Willow Ware kitchen suppliers. I had not heard of the women's movement. My knowledge of it as a force came some years later.

I was raised the youngest of fifteen children and was told I was as good as anyone else and usually better. I am more assertive than other members of my family and it is probably true that a certain aggressive consciousness of identity tolerated in my time was not tolerated earlier. I profited from the time I was born into. And these days young Aborigines are much more aware, a welcome sign.

During 1973–5 I lived in a de facto relationship in Sydney, then decided to move to Wagga Wagga to improve my lifestyle and that of my child, particularly our housing. I also wanted to escape what had become an increasingly violent relationship. The move was the beginning of a whole new existence for me. At this time my only income was the supporting mother's benefit. Then I was fortunate to get the health worker's position at Griffith in New South Wales. The job was with the Health Commission and I worked with the local Aborigines and those living in the outer-lying areas. Working with my own people gave me a sense of well-being and fulfilment I had not previously experienced. I gained insight into the problems of Aboriginal people, and being involved in helping meant I enjoyed the work tremendously, despite constant exposure to deprivation and inhuman conditions. I felt I was doing something real to help.

You can understand the local black community of Griffith being a little upset that a black from Wagga (some 150km away) should be selected a health worker in their area. This problem was quickly overcome. My name was a great help: Williams can be an advantage (and sometimes not) in Aboriginal communities from the Northern Territory to Western Australia. I had some hassles with the white office staff, but was sure to let them know I considered myself the expert and would not allow them to make me a puppet. My attitude made the blacks proud.

The community I worked in suffered beyond human endurance, subjected to all that is preventable. Health problems were, and remain, many. Heart disease, liver disorders, middle ear infection, malnutrition, alcoholism. Overcrowding in the ten small cottages well below standard was as high as twenty-five to one house – a conservative figure. The women were obviously the stronger of the two sexes. The families were kept together with the best know-how possible on the women's part, but to see the hardship was saddening and frustrating.

I was humbled on many occasions. One man in particular, an alcoholic, would always send for me when he needed to get to hospital. He wouldn't go for anyone else. It didn't matter how drunk or how sick, where he was, or what time. He knew I'd make sure he got the right treatment – by that I mean treated like a human being as well as having his physical needs taken care of. Each time he recovered, he would bring me something to say 'thank you' and tell me there should be more like me. He died. So too did others, young and old. Deaths upset me and made me angry, especially when small efforts could have saved life.

The health worker programme brought workers together several times annually for seminars and lectures. This provided the strength to go back and continue, for when working we all felt great despair. The get-togethers also provided many happy times. There is nothing like the black sense of humour. A dear friend, Condo as she's known, gave us plenty to laugh about. You have to be able to laugh at circumstances in order to survive, and she provided all the comedy we could handle. Through this programme, many were educated. Some were much older than I. Condo, in her nineties, couldn't read or write. Before I left she came through the course with flying colours. That was a great moment for all of us, when real achievements showed through. The programme gave me a chance to achieve what I thought important, too. The main task for me was to provide a support system among the young and impressionable, working within existing institutions with integrity to show we are a worthy race with a multitude of skills. The main goal, to promote the worthiness of being Aboriginal.

Then, in 1980, I decided to marry. I had to resign and moved to Canberra with my husband. He, bless him, is not only white but a welfare officer. Among many Aborigines this automatically gives him an approval rating of about three, on a scale of one to ten. Never mind. We are quite happy and have a lovely black (well, almost) baby.

Living in Queanbeyan, near Canberra, in that year a group of us set out to show a different side to young blacks. Always we've been

promoted on postcards, tea-towels or coasters standing on one leg leaning on a spear and (not forgetting) with a kangaroo. While holding
our culture in high regard, we are tired of being seen only in that way.
We set out to show just how beautiful black can be, organising a black
modelling show. The women's movement didn't grant full support,
the reasons probably being cosmetic beauty is not desirable if you are
a woman. (A little like not wearing a bra to prove a point and suffering the physical pain of being a little too large.) Our aim was to show
we are able to achieve in any field. We taught basic modelling and
staged a fashion parade with an audience of 700 at a local shopping
centre. It was a proud moment. All our models looked superb and carried off the show with great style. Although it didn't go on to bigger
things, we proved a point. And we aren't ready yet for the world of
big fashion. It's hard at this stage to worry too much about the cloth-
ing that makes the body look extra good, when it's difficult to feed
the body to be healthy.

It's one thing to get a job in an Aboriginal organisation, but it can
be daunting for an Aboriginal to apply for a job in an all-white organisation, in competition with able white applicants. When I applied for
the position of co-ordinator with the Queanbeyan City Council family
day care programme I was unsure of myself. The post had never been
held by a black. But the council showed their good sense in selecting
me. Working with the programme, apart from the commitment I have
to everyday questions and the direction of activities, I believe this
appointment will stand me in good stead when I return to an Aboriginal organisation, which I intend to do eventually: my life should be
there, doing what I can.

During my time as co-ordinator I've taken on another role, becoming something of an Aboriginal liaison person: Aborigines come to me
for help and advice, and I can help through what I have learnt of the
system. Queanbeyan has approximately 800 blacks. Accommodation
is cheaper than in Canberra. Many blacks work in Canberra and live
in Queanbeyan, yet for this large population there is not one Aboriginal person attached to any government department. This being a
transient town, I see people from Griffith, Wagga, Condoblin, Melbourne, Western Australia, Sydney, as well as Canberra. I am well
known throughout the area, so agencies use me too – if there is a
problem with one of the pupils, the schools come to me; also the health
centre, Youth and Community Services Department, the police, hospital, the council, CES, social security, and women's refuges come to
me. I enjoy doing anything, if asked. As well, Aboriginal people help

me. This is the part of the job I welcome and relish. If an Aboriginal person comes in on a day I've had enough of the whites, it's such a refreshing change. It allows me to recharge my batteries. Dealing daily with white people, I find this recharging necessary. At one stage I had so many Aborigines coming to see me I could sense some objections and decided I should let my boss know in case of repercussions. I need not have worried. I was told so long as I did the work I was paid for, my 'liaison role' was okay.

In December 1981 I was appointed by the Minister for Health as director on the Queanbeyan Hospital Board. My experience in community work and being Aboriginal helped. The following year, in December, I was nominated as chairperson by two other women directors, and was elected by majority. I had no idea of the flack in store for me. My election upset a few people – some on the board. At that December meeting the tension was high. I was stunned. This was the first time I had experienced such strong feelings against me. I asked the chief executive officer to continue chairing the remainder of the meeting.

The board wasn't to meet again until February 1983, due to the Xmas break. That left me two months to prepare myself for the big test. Being a small community, news travels fast. People I thought would be happy with my new appointment now presented a complete turnabout. Some showed outright rudeness, ignoring me. Some were disgusted I would even consider myself capable of performing the duties of chairperson. Others urged me to resign. To avoid further abuse I found myself walking the back streets and staying home. Just when I thought calm had arrived, I received a letter from my predecessor. My first reaction on reading it was shock. I read it many times before the words sank in. Before the letter arrived, I was under tremendous pressure to resign. Now I was angry. This man had such a nerve to send me what was an awful letter. Little did he realise his words would have the opposite effect of what he intended. I would now do the job and do it well, in fact better than any of my white male predecessors.

I received support from my husband and family. They along with the black community are very proud of me. The four women voting for me on the board were supportive, as well as some women outside, members of the women's movement. Although I strongly appreciated their support, I knew the order in which I had it was as woman, then as black, then the democratic vote, while I at all times am black first, woman second, then the democratic vote.

This was the first time a black Australian had held the position of

chairperson of a hospital board. In the past, our only position in
any hospital was as patients (if we were allowed in) or domestic staff,
cleaning the floors and treated very much like the trash we cleaned.
It's a jump from the floors to the head of the table. I consider my
appointment a great advancement for the Aboriginal cause and hope
many will follow my lesson, learnt through this ordeal: that opinion
has not changed. It's still very clear that if you're black and don't rock
the boat, you might be suffered, as a token. I am not a token, and
won't be.

Over the years the Catholic church has funded me as a delegate to
their Justice and Peace conferences. I was with our renowned Mum
Shirl visiting the Sisters of Justice Mercy Convent in Canberra when
asked to represent them at a seminar in Perth. I thought about being
bogged down with religion and nearly decided not to go. I need not
have worried. No one tried to convert me and I came home with lots
of new-found knowledge. I presume I'm invited to the conferences for
my provocative viewpoint; I know it is not for my religious background.
    At the Western Australian conference I saw at first hand just how
badly blacks are treated in that state. We were to spend a day visiting
organisations such as St Vincent de Paul and the Salvation Army, half-
way houses. I had no interest in seeing these places and went to as
many Aboriginal organisations as I could. My days there showed me
a lot. I visited the Aboriginal Legal Services office and from there,
Bob Riley was my guide for the remainder of the time. The Perth
Children's Court had sixteen courts in session at once and mainly all
Aboriginal kids. Their treatment was appalling. It seemed common
practice for police to lock them into lockers and bash the outside with
bats.
    We went to a settlement roughly 5 kilometres from inner-city Perth.
Five vans had been donated by a mining company – with one toilet,
one washing tub, one shower and one light to service all the families
living in the vans. That visit above all was upsetting. The babies were
sick. The adults showed such loss it is difficult to describe. They are
terrorised by the police. The young women are raped; bashings are
common. Just a little way through the scrub was a park area where
the practising Klansmen bashed Aborigines to the point of death. I
was devastated with what I saw. I met a woman about forty years old,
who thought I could do something. If only I could. It was hard for
her to understand I was there for my own interest, and was not con-
nected to a higher power, or its messenger.
    After visiting Western Australia, I think we over here don't have

any problems at all. To see such apathy about the destruction of Aboriginal culture was so clear in WA, even more so than in the Northern Territory or South Australia. Although bad throughout the country, that destruction showed dramatically in Western Australia.

Later, from a conference in Alice Springs the one memory that stays with me is that the locals consider us of the quarter-cast or half-cast to be white. A strange feeling for me – then I knew what it felt to be of no race at all. It is a sad day when blacks reject you because of your percentage of white blood, however small.

In some ways I have adopted the women's movement and in some ways the movement has adopted me. This has been to my advantage on occasions, but I dare say it works both ways, and the advantage has been reciprocated. I appreciated the support of feminists through the hospital board episode, and their continuing solidarity. But it helps the feminist movement to have me to promote to the position.

Though I know some strong and caring feminists, I have some negative thoughts also. Thinking about the way the women's movement operates, having worked with women's refuges, it seems to me that the obvious good of having refuges is often spoiled by 'feminist' power plays and double-dealing. Among the enlightened and liberated women of the 'movement', there continue to be patronisers and those who would use Aborigines for their own purposes.

Although this is not a forum for the black cause, land rights, or the 'white problem' which is the basis of all problems facing Aborigines, I feel strongly that the women's movement should support Aboriginal issues. And that this support will reap benefits for all disadvantaged Australians. My daughter Bianca is a child of great spirit who wears her Aboriginality proudly. The women's movement has made huge gains through the 1970s and into the 1980s, and it is a combination of this pride in being female which is promoted by the movement, and the pride in being black which comes with the land rights movement and black movement generally, that has led to my daughter being able to be proud as a woman and as an Aborigine. But much work remains to be done. Often the women's movement is unable to see where importance lies. Not long after returning from my WA trip, members of the women's movement asked me if I would march in an Anzac Women Against Rape march on 25 April. How dare they even ask. They were objecting to what happened in the past – yet live in a country where it's still happening today. Will they march for the black cause, for the cause of black women?

Australia's history of racism and sexism is so bad we must believe things will improve. The groundwork for a more sharing and equitable society has commenced; agitation by women and blacks has led the way to achieving the goal.

I am determined to help by succeeding in positions I hold and aspire to. The knowledge and skills I am developing in the white world will be useful when it is time for me to return to working with black Australians. I am learning skills through feminist friends, too. Still, I believe that black Australia's main concern, women or men, is racism, not sexism.

Part Two

Moving between
Two Worlds

8 | Elizabeth (Biff) Ward

Born 29 November 1942, Elizabeth (Biff) Ward is the author of *Father-Daughter Rape*, published by the Women's Press in 1984. She is also a poet and is working on a novel. She was 'pleasurably involved' in organising the Mt Beauty Women's Liberation Theory Conference of January 1973, and the Anarchist Feminist Conference of October 1975. For her, the Women for Survival protection camps at Pine Gap in 1983 and Cockburn Sound in 1984, in which she was involved, are important events in Australian feminist history.

Having spent most of her life in New South Wales, Elizabeth Ward moved to Alice Springs in 1982. She now lives in Adelaide where she works as an equal opportunity officer in the Department of Education.

On Being Late

I am late in writing this. Yet lateness signifies not tardiness, not disorganisation nor unwillingness – it signifies what has happened to me in the process of becoming and being a women's liberationist.

I became a women's liberationist in January 1970 when I had my first contact with other women who identified as such. I was then twenty-seven years old, living in Canberra, near the high mountain country and the beautiful south coast of south-east Australia. Although I appreciated the proximity to 'natural', that is, non-city, places even then, that appreciation was to turn into something much larger, much deeper, and much wider than I could ever have imagined back there in 1970.

At that time I was living with a man with whom I had, until then, shared as much of my life as I could for five years. A year before I had given birth to twins, a boy and a girl. My daughter of my first (and only legal) marriage, six years older than the twins, lived with us too. The man and I both worked as high school teachers; I enjoyed my work and gave a lot of creative energy to it. But for both of us, throughout those five years, our primary focus was the Movement against the Vietnam War. I developed comprehensive organisational skills, learning many conflicting left-wing theories about 'mass actions' and street demonstrations. All my real friendships, my social and emotional life, were to be found within this political matrix.

Indeed, it was within this anti-Vietnam war world that I first met women's liberation: a session was included (for women only) within a national anti-war conference in Sydney. What engaged me utterly at that session was when a woman spoke of having always believed she was as good as a man (intelligent, articulate, fit and healthy, interested in politics, not babies and dish-washing liquids). Kethunk, as they say in the comics, went my guts – midriff or solar plexus, actually. Because before she said it, I knew what came next: This means that you think being a woman is not good enough, and yet that is what you are. You are hating yourself.

So, to touch on lateness again (and we'll come back to it), I began to realise in that moment, an epiphany of painful magnitude, that I had been being *something which I was not*. I had been denying what I was. And let me tell you, in being something I was not, in trying to be accepted as an 'equal' with men, I was *never* late. I couldn't be, because I never listened to myself, my psyche, my body, my feelings. I gave myself almost no space at all. I was too busy being the perfect 1960s working wife and mother which meant doing *everything* in the house; as well as working in the paid workforce with feeling and commitment; as well as doing everything I could, and more, for the anti-war movement, the left, the (male) revolution; all of which meant being utterly reliable, punctual and efficient, fitting into other people's time-tables all day everyday, overlapping and interweaving, being punctual for the rest of the world.

I've already indicated that becoming a women's liberationist meant that I no longer shared the everythingness of my life with the man I lived with. I *tried*. I tried very hard to share with him what was happening to me. I tried so hard that he decided women's liberation had more to offer the world, the cause of revolution, than his particular brand of marxism. But I couldn't really share with him because he was, after all, not a woman. The only people who understood (we didn't 'understand' much at all, really, at first; we simply flew together on the greatest high we'd ever known) were the other women who were going through the same process. And their numbers grew all the time. There were more and more of us. My world changed. Very quickly (by January 1971 certainly), the primary focus of my life was the Wednesday night meeting of Canberra Women's Liberation.

Our meetings were really the much-touted 'consciousness-raising' variety, although we never called them that. We kept minutes: a new beginning of women's consciousness about historical records, based, never let it be forgotten, on *taking ourselves seriously as women*. We determined topics a week or two ahead, and then a woman, or maybe two women, would volunteer to prepare a paper for discussion: and discuss we would – personally, theoretically, politically, emotionally, and personally again. In those early days there was no body of feminist literature: only de Beauvoir, Friedan, the snippets of research which we dug out of diverse hidey-holes. Mostly we developed our theory out of our own lives. Then came Greer and, more importantly for those of us already convinced, Firestone, and Morgan's anthology *Sisterhood is Powerful*; and we were away, sailing high on what was clearly an international journey of discovery. It was an un-covering, a recognition of the nature of patriarchy which meant, since we were our own evidence, personal change and political intervention.

Rather than discuss the ideas, the public politics represented by the absolute explosion of skilled and articulate women into the bureaucracies, the arts, the unions, the professions, everywhere, I want to stay with the more immediate, un-public changes that went hand-in-hand with the beaming, serious, laughing, angry public faces of women's liberation.

I am recalling now the first time I went away with a group of women (the first time in my life) for a weekend to the coast. It was July 1972: bitterly cold in Canberra, pretty nippy south of Bateman's Bay. There were eight or ten of us in a house in the bush, the surf pounding on a crescent beach down below, the sound of the waves reaching us through healthy banksia and high gum trees. The first, the Friday, evening, we ate and drank by the fire. About 1 am we made our move for the beach, ostensibly for 'fresh air'. Most of us quickly shed our clothes and went swimming, as drunk on the experience of being only women together, as on the alcohol. After swimming, I began cartwheeling (nearing thirty and unfit since having my twins) and I ended up cartwheeling up the entire length of the beach and back again. At the time I wondered why I'd never done it before; later I realised that because there were no men there, I could do it because it didn't matter hòw I *looked*. Sure, I was sore next day, but we swam lots more and walked, and I dated the fitness I felt for years afterwards from that night: it was based on *allowing* my body to do what it wanted, rather than behave in the ladylike, unathletic way accorded a woman who was thirty-ish and mother of three.

A few years later, I remember a moment, about midnight, a warm summer evening, when I was riding my bike (named Mary Poppins, no gears, full 'lady's' bike) home from visiting a friend. Dressed in singlet and jeans, barefoot, I tried to ride no-hands as I had as a kid. Flying past my children's primary school, I hugged myself and whooped as I felt my trusty thighs control Mary Poppins. Then suddenly I did a double-take, as they say in the television comedy scripts (except this was no comedy), and plunged into a real, existential crisis about who and what I was. Now thirty-three, a voice shrieked in my head: 'You're not a proper Canberra mother! Proper mothers don't behave like this!'

That took a year or two to ally: checking with my children that I didn't embarrass them, worrying about it, but not actually altering the path I was on – it felt too good. Eventually I realised that I was only dealing with the fairly resistant eradication of my own childhood expectation of how thirty-three-year-old women behaved. They certainly didn't ride bikes no-hands at midnight in bare feet in the 1940s and early 1950s as far as I knew. Nowadays (at forty-five), I revel in the changing face of women. The increased freedom – emotional, sexual, political and physical – has produced a new kind of agelessness among women, those women who can take advantage of these freedoms. And the extraordinary thing is that this is true even of women who work in the hardest of all feminist occupations: in refuges and rape crisis centres. Such a woman may one day look 135 years old, but next day she'll be mistaken for twenty – she's actually thirty-seven. It's proof enough for me that, in spite of the unending oceans of pain and atrocity uncovered by feminists, working with and for other women (and therefore yourself) is the healthiest way to live.

Over all those years of the 1970s, I went more and more often to the country and the coast: usually with other women, occasionally with mixed groups or my lover of the period, often with my children, and sometimes alone. Gradually the alone times became the most precious. I began to discover the joy of solitude, the richness of quietening and listening to the wind and the grass growing and the earth breathing. I had, I realised one day, been there before: as a young child, sitting in a special place in a special tree. I had come full circle, but was still travelling.

I had started keeping a diary, a journal, in 1972: another sign of a woman taking her life seriously. On those alone times, I took to writing more and more. By 1975 I was writing poetry often. Some poems 'happened' to me, demanded to be written, appeared to be word-perfect first time: committing them to paper was a new kind of intense, ecstatic experience. I never went away, even for a night, without my diary and writing pad.

From 1974 to 1977 I worked at an alternative school, a government school, known affectionately as 'SWOW' (the School WithOut Walls). Over time, a type of creative writing lesson evolved, during which I, with six to fifteen students, would 'go' somewhere: usually a quiet 'natural' setting (though once we went to the hospital, another time to the kafkaesque empty drive-in), and there we would write, silent and companionable. Then we would gather in a circle and read each other what we had written. This mode became a process which I emulated in my 'private' life, my trips alone to the country: mountain, valley, forest, river or sea. I began to *see* as I never had before. I became able to monitor my feeling the slowing down, the tuning in. A deeper reaction. A new way of being.

In late 1977 I resigned from teaching. I spent a period as a pensioner; I was responsible for a three-hour community radio programme; I

travelled in the USA and Mexico and New Zealand; I returned penniless, got a job at the Canberra women's refuge and bought a decrepit
1965 Holden whose name is Maggie. I mention Maggie because she
was so utterly disreputable on the surface, so utterly reliable where
it matters (guts and staying power), and because she has been my companion on many alone and many shared trips exploring natural places.

Which brings me almost to the early 1980s. In 1980 I was having
breakfast with Lizzie (with whom I shared house/home) and Virginia
(visiting from Sydney), when Pat called in on her way to work at the
refuge (it was one of my days off). Somewhere in the ensuing gabble,
Pat said she wanted to visit central Australia that winter. My whole
being spronged! Before Pat left, she and I made a pact to do it. Lizzie
and Virginia were keen too. In the event, Pat, Virginia and I went
(in Maggie) and the fourth woman was not Lizzie, but Obi.

On that trip I experienced, I knew, a new dimension: the physical
universe, the world of rocks, trees, weather, colours, water, night and
day, grasses and flowers, embodied meaning. She was the reality; I
a phantom, allowed for the short time of my lifespan to read her if
I could. Schooled thoroughly as I have been in patriarchal thinking
processes, I tried to explain to myself what I was seeing. I said that
the physical universe united female sexuality (fierce joy), spirituality
(profound certainty), and nature (perfect form). When I returned to
Canberra, I saw the country I loved anew: my seeing went layers deeper
than before, created new connections. I eventually stopped trying to
'understand', explain. All the answers we need are there for the finding, in the physical world which has no words.

I determined to return to central Australia within two years (the time
scale being determined by pragmatic affairs like parental responsibilities, work commitments, and money). And I did it, twenty-three months
later, with two other women. This time we saw more of the country;
we wrote and drew and filmed and talked. And the joyous certainty
I had felt on the previous trip expanded and deepened. My joy was
so intense that the demon of rationality asserted itself in the form of
fear: fear tried to strangle my joy, arguing that I would disappear into
it and be called mad. I guess my joy swamped the demon in the end,
because at the end of the trip I decided to live in Alice. Just like that.
Fifteen years in Canberra, loving the nearby, daily visible, high mountain country; having cast deep roots into the life and being of that
peculiar city; knowing nearly all my beloveds were there or within
reach on the east coast, I decided to leave.

Being in 'the Dead Red Heart of patriarchal mythology' (to quote
one of my own poems), I recalled (at the ineffably feminine point of

baking biscuits on a Saturday morning) that as a child, around eight years old, my first-ever expression of what I would do as an adult was 'to marry a man who lives in the Outback'. Recognising that the first part of this wish was functional and therefore irrelevant and that the second part was the substance, I was struck with an epiphany that almost equalled my realisation that I had spent a great deal of my life trying to be what I was not. I felt/thought/heard a yell: 'You've done it! You're here!'

How and why, where that eight-year-old desire came from, I know not. What I do know is that the process of trusting the modes down-graded by patriarchy – dreaming, feeling, desiring, connecting, intuiting – produces deeply satisfying results. It is women's liberation and all the wonderful women I have known therein who have given me both permission and a framework within which to take the risk of following my own star – even when I don't understand why we're going where we are. So being 'late' comes to be seen for what it is – merely a patriarchal label used to denigrate the practice of wait-ing, waiting for the time, the direction, the right time and place to be, and do what has to be done.

A recent and pertinent example of waiting for the right direction and then seizing the time, has been the evolution of large Women Against Rape marches on Anzac Day (the quintessential celebration of patriarchy and its acolyte, war). In Canberra in 1980, fourteen women out of a total of sixteen were arrested for even being in the vicinity of the RSL (Returned Services League) march. So in 1981 an historic event occurred. Not only did over 300 women get out to march but also sat down, waited, gave time for discussion and adjust-ment and group decisions when confronted by a wall of police. Having decided to move forward, sixty-one were arrested. In 1982 over 600 women marched. The evolution of this movement grew from a gradu-ally deepening analysis of the role of rape in keeping women as a class under control; and from 'waiting for the time' to irrevocably put rape on the public agenda, biding in awareness, in order to move forward at the point of greatest authenticity.

Being in Alice Springs led to fantasising in a fairly non-specific fashion (though nonetheless passionately for that) of the demise of Pine Gap. It seemed apt, somehow, that having settled in Alice Springs because of the unutterable beauty and inchoate familarity of the coun-try, there's a first-strike nuclear target just down the road. Apt, because I believe fervently that to behave according to the war-mongers' view of the world (that is, not to live in central Australia because of Pine

Gap) is to accept the inevitability of the holocaust – which I don't. To fight against it is to believe that sanity (non-patriarchal love of life) will prevail. And where better to fight the nuclear sickness than on the doorstep of its principal edifice? Fighting often has elements of waiting. Beauty and the Beast: the desert, with the help of her friends, will, one day, swallow Pine Gap, and stories will be told of the strange place that used to be.

The one important thing I have yet to mention has been the discovery, in recent years, that I am a writer. Through my work at the refuge I became intensely concerned about child sexual abuse, née incest – which I began researching a little, and ended up writing a book about, in which I attempt a re-naming: *Father–Daughter Rape*. Alongside the horror of the subject, the pain and anger that went into the writing, I found an excitement, a centred-ness, in the actual process of writing, such as I had never known before. One can never truly say 'If x had not been, y would not have followed', but I feel certain that without women's liberation I would not feel like a writer. I have grown in feminist soil: it/she determines what I am today.

I am writing this a month over the due date. Tomorrow I'll type it up. It is so because I had to wait until I knew what I needed to say, was meant to say, and how to say it. It may need a little pruning, or water, or sun: but it fell into my lap. As all things will, if we learn how to prepare for their ripening.

9 | Elisabeth Kirkby

Elisabeth Kirkby was born on 26 January 1921 in Bolton, Lancashire in England, and was educated in Nottingham. During the second world war she served from 1942–5 with the ATS, undertaking NCO training in 1942, and played in various wartime productions, including *Stars in Battledress*. She arrived in Sydney in 1965, via Malaysia, where she held various positions in Radio Malaya and Radio Malaysia from 1953–64. Until 1972 she wrote and produced various programmes for the ABC, including *Learn Indonesian*.

Elisabeth Kirkby is state leader of the Australian Democrats in New South Wales, vice-president of Worldview International Foundation and president of the Society of Australian Film and Television Arts and Sciences, as well as being involved in other activites.

When the Air Force Holds Cake Stalls

1972 was the year of the Whitlam government and also the year of *Number 96*. After twenty years of working professionally as a writer, director, actress and radio commentator, suddenly I was caught up by the power and influence of television. I became Lucy Sutcliffe of *Number 96*, the popular television soap opera, and although I did not realise it at the time, I developed a public image as 'Lucy' which remains years later, although my life and career have changed totally.

Then I had children in their teens, one of them still at school; my public image affected them. It affected my husband, already known for his book *Everywoman* which was even then a world best-seller. So, inadvertently, the emergence of 'Lucy' changed our lives. There were newspaper and magazine articles about the 'family' life of TV 'star' Elisabeth Kirkby; interviews with the son and daughter of 'famous' parents. Luckily, my youngest son escaped this part of the media scrutiny. Hopefully, we all coped with it reasonably well – although I would have far preferred to be known as the outstanding Portia or Lady Macbeth. I was never ashamed of the soap-opera image, but it did not seem to make me either a star or famous in my own terms. It certainly made me a household name in Australia and as the character was real, hardworking, tough, and a 'survivor', the 'Lucy' label was one for pride. However, it was a long way from politics or even the women's movement.

In 1972, I was a council member of the International Association of Women in Radio and Television. I became president in 1976. I was on the New South Wales Council of the Australian Institute of International Affairs and a vice-president of Australian Actors' Equity. I remain a member of Actors' Equity, and on the Council of the Actors' Benevolent Fund, and a member of the International Association of Women in Radio and Television, a vice-president of Worldview International Foundation, and member of the Women's Electoral Lobby.

Although in 1972 I had supported the Labor Party through the *Make It Australian* campaign to increase local content in both film and television, I do not think I clearly perceived the need for a 'women's movement' as such. My profession had meant I had never been actively discriminated against. My hours of work, conditions, pay and promotion prospects were the same as for a man in my profession. Acting is always uncertain, so job security was never one of my goals. Actors do not get superannuation, so I did not expect 'equal' superannuation rights either.

Leaving school as I did, just before the second world war, then gaining equality with men during the war years, lulled me into the true sense of false security. Because I had achieved a reasonable measure of equality and had pursued my career throughout my marriage, considering myself 'liberated', I was far too complacent and had no real understanding of women's issues. I was active and vocal in my opposition to the Vietnam war. I campaigned vigorously for better conditions in my own profession, but I was not identified with the women's movement in any real sense. I was a 'political animal' because I had definite ideas on law reform, child-care, health, education and a range of social problems. Yet in the early 1970s I did not see that the solutions lay mainly through women's organisations.

The turning point came in 1975, for me as for many other Australians, through the dismissal of the Whitlam government. I became actively political at that time, although I knew I could not join the Australian Labor Party. A party in which members were so hamstrung by caucus decisions had never been acceptable to me. Nor would I have been acceptable to such a party, as my need to express my personal feelings on a variety of delicate issues such as nuclear disarmament, capital punishment, abortion, homosexuality and rape, would have been anathema. In 1977 I joined the Australian Democrats because it was obvious by that time that a third force was needed in Australian politics. The polarisation of the two party system, the lack of credibility of the leaders of both political parties, and my overriding conviction that a new party with new priorities was long overdue made it inevitable that I became an Australian Democrat.

So, my lifestyle changed again. I had left *Number 96* in 1975 to have more time to devote to a small property in the Lower Hunter Region, to establish a garden and to return to the theatre. In 1977, the theatre had to take second place, the garden became a hobby for leisure hours – not a full-time pursuit – and I started on the long, tough road to gain parliamentary office. I stood for the seat of Hunter in 1977, the second safest Labor seat in federal parliament, gaining 12 per cent of the vote. I was voted to the number two position on the Democrat Senate ticket in 1980 and stood for the state seat of Cessnock in 1981, the second safest Labor seat in the New South Wales parliament. Between 1977 and 1980 I began to realise it was vitally necessary 'to get political' to achieve the ends of the women's liberation movement.

Unless I fought for myself and my own career, I would be valuable as a candidate only because I was a household name. I would still have to fight for pre-selection for winnable seats, or for a winning position on an upper house ticket, by proving I was better than the male contenders. Only then did I face the covert discrimination against women in a patriarchal society – even when the avowed aims of parties and policies state that they oppose discrimination. I had to temper my women's liberation enthusiasms so that the label of being a 'radical' feminist would not jeopardise my future or that of my party.

I read, talked with, and met many feminists. 'Sisterhood is powerful', but I am alarmed at the splinter groups that emerge. I am convinced that 'single-issue' lobby groups and/or parties lose more than they gain. Such groups probably cannot be avoided, but there must be strong affirmative action to weld them into a network of concerned women, expert in a variety of fields and powerful enough to work in unity towards the common goal. For me, the priorities of the major political parties remain wrong. There is still no overruling determination to end discrimination, not just against women, but against all underprivileged groups, including those of ethnic origin, black Australians, unemployed teenagers, and of course the aged.

Women in Australia are now 51.4 per cent of the population. Yet they continue to be discriminated against socially and professionally. Many of the reforms that women have worked for over the past years are continually amended; their real meaning is eroded. Anti-discrimination legislation without 'teeth'; no improvement in the availability of child-care to allow women to compete on equal terms in the paid workforce. Rape counselling services, family planning services, women's refuges and a whole range of community welfare projects fight for funding. In a recession, governments see such projects as soft options, areas where cuts can be made without losing votes. There is a growing feeling that women should return to the home, should confine their energies to child-bearing and child-rearing; obviously sexism is increasing.

Regrettably, many women continue to foster this scenario. Even when aware of the reactionary forces threatening their hard-won rights, they accept. Far too few women want to fight back; perhaps it is part of the apathy of recession that makes it easier for them to retreat than to continue the struggle. And I see great danger in this acceptance.

It is more essential than ever that the women's movement grows in strength. I am also beginning to be convinced that a woman's political party may be the only answer in the end, unless the present parties change radically. The meagre number of women parliamentarians, the small number of women candidates, strengthen this conviction.

I find it hard to understand the rhetoric of reactionary groups like the Right to Life Association, pontificating about the rights of the unborn, the evils of abortion and homosexuality, yet making no statement at all about the increasing number of young women under the age of nineteen who are registered neither as unemployed, employed, nor in full- or part-time education. According to Yvonne Preston of the *Sydney Morning Herald*, they 'are simply disappearing into domestic work, or into the exploitation of casual work, developing no skills, or real work experience, let alone entering on a career path'. She continues: 'Despite all the changes that have occurred in the past decade, women are still seen as a reserve workforce, plugging gaps, taking part-time jobs, providing labour as and when and if required, on the cheap.' I am appalled that no male-dominated political party seems to understand that as long as women are in the position so vividly described, there will be an increase in prostitution, child pornography, drug abuse, and mental illness. Political women cannot wipe out all social evils, but political women, once having gained sufficient power, can raise the status of women and legitimate many of the problems facing society as a whole, because they have different, more important priorities.

The result of the 1970s, the early 1980s, and my activities? I can only answer that question personally, because publicly I have been able to achieve very little. In personal terms, I have gained immeasurably. I am more tolerant, more compassionate, more understanding and more determined. I have gained the strength to stand alone, because the pressures of these years on my family have caused a complete reorientation of my personal life. I am lucky that this has happened because I know now I can devote myself totally to my career without any sense of guilt. The years of compromise and of believing family should come first (because that was my conditioning) are over. Now, I am a 'different person', and the women's movement and a new political career are largely responsible. I would not want to go back to the early 1970s, to where I was 'at' then, to be bound by the constraints I put on myself and allowed other people to put upon me.

Of course, I have been disillusioned by the actions of other women, but I have been even more disillusioned by the actions of men, both personally and professionally. Not only do I believe it is possible for women to work together to achieve the desired ends of the women's movement; I believe it is essential. No one else can achieve these ends but us. We have to learn to communicate, to negotiate, to compromise and to fight. All that can really defeat us is a lack of will, and to lose that will would lead to a shameful defeat indeed.

In 1972 I believed the Chinese proverb:

> If you want to be happy for an hour, drink wine.
> If you want to be happy for two days, get married.
> If you want to be happy for a week, kill your pig and eat it.
> If you want to be happy for ever, plant a garden.

In 1975, I was on the point of 'opting out' and adopting an alternative lifestyle. Now, I know this is impossible. There is still too much to do, too many people to convince, too few people who really care. So now, I follow another proverb brought to my attention by the Women's International League for Peace and Freedom: 'It will be a great day when our schools get all the money they need, and the air force has to hold a cake stall to buy a bomber.' History makes it all too apparent that men have never had the will to work for peace. This is another and even more important goal that women have set for themselves; they will have to pioneer in this field, too, if the world is to be safe for the men and women of the future.

How women can begin to operate more effectively is a problem needing careful and urgent thought. We are underrepresented in the higher echelons of the bureaucracy – on the boards of statutory bodies and on councils, commissions and committees. There has to be a greater and even more determined attempt to ensure our views are given a fair hearing. Regrettably, we have not been heeded in the past. The dismantling or demotion of the federal Office of Women's Affairs and the way in which recommendations of the National Women's Advisory Council were ignored by the Fraser government, and the accompanying lack of funding for women's access to education, training, secure employment and housing were all matters of highest concern.

I have reservations about the strength of women in the ALP. The first ray of hope was the election of the Australian Labor Party under the leadership of Bob Hawke in 1983. The avowed policies of the federal government are to lift the status of women. The ALP admits the costs of inequality. They underline the dangers of poverty, dependence and ill health. They insist that unemployment leads directly to 'poverty, and the waste of human talent and potential; and fosters anxiety, powerlessness, divisiveness and dependency'.

I suppose we should feel ashamed that a party dominated by men should be first to point out the devastating personal consequences of unemployment. And even if the party only grudgingly admits that loss of income, security, skills and esteem damage women as greatly as men, at least they are now on record as saying that 'the loss to our country in this loss of human potential is incalculable'. I echo that statement as a woman and as an Australian Democrat. I applaud the ratification by the Hawke government of the United Nations *Convention on the Elimination of all Forms of Discrimination Against Women* and the introduction of affirmative action in employment. This programme must be made effective, because it is only thus that we will be able to wipe out the inequities of the past and become secure, self-supporting and fully productive.

I hope that by the 1990s, the voice of women will be heard. Certainly, I and my party will work with the Australian Labor Party toward that goal.

10 | Elsa Atkin

Elsa Atkin came to Australia in 1960, holding a triple matriculation in English, French and Arabic. She was born in Iraq in 1944.

Elsa Atkin is a longtime member of the Women's Electoral Lobby (WEL) and Women in Management, a foundation member of the Women's Network, and was co-convenor of the Women's Sub-committee of the Ethnic Communities Council and a member of the Steering Committee of the Women and Arts Project in the New South Wales' government. She is actively involved in the women's movement, ethnic affairs, and equality of opportunity for disadvantaged groups. Currently full-time Head of the Equal Opportunity Unit at the Australian Broadcasting Corporation (ABC), she is studying part-time for an MA degree in government at Sydney University.

In Retrospect

In the early 1970s I was a young wife with a little terrace house in the gentrified part of Sydney, a baby in nappies and a devoted husband beginning to develop what he hoped was a promising career: a nice, neat, tidy package that was just not enough. Within me was a growing need to do more and to be more.

My husband and I had a general understanding that I would quit work when we had children and stay at home at least until they were of school age. At the time, that was acceptable to me. Why? I now realise that my whole conditioning as a woman (and an ethnic woman as well) made me believe I should want this desirable package regardless of whether it satisfied me or not. It didn't.

I was born in Baghdad, Iraq, where I spent all my childhood and most of my teenage years. Though non-Catholic, I was educated at a French convent, so was heavily influenced by the code of ethics and beliefs of the Catholic church. I grew up in a 'comfortable' home with parents who maintained traditions which dictated that they rear their children under a very strict code of conduct and morals. They did, however, place a great deal of importance on education for both boys and girls. I was more fortunate than other young women living in Baghdad then: generally women were considered and treated as second-class citizens. Convention dictated that as soon as a boy was born, the parents assumed the name of the boy and from then on they were called 'father of' and 'mother of', irrespective of whether there had been girls born before or after him.

The country was politically volatile where demonstrations were, to me, a way of life. They ranged from being anti-British, to anti-Russian, to anti-Israel, to anti-imperialist, to anti-communist and so on. The political winds changed constantly and unpredictably and I can remember going to demonstrations, shouting slogans and having no idea of what I was saying or why. We, as school children, were forced to take part in these demonstrations by factional groups of young people who would come into the schools and intimidate us.

In 1960 I came to Australia with my family to join my brother, and

here I stayed, out of choice. Although it was voluntary, the early years
in Australia were difficult. Being from Iraq of non-Moslem background
I didn't fit into any of the other ethnic categories – categories decided
either by the Australian community or the various ethnic communities. Unlike the Greeks or Italians, for instance, who immigrated here,
we didn't have around us other Iraqis, let alone Iraqis from a similar
background, who were already established and could act as a support
system. So here I was in a new country feeling a lack of confidence
as a person and as a woman. Australian men and women in the 1960s
oppressed women, they oppressed ethnic groups and foreigners. The
difference in culture and traditions was, to say the least, a shock both
mentally and physically.

My experience of alienation in Baghdad because of leading a European lifestyle in a middle eastern culture paled into insignificance
against the alienation I felt in the first stages of my life in Australia.
I felt misplaced. I felt conspicuous. I felt as though there was nobody
who was 'like me'. To try to fit in somewhere I found myself having
to reject all my own culture and taking on the Australian ways: I lived
with contradictions of issues within me then and, to some extent, I
still do.

In order to survive in 1960s Australia, I deliberately broke with all
my previous traditions. I consciously made the decision that I had to
become an Australian in every respect and did the full 'assimilation'
bit. I completely stopped corresponding with Baghdad friends, speaking languages I'd grown up with, enjoying food that I'd always relished.
With my Iraqi political experiences behind me, I welcomed and enjoyed
the new freedom of political inactivity on my arrival in Australia and
did not feel an urge to participate in any demonstration until much
later, in the early 1970s and the anti-Vietnam war pull. I married an
Australian in true 'wasp' tradition – white wedding, church, reception
and all the trimmings. Then in the late 1960s we spent two-and-a-half
years in Europe and I made contact again with European ways. I re-
discovered the beauty of speaking French, German and Arabic and
also discovered it was acceptable to communicate in a language other
than English. I went ahead to learn Italian too.

I no longer felt 'out of place'. I realised I could return to Australia
and not feel out of place there either. I could be an Australian woman
who had a non-Anglo-Saxon background. The setting in 1972 was of
my being in the early throes of motherhood, of being proud of my
identity, and of no longer feeling shy and hesitant about my ethnic
background. I was also beginning to feel a strong bond with Australia
and Australians, and a love of the country and concern for it and its

people. In one way, it was the first time in my life that I felt a real sense of belonging.

Having left behind a solid career in office administration, I was living the life of a young family woman who had come to terms with an ethnic background but who was continuing with most of the traditional women's roles and attitudes common to all nationalities at some level. Within myself I was not satisfied, but I believed that I was what I had to be. Eventually I had to do something to satisfy the gnawing needs and decided to combine early motherhood with university studies, at first by correspondence. The decision to return to university in 1972 was, on reflection, critical. I recognised my own needs and did something about them.

Another key factor was that I became acutely aware of male chauvinism. One strikingly memorable personal event of 1972 was suffering a very painful (both emotionally and physically) miscarriage. During the stay in hospital the doctor interacted almost solely with my husband. There I was in pain, it was my body, but the doctor really only discussed matters with my husband, with me in the room being of no more use than a bystander in an event of some significance. (We refused to pay his bill for 'professional' services and heard nothing more from him.)

This, and other events, made me angry enough to react, realising that only by my meeting the challenge would I change the unfair situation. Initially my thoughts were for me, but as I discussed the problem with other women, similar stories emerged. I realised attitudes and values placed traditionally on women were a concern for all women; they were universal.

The 'blame the victim' attitude came back to me in other guises. I will be forever haunted by the face of a woman I knew as a child. The face full of agony and despair belonged to a Jewish friend of the family who was raped by Arabs in Baghdad, during a pro-Hitler civil disobedience. As a consequence, the woman was abandoned by her husband because she was 'sullied'. Her children were taken from her to be reared away from the person who had 'brought' so much shame to the family. I can still see her coming over to visit with her elderly parents, always walking two steps behind, always sitting two steps apart from the others, for fear of contaminating.

I joined the Women's Electoral Lobby soon after its formation and I remember the thrill of associating with women with a similar, at times higher, level of awareness and a strong sense of purpose. That I was not Australian-born was irrelevant. The women's liberation movement

and its issues united all women concerned with changing society's
unjust attitudes to women regardless of nationality. It frightens me
still that in spite of hundreds of years of different cultural traditions
in so many different countries, the issues concerning women are virtually universal and therefore so much harder to change or eradicate.

I remember the lobby groups formed for child-care, abortion,
women's refuges, media action and how, with our babies crawling
around us, we prepared and worked at a successful campaign to have
a woman, Carole Baker, elected into local government. She went on
to become the first woman mayor of North Sydney. While the kids
played we consumed umpteen cups of tea, wrote newsletters, speeches,
organised suburban letter-drops – all activities going into a political
campaign. We also collected information on which politicans were and
were not sympathetic to women's issues. If there was a politician in
an area, if there was a political debate taking place, our telephone network would go into operation. And it was very efficient. I remember
getting phone calls with directions to get to certain places with my
own and any other children I was minding, to demonstrate or lobby
for child-care grants, women's refuges and crisis shelters. I did so willingly, and so did many others.

Things were starting to happen. Politicians were actually starting
to pay attention to women's issues. Apart from the sense of achievement we had, how much more stimulating, interesting and invigorating
such activities were than being at home doing the never-ending washing or cooking. When any guilt feelings overtook us as either a group
or an individual, there was one woman who would constantly remind
us that no woman she knew of had, as part of her epitaph, 'she kept
a clean house'. That certainly brought things back into perspective
and once again our priorities were sorted out. And it was then, when
my children were very small, and in my longing to get away from the
house, that I took on a one-day-per-week teaching job which earned
me $16, of which I paid $13 for a housekeeper and $3 for petrol there
and back.

In the 1970s I was going to open forums, organised through WEL
and other women's groups, where all aspects of women's lives and issues
were discussed with no embarrassment and with a sincere feeling of
wanting to share and improve. The power gained from my new-found
knowledge led me to question what I had earlier taken for granted.
The more I questioned and analysed, the more shaky became the
criteria for acceptability. I was happy to be among women; I was feeling uplifted in the knowledge that other women felt the same injustices

I felt and were doing something about them. I saw it was necessary to become political.

The Whitlam years brought with them progressive and humane social welfare and cultural policies. They focussed on the fact that it is possible to make gains, but also made me realise how precarious were the gains and how easily lost: the Whitlam dismissal brought home to me just how quickly any situation can revert and while it made me cynical about our so-called democratic process, it also made me more determined to keep fighting the issues and more eager to increase my understanding of the political system.

At university, setting out on a new path I studied politics and met women of various ages and backgrounds who had similar interests. We developed a large support system as a result. We needed to discuss with others who understood the difficulties of being a wife and rearing small children while undertaking the rigours of university study. Together we also learned to laugh as we recounted putdowns by other women and the 'let me make you feel guilty' statements by family and friends who were forceful in their opinion that we were inadequate mothers and wives. At the time I convinced myself that their motives were to put me down because they were weak and were jealous of my ability to cope. On reflection I believe that I simply represented a threat to their beliefs – acquired from early conditioning. For them to accept me and my activities, they would have had to question their own parentally ingrained philosophies, attitudes and values; they would have had to break with convention, and were not ready to do so. I looked at my attitudes and made changes, and believe that at some time everyone is faced with having to question long-standing attitudes. Meanwhile, I support all women no matter what stage of development they are at. I realise now a great deal can be achieved in working through the system and strongly believe in giving support to women at the top, holding positions of power. People can always grow, and rather than demean women who have made it, or always being on the lookout for symptoms of sell-outs, I am for raising their consciousness and developing in them a sense of accountability to feminism.

After completing my BA and intent on getting into the main stream to change society, I worked for more than two years at the director/policy planner for Co-As.It, an Italian welfare centre. At this point I had to look at all forms of discrimination and soon realised that discrimination of any kind has similar effects on the person concerned whether they be from a black or ethnic community, a handicapped person or a woman. (Women who are black, or ethnic, or handicapped suffer double discrimination.) Working with the Italians heightened still further my awareness of discriminatory practices and issues. It concerned me that most Italian women were so entrenched in the Italian female role that I knew if I tried to force feminist issues on them they would scuttle further into a corner.

To reach them and break their isolation, we first invited them to various functions which appeared on the surface to be a get-together of Italians to enjoy Italian music, food and the like. We all did enjoy this, but at the same time we began to gently elevate their level of awareness of the various issues that concerned them as individuals and as a community. We invited speakers to the luncheons who, through interpreters, informed them of baby health centres, social welfare agencies and where and how they could get help with any sort of problem. As we gained their confidence, they started to open up and talk about their problems, from incest to complete male domination in the household. Some went on to form self-help groups. We were told we would never reach the women, but we did; the programmes we devised were successful and other ethnic and community centres copied our initiative.

It was relatively easy to become involved in ethnic issues after experiencing some of the problems which are day-to-day fact for foreigners at some time, but at no time have I let my ethnicity become my profession. From ethnic issues and women's issues, the concern and involvement in other discriminatory practices towards other disadvantaged groups was an obvious transition. Earlier, I was a contained woman holding beliefs handed down to me by others which I accepted. After the 1970s, I was a woman who had developed her own beliefs and attitudes and was actively working to help shake other members of society out of their complacency and ignorance. My foremost concern now is that women must have the right to choose the life they want: pointing out that while a woman's right to work for wages has been challenged, not much challenge has been staged by society about women's right to work for nothing as a housewife and mother.

In 1980 I was appointed to the Wran government's Women's Advisory Council. This two-year appointment left a significant mark on me. In the highly political environment in which WAC operated, I learned more about political manoeuvring than at any other time. In 1981 I became involved in the women and arts project, the aim being to focus on women's achievements in the arts and highlight problem areas, such as employment training opportunities and recognition. The project culminated in 1982 in a state-wide festival of women's contribution to arts, but most importantly, it gave women confidence, helping them develop a recognition of themselves as artists. That so many women were involved showed again that women from disparate polit-ical, social and cultural groups can work together through the process of change to achieve a desired end – a vital part of the development of feminism. For some, it was the first time they had ever been 'in' women's issues.

Today I see a huge contrast between Mrs Atkin of 1972 and Elsa Atkin of the 1980s. I remain a wife and mother, but am an individual. I am officer for equal opportunity with the Australian Broadcasting Corpo-ration. I was appointed in 1980 to the first position of its kind in the federal sphere. I am concerned with the handicapped, Aborigines, eth-nic groups and, of course, women. I am a feminist who is learning about the community at large and, most importantly, about myself and my place as a feminist within the community. There is no question that my involvement in the women's movement helped me gain a true sense of myself, having a profound effect on the way I lead my life today, the rearing of my children and my relationships with people generally.

Throughout my involvement in and development through the move-ment, I have had the support and understanding of the man who shares my life. He has developed with me and had I not had his understand-ing and his own commitment to feminism, I would not have been able to develop in the same way. My family is the source of strength and security, the love and caring that I so much need in order to exist. For me, the women's movement is about helping both women and men to change their attitudes, and while my total commitment to equal-ity of opportunity and feminism has given me the impetus to struggle to change society, I am at the same time struggling to change myself and my relation to society. At first the struggle was within my family as I endeavoured to change the patterns of behaviour of all of us and tried to reach a satisfactory agreement on the redistribution of labour and benefits at home. One important outcome has been the making of a conscious decision by us as parents to ensure that feminist princi-ples prevail in the rearing of our two boys.

My growth through the 1970s and today has been contributed to by other outstanding women through the women's movement. Today I find I can deal with women's issues on a far more objective level. I no longer feel a burning anger at statements that women have now 'got it all and don't need any more'. Happily I can say that by being able to deal with those issues objectively, the results are far more posi-tive. Confrontations and angry outbursts, I find, simply lock the person further into the held belief. Objective discussion, presentation of facts and figures gives the person information to think about without threatening the security of his or her life. The results of my work have been far more significant with this stance. Also, though I am constantly engaged in consciousness-raising, which I see as a vital political activity, I have come to believe that formalised change has to be also through the conventional political process to enable society to *accept changes to itself and to the individual.*

With radical political change, there are always two sides. Looking back through the 70s decade, I believe that while the women's movement sharpened my awareness, gave me a sense of belonging and presented me with a number of positive female role models such as Wendy McCarthy, Joan Bielski and Gail Radford to name but a few, I have come out with plenty of bruises and some bad wounds inflicted by women. These are the women who, perhaps in their eagerness and haste to achieve change, were impatient with other women who were treading more carefully, partly because of ignorance and partly because they wanted to achieve the same ends by different means. My involvement in the women's movement has subjected me to having to suffer intolerance, dirty tricks, funny power plays: all tactics of intimidation carried out by disparate groups of women or individuals under the guise of sisterhood and in an effort to reign supreme. Luckily I realise this was all part of my process of growing, without which I would have been a much lesser person. The women's movement is large and resourceful and its influence and advantages far outweigh the disadvantages. I care about the movement and will continue to care, but after my experience in the 'new' women's movement, I will be a lot more cautious about taking on issues under its banner.

11 | Marjorie Luck

Marjorie Luck (previously Levis), born in 1939, was raised and educated in Devonport,Tasmania. Among the various jobs she has undertaken are teaching, running an alternative bookshop, welfare work in women's services and housing services, and textile work in Arts in Working Life Projects and Community Arts Projects. In 1985 she completed a Master of Humanities degree in Tasmanian history. As president of the Australian Social Welfare Union (Tasmanian Branch), Marjorie Luck is involved in trade unionism in Tasmania and is particularly concerned about the role of women in trade unions.

Marjorie Luck spends as much time as possible at her family shack at Hawley on the north-west coast of Tasmania.

Not a Dinner Party

A revolution is not a dinner party, or writing an essay, or painting a picture, or doing embroidery; it cannot be so refined, so leisurely, so gentle, so temperate, kind, courteous, restrained and magnanimous.

Mao Tse Tung

My interest in the women's movement was not sudden, although it took the statement of a Women's Electoral Lobby guest speaker at the local school's mothers' club, with all its blatant discrimination, to shock me into joining WEL Tasmania in November 1972: 'Women who sell men's shoes get paid less than men who sell men's shoes. Women who sell women's shoes get paid even less' (WEL guest speaker to the Taroona Primary School Mothers' Club, November 1972).

My mother's family is full of strong, politically radical women who developed my socialist consciousness and, to a lesser degree, my feminist consciousness. Despite this, my early ambition had been to marry, be a perfect wife and mother, and live happily ever after. By 1972 this was not quite working out. I was aged thirty-two, with two small children and a marriage which had become meaningless.

WEL began to dominate my life. Not in the paid workforce, I was able to devote my energies to political lobbying and campaigns on women's issues. A whole new world of women opened up. Yet there were many hurdles. My background and education led me to respect the law and believe that, mostly, people received equitable treatment before it—a myth soon to be dispelled. I had also embraced the erroneous belief that if people had the drive and ambition, they could achieve their goals. What a lot I had to learn about sexism! I had to come to know myself and know that the personal is political. The road to radical feminism was slow and hard.

Early WEL meetings were traditional, with the formality of a constitution and office bearers. Yet we set up less formal action groups dealing with child-care, discrimination in the workforce, abortion and contraception. Although I worked closely with women, our communication at this stage was usually confined to the particular issue on which we were working. One night, after a WEL meeting, eight of us sat around drinking, when one after another we confessed to having had an abortion. The barriers separating us began to dissolve as for the first time we talked about our personal lives. From that moment, for me, there was no going back.

The Hobart Women's Shelter was initiated by WEL at a public meeting in 1974. My organising role introduced another enormous change to my life and attitudes. For the first time I came into contact with the violence suffered by many women. I had difficulty relating to the battered women seeking refuge in the shelter. They were totally outside my experience. Their rough honesty and blatant pain made me feel superficial and inadequate, which I undoubtedly was. I lacked the right words of comfort and the capacity to relate. An uncomfortable alien, I hung in there, determined to learn about and understand the misery of some women's lives.

I met the woman who was to radically change my life at this time. Sue Edmonds was like a flash of lightning racing through lazy parochial Tasmania. Through her compelling marxist feminist analysis, she put into words the ideas I had wanted. Suddenly we were having dynamic women's shelter collective meetings, and learning to understand and love women and understand and love ourselves.

For the next three years I dwelt, by choice, almost exclusively in women's society, and was part of the joys, the traumas, the triumphs and disasters of working in a women's movement that was finding itself. Women's conferences on the mainland added to the complexities; nonetheless they were stimulating and exciting and not to be missed – at least for those of us fortunate enough to be able to pay the exorbitant airfares across Bass Strait. It was marvellous to share the vitality and enthusiasm of a large number of women from all walks of life. One of the most stunning conferences was the first Women and Labour Conference held in Sydney at Macquarie University in 1978, mainly at the instigation of Sue Bellamy. Two thousand women turned up to talk; tell about their research into women of the past, about feminist theory, contemporary women and contemporary women's issues; to infuse one another with enthusiasm. At one session, women shared their experiences and knowledge of their grandmothers' lives, their mothers' lives and their own lives. Most women in the room were openly weeping as other women told us of the agony of their experiences.

Although the Tasmanian women's movement owes much to mainland feminists, particularly through the exchange of ideas and support which came through going to conferences like Women and Labour, we were at times subjected to visits from our mainland sisters who felt we needed shaking out of our apparent lethargy. Their expectations of us on a personal level were out of step with the way our lives were lived in Tasmania. Their demands that we should come out loudly proclaiming our views on various issues were inappropriate; they had not grown up in our milieu – we knew the local scene and how capable the locals were of absorbing new, feminist ideas without being alienated. These mainland women did not stay around for long: they attempted to shake us up in a variety of ingenious and public ways – leaving us to clean up the mess and try to put back the tatters of our lives. Out of that terrible trauma – which we went through on a number of occasions – we in the Tasmanian movement became very close, forging bonds that will never be broken.

In 1973 I entered the paid workforce, first as a part-time teacher, then as partner in a feminist bookshop. Being in a fairly independent position enabled me to be outspoken on women's and social issues at times when other women had to be more careful because of their jobs or family responsibilities. Tasmania is so insular and conservative that it is amazing that the women's movement has had any impact at all, but it has. I have spoken out on emergency housing for women, rape law reform, wife bashing, abortion rights, incest and other related matters. The public response has sometimes been of outrage or shock, yet at other times there has been strong support for positive change in those areas, as during the National Conference on Rape Law Reform held in Hobart in 1980, when I spoke formally, putting a strong feminist view on rape law and the way it distorts women's actions and supports the men who rape. Somehow the media managed to cope well and present a reasonably accurate picture.

Through the years I moved forward, my development helped when I went back into my family's past, finding my roots. My uncle, the only living great-grandchild of the first Luck (born in 1824) to settle in Tasmania, called a family reunion. He and I decided to research the family's background. (This led to the revelation that my great-grandfather had been sent to Tasmania as a convict at the age of seventeen for the theft of a pair of clogs, a fact which he had carefully concealed during his long and successful life.) Concentrating on the past, it became necessary for me to examine my relationship with my father. That led me to examine my feelings for the other men who have influenced my life. Generally, the result has been positive. I had two superb role models in my mother's brothers. One of them introduced me to books. Keen on women's education, he believed 'there's nothing you can't do if you really want to'; this gave me confidence in myself and my abilities (although now I can see external factors prevent some people from 'doing what they really want to', rather than their own supposed inadequacies). Though he and his brother were politically conservative, they influenced me to stand up for what I believed in. My ex-husband, too, was terrifically supportive in extending my education, especially with regard to women working; on this he had no reservations and gave me strong encouragement.

My father taught me to love Tasmania with a passion which surprises even me. However he would not have agreed with my involvement in the Australian Labor Party, although he accepted (not very gracefully) my mother's radical political philosophy. Early in 1975 I joined the Labor Party with the specific intention of carving myself a political career, but I found the women's movement far more interesting and more valuable to me in the development of my feminist socialist consciousness. I abandoned all thoughts of a political career which was, at the time, totally irrelevant to my life.

However in 1980 I became involved in the federal election campaign of Fran Bladell, standing for the seat of Franklin. My interest in the Labor Party was rejuvenated. During the 1982 state election when the twenty-year reign of the ALP ended ignominiously, I took advantage of the speed of the campaign to stand as a candidate. It was a short, three-week campaign, which I called a 'fun run', and it became an amazingly exhilarating experience. The most heart-warming part of the campaign was the dedication of the women who worked with me. In Tasmania under the Hare-Clark system, seven or eight ALP candidates were running in the electorate and the usual practice is for the candidates to work on their own; most do not get the support I did. Someone said she would do all my press releases. An older woman from next door came door-knocking with me every day. There was always someone ready to go door-knocking whenever I was ready. Women worked at keeping me safe and sane, feeding me lunches and dinners between campaigning. Tina Baines was dedicated and Margaret Thurston, my campaign manager, ran a smooth and supportive organisation.

Looking at my life now and back in the 1970s, there is little similarity between then and now. I still live in the same house with my two children, our dogs and cats, but in most other aspects my life is completely different. At the beginning of that decade I was using my husband's name. After our marriage ended I wanted to change my name, but was reluctant to use my birth name, as it is fairly well known as a conservative Tasmanian name. By 1981 I was able to resume it with equilibrium because I had come to terms with my background and consequently with the world of men.

As for my political campaigning: although it was a rich and rewarding experience, I wouldn't want to do it again. During the election campaign, my waking nightmare was that by some mischance I might get elected. The campaign forced me to look very closely at the dangers and pitfalls faced by politicians: how does one maintain integrity in the face of the wordly temptations that our political system embraces? how does one keep close and loving friendships in a system that alienates people from politicians? and how is it possible to escape the trap of seeing people as votes, and not as people? There has been little discussion on these questions within socialist parties and less, if they are even seen as relevant, in conservative parties. New wave feminism has achieved much in the way of raising society's consciousness on many levels, but we have made very little progress within the political structures. It is not sufficient to have women politicians. We need party machines that are feminist orientated. At present the marriage between feminism and socialism is uneasy. If women are to become influential within the whole political structure, we must consolidate what gains we have made. The influence of individual women politicians and individual women in other areas can be too easily lost. When I watched the state funeral of Leonid Brezhnev and saw no women among the government leaders, my heart cried out: 'Where are you Kollontai?'

More joyously, I have discovered my own creativity. If I had been told in the 1970s that in the 1980s I would be completely absorbed in creating tapestries, I would have considered it the wildest flight of fantasy imaginable. For over twelve months I designed and stitched tapestries into which I put the interests of my life. I began with a family history for my daughter, using symbols to portray members of her family. During the 1982 election campaign I created a tapestry which celebrated that great adventure. In 1984 I sold my bookshop and am now making the tapestries full time. For friends, I have made tapestries using Cretan, Egyptian and Greek history and mythology. This too is a part of our revolution. In embarking on this art form, I feel at one with the women of the past, who stitched into their creations the stories of their lives.

12 | Liza Newby

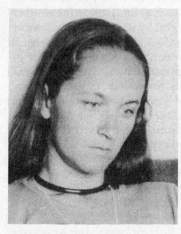

Liza Newby was born in London in 1946, of Norwegian–English parents. At eleven, her family emigrated to Australia, settling on a farm in Harvey, a small country town in the Darling Range foothills, 130km south of Perth, where she grew up.

At the time of writing, Liza Newby was lecturer in law at the University of Western Australia, and had studied and lectured abroad in England, Canada and the United States. She has researched and written on legal issues relevant to women, particularly rape laws, and on criminal justice policy for Canadian Indians and Australian Aborigines. In 1983 she was an inaugural member of the first Western Australian Women's Advisory Council established by the Labor government, and in 1984 was appointed as the first state Director of Women's Interests and adviser to the Premier on Women's Affairs by the Western Australian government, a position she held while on leave from the university.

A Sense of Place

I have found over the years I tend to become restless or unhappy when things settle for too long into predictable patterns or comfortable routines. With rather belated insight, I have begun to understand that whatever has happened to change things for me has had less to do with 'chance' or 'luck' (conventional explanations for women's life experiences) than with my own desire to resist 'falling into a rut' which, whenever monotony threatens, leads me to head off in some new, interesting, and more challenging direction – whether this be further study, changing jobs or countries, getting married or divorced, having babies or not having them – or even something as mundane as moving house! (One of the more delightful revelations of approaching middle age for me has been the idea that the seeking of 'change' for its own sake is not, as I had thought, a temporary stage on a journey to full adulthood and 'settling down', or a sign of 'immaturity', but in fact can be a desirable and exciting end in itself.)

True, my life altered direction fairly dramatically in the early 1970s, as it did for many people. Also true that in this, the philosophies and emotional support of feminists were a major catalyst. But, with the benefit of hindsight, it seems a little naive to lay it all at feminism's door. Probably, even without the women's movement, something had to 'give' around about then – I couldn't (or wouldn't have allowed myself to) stay as I was. Then again (as is always so) – no doubt the inspiration to rebel was buried somewhere in my childhood – people don't just slough off an old life and take on a new, just like that. Perhaps things would have changed anyway. But certainly I was very lucky that it all came together, right at that time, so that when I was ready to break out there it was, a movement, a philosophy, support, a *raison d'être* giving me a place in which to do it, making sense of it all.

I was part of a conventional, quite affluent, middle-class family. My parents were Scandinavian, and I was born and spent my early childhood in London. When I was eleven, we emigrated to Perth. These two events produced contradictory influences. On the one hand my European background provided me with much broader horizons than

109

usual for Australian girls at that time. I loved to travel; by the time I was fifteen, I had visited (even if only briefly) all major continents on my way between Australia, England and Norway, where the various branches of my family lived. My parents were literate, articulate, and accustomed to living at the hub of political and cultural events. I grew up with books, reading, discussion as much a part of life as breathing. Contrarily I – we – lived in a small, isolated and parochial city, from which the major influences on a world stage were felt distantly, and in which, at least in the fairly narrow circle of people whom we knew, life was comfortable, politics were conservative, and a woman's course was quite definitely settled in the direction of marriage and motherhood.

To do them justice, my parents were not conventional in that regard. They did not, like most of their friends, believe that education was 'wasted' on a girl. I remember their firm insistance, when I showed interest in careers of nurse or secretary, that 'a girl should never learn to type – or she will always be "just" a secretary' and 'if I was interested in that sort of thing it was a waste of a good brain to be a nurse, I should be a doctor'. It was always taken for granted I would go to university. The problem was, what they said was not how they and their friends lived. However hard I try, I cannot recall one, not even one woman among my mother's friends, or my friends' mothers, who worked or had a career for its own sake. Women who had jobs (like teachers at school or the divorced mother of a friend) did so because they 'had to'; they were for one reason or another obliged to support themselves because they had no 'man' to provide for them. Marriage and motherhood were the only real female careers I saw. The alternatives to which most of my contemporaries at the private girls' school I attended aspired – teacher, nurse, secretary, librarian: traditional female occupations – were regarded as temporary stepping stones to that end. Similarly, I have no memory of ever having heard, either at school or at home, anyone genuinely profess a non-conservative non-liberal political point of view. It is not that these alternative influences weren't there if I choose to look, but I never seriously considered that there was any other way of looking at things, so comfortable, cocooning and self-sustaining was the cushioned environment in which I grew up. Even after leaving school and doing well in law school, I still had no real sense of what I would do apart from marrying and bearing children – so that, when towards the end of my third year I fell pregnant to the man I had been 'going with' more or less since I started university, I abandoned my nascent legal career without even a backward glance, scurrying happily off to England with him to fulfill my 'destiny' as wife and mother. How, I hear you ask, if things were as conventional as all that, did you end up doing something as radical as going to law school, one of four girls in a class of ninety? The answer is – I'm not really quite sure; it had something to do with having no sciences, and a BA being too 'ordinary' (everyone did Arts) so law was the only alternative and the male-female ratio was definitely in my favour!

That was 1966. By the beginning of 1971 I had achieved everything I thought I wanted: two beautiful tow-headed children, plenty of friends, nice suburban house near the beach, and marriage to a successful, intelligent, ambitious man who was 'going places' and would take me with him. I was just twenty-four years old. The problem was I really wasn't very happy and didn't quite know why. The question was what was I to do with the next fifty years?!

Now, it is amazing to me that I could have come into young adulthood, despite all the advantages of my upbringing, with so little real sense of myself and my place in the world. But the fact remains that I genuinely, in my early twenties, had not in any concrete sense 'seen' beyond the realisation of the immediate goals of marriage and motherhood. I simply assumed, I suppose, without ever thinking about it much, that I would continue as I saw the women around me continue – rearing children, participating in community affairs, travelling overseas from time to time, running a home and family, possibly taking a few courses at university, being almost completely dependent for our continuing lifestyles on the income and status of our husbands.

However it didn't take more than two or three years for me to discover that this prospect bored and depressed me absolutely. By the end of 1971, things had changed fairly dramatically. I had re-enrolled in law school, joined a newly formed women's political group (forerunner of Women's Electoral Lobby in Perth), taken a lover, and read Betty Friedan's *The Feminine Mystique*, so discovering 'the problem which has no name', and that I had it! I still recall the sense of excitement and revelation I felt, shared by millions of women before and after, when I found myself reading about myself, my own life, discovering that I wasn't alone, there wasn't something wrong with me.

For the next three years I was a law student. For many women, law school has been an intimidating and potentially radicalising experience. It was at that time an intensely male environment in which women could be, and often were, treated as interlopers. There were few models of women lawyers for female students to emulate; in the small conservative law school I attended, the large corporate city firm (whose partners were all male) was the only obvious career path – legal aid, social welfare law, poverty legal clinics were ideas of the future. However much of this passed me by. I remained relatively uninvolved in student and university life. For one thing I was older than most of my fellow students. For another, I had too many other activities outside the university absorbing my energies. I was still married and had two very young children; I was becoming more and more intensely involved in the political activities of a women's group; and as a by-product had my own personal struggles. I went to lectures, did whatever study was necessary to pass reasonably well, and retreated to my 'other' life.

By the end of 1973 I was coming close to graduation with still no clear idea of what to do next. I knew only that 'conventional' legal practice, 'black letter law' as it is known, did not appeal to me. Law is traditionally taught and often practised as a series of rules and precepts divorced from the social and political context. I could not match teaching and practice with a growing radical sense that law and legal rules were an inextricable part of a system full of injustice and oppression. (By that time I had finally caught up with the 1960s!) In any case, the demands of the articles system (a full forty hours in a law office each week plus early morning and evening classes and study) were, I felt, out of the question for me, with full domestic responsibility for running a household and children, and little money to pay for extra help and child-care. So I resolved on an academic career.

Then, I started to drift away from close political involvement in the more organised activities of the women's movement, not through any disenchantment or rejection of their policies or direction. Rather a pragmatic decision grew on me as I realised how finite was the time I had. My original group broke up and transformed itself into WEL. I am not a very good organisation or committee person. I had found rewarding the period of intense consciousness-raising, and political discussion and lobbying we had spent together – for all of us our first real venture into the world of public affairs – but I was not prepared to take on the commitment to a new group. It was, I suppose, a matter of priorities. Women face this dilemma all the time. There are not enough hours in the day for all we want or have to do. I was working more or less full-time, and evenings and weekends I needed free from structured demands – for family (and housework!), friends, reading, discussion, music.

Leaving Perth in 1975 with the two children, I travelled to England and a graduate course in criminology, one of the only social science disciplines which treats as relevant, and will take on, lawyers at graduate level. I could break out of the narrow confines of traditional legal studies, and equip myself for a university job. So, at the fine old age of thirty, I was living the life of a graduate student. I shared a house with other students and it became a focal point for the whole graduate year. 'Pubbing' and parties, late night discussions, intense intellectual debate in what was one of the leading radical schools in its field in the English-speaking world – I loved it. The course at Sheffield was primarily marxist in orientation, and my study laid the intellectual foundations in radical social theory and feminist philosophy, to remain the cornerstone of my academic work and political convictions ever since. It also added empirical evidence and theoretical coherence to what had hitherto been rather inchoate feelings of social injustice, and the oppression of a class and gender divided society.

This year was also the end of my marriage. My husband did not come with us to England, and when I returned to Australia fifteen months later, we decided to separate permanently. Although he had always supported my activities, both financially and emotionally, it was clear that our lifestyles, values, and long-term goals were diverging sharply. We divorced soon after.

The next two years were hard. I was not conscious of it at the time, but in retrospect, the absence of tension now highlights the strains I felt then. I was a single parent, alone with two children and, although in my early thirties, I had yet to learn how to live as a completely independent and self-sustaining person, economically, emotionally and physically. I was embarking on a new career, in my first full-time job, in an environment not particularly supportive of women or of the radical sociological approach I wished to take to the study and teaching of law. I remember two incidents in my first year. I walked into the staff common room on the day I started work, to the remark 'O my god – the women are taking over the law school.' (I was one of two women on the staff.) Then a group of women students and I put together a women and law course and presented it to the faculty. We had a good course outline, and the student numbers to take it, but I was blissfully unaware of the politicking involved in being a successful academic. We didn't make it past the first review committee. Things have improved. Three years later there were five women on staff, and the faculty was supportive of my work, particularly with generous travel leave and research money.

My personal life was also in a fair degree of tatters. For the first year I was numb – shell-shocked, I suppose. And in the second, I bounced from one unhappy love affair to another before I learned to accept, and enjoy immensely, the independence and freedom of being single. This time really brought home to me the tremendous importance of the emotional solidarity between women that is part and parcel of the meaning of the women's movement for me. I was emotionally fed and sustained by my women friends. I recall one period – the only one where I came close to cracking up. A love affair had ended, I was at a low ebb, and I went on a Valium-sleeping-pill binge – not with any real suicidal intent, but just to temporarily obliterate what was happening to me. Quietly they took over, tiptoeing in to see if I was all right, otherwise leaving me alone to work it out for myself, providing meals for the children and seeing them to and from school for three days, until I was ready to pick it all up again. I have never forgotten that.

The challenge of those years, and one that has remained an exciting part of my life ever since, was the endeavour to create on my own terms, independently of any man, the kind of life and lifestyle I wanted to live. To juggle competing priorities of work, family and my own needs. To generate 'space' for myself and make a worthwhile contribution to the problems of social oppression and injustice I regard as important. To travel and be secure and confident with myself. Some things had to go. There was no time for the kind of intensive political commitment involving extensive evening and weekend work. After five years, I gave up working as an abortion counsellor and law reform campaigner and decided not to join or rejoin any of the other active women's groups.

Other new interests emerged. In 1978 I spent six weeks trekking, alone, in Nepal and India, having first-hand experience of poverty in the third world and the tremendous gulf between our world and theirs. My own discipline of criminology, and the structural links between women's oppression and other disadvantaged groups, led me to Aboriginal issues. Problems of Aborigines (and later North American Indians) in our legal system has become a major part of my professional work and an alternative focus of social activism. Arising from that, in 1980–81 I spent eighteen exciting months working and travelling in North America with my children, first in Arizona as visiting law professor, then in Canada as consultant to the federal government. There I met the man with whom I currently live, conducting the 'original' long-distance relationship commuting between Canada and Australia!

The years of the 1970s women's movement were enormously rewarding and challenging for me, and in the political arena for women generally. I have seen issues treated initially as the outrageous demands of a few aberrant radical females become part of the mainstream political platforms of both parties. I look back to younger women, hoping that I and others like me can provide the kind of example, inspiration, and mentorship that we did not have, back then. I look forward to the calm, sensitive, wise faces of older women, and think, 'I would like to be like that when I am fifty, or sixty, or seventy.' The changes that happened to me are not unique. My experience is repeated by thousands of women similar to me. Having achieved what we have, the greatest challenge for the women's movement now is bringing our values about the balance between family, personal life, and work, into general acceptance. We have made it into the paid work world, but that world is a man's world. We are still forced into choosing between family life and career as our primary goal, or trying to become superwomen and combine both. As the 'nurturers' responsible for family life, we lose our competitive edge in the public sphere; as career women, we have to sacrifice our values about the importance of personal relationships. There are a few men on our side of the fence, but not enough. Most men still do not face, or understand, this essential dilemma. Resolving it, for both men and women, is to me one of the single greatest contributions feminism can make to the quality of our lives.

There is also a dangerous lack of awareness among many women's groups active in the public arena of the class as well as gender divisions implicit in oppression. Middle-class women like myself have no conception of what it is like to be black and female, or migrant and female, or working class and female. Many issues about which feminists are most outspoken do not address the concerns of these women at all. I see in the still existing pressure to conform, on my teenage daughter and girls like her, evidence of real failure on our part to reach and effect any broad-based change in the lives of non-middle-class Australian women. Rape is another area where, when women tend to blindly call for heavy penalties and more punitive sentences, they are quite oblivious to the fact that, in a class-divided society, the burden of penal sanctions falls disproportionately on poor people and disadvantaged minority groups. By their actions, such feminists run the risk of simply adding to the oppressive capacities of state social control.

The future will be as exciting and as challenging as the 1970s and early 1980s. It will also be different. The euphoria of the early 1970s gave way to the realities of recession and unemployment in the 1980s.

Women activists generally felt threatened in the late 1970s; women felt they had to work hard just to hold onto what they already had. At the same time, the influence of 'women's issues' and 'the women's vote' on political affairs appeared to be growing stronger. The 1983 and 1984 elections bore this out. But women must continue to fight for more, while fighting to retain what we have gained.

At a more personal level, I look forward to an increasing involvement in these issues over the next decade. I feel as if I have taken a great deal more from women than I have contributed – emotionally, intellectually, and politically. Now, I am intent on giving some of it back.

13 | Vera Levin

Born in China of Russian parents, Vera Levin is fluent in several languages acquired while living in the United States of America, Canada and Israel. At the age of fifty she graduated in 1980 from the University of New South Wales as Bachelor of Arts and completed her studies in law to be admitted as a solicitor of the Supreme Court of New South Wales in December 1983, just four months before her fifty-fifth birthday.

Shortly after admission to practice, Vera Levin commenced work in the family law section of the Australian Legal Aid Office in Sydney; after eighteen months, she was offered and accepted a permanent position. She is now practising with the Legal Aid Commission of Victoria.

Vera Levin has two daughters and a son.

You'll Be Fifty Anyway

After twenty-one years of being a housewife, a mother of three and my husband's helpmate as his career blossomed, in 1972 I found myself back in Sydney. My husband's career demands meant we had to move home and family almost every year. Now I was determined to stay put and allow myself the luxury of living in familiar surroundings for as long as possible. Most importantly, I wanted to give my children the opportunity of having some continuity in their education.

The return to Sydney coincided with my second marriage to someone who in personality and character was the complete antithesis of my first husband. The outstanding problem was to earn enough money to support our family. Using administrative and secretarial skills grown rusty, I found a secretarial job. Part-time work was rare then, but I was determined to be at home when my two younger children came home from primary school. After a year in the job I became secretary to the managing director. Once more I was helpmate (albeit paid) to a burgeoning career.

I was born in pre-war China in the town of Harbin, daughter of well-to-do Russian-Jewish parents. My education began in an English school for girls, my high school years being spent in a boarding-school run by American missionaries in Shanghai. The combination of a bourgeois European family, living as a privileged minority in China, and the parochial schooling meant a fairly cloistered, somewhat unreal upbringing. The contrast between these early years and my next twenty years as a married woman, living much of the time in the larger cities of Israel, Canada, the United States and Australia was varied, but allowing for differences in the status of women in each of these societies and in cultural values, one subjective experience remained constant – my awareness that my view of a woman's role and its potential was not widely shared.

When Betty Friedan's *The Feminine Mystique* appeared in the 1960s, I realised I was not alone. For years I had been telling anyone who would listen that a trained orang-outang could do the housework and that, despite an abundance of love for one's children, for an intelligent woman to spend practically every waking hour with the goo-goo-ga-ga set was difficult and stultifying. Waiting for the return from work of one's only adult companion, to find he wanted to have his dinner and fall asleep in front of the TV because he had been with adults all day, seemed degrading and unfair to both parties.

Few people agreed with me. I felt more guilty and more of a misfit. So, if nothing else, early feminist literature gave me a sense of community with other women, at least vicariously. Although some women of my 'vintage' and position agreed with some aspects of feminism, most of my contemporaries in the late 1960s were too involved with furthering their husband's careers – and through that their stations in life – to regard feminist activities with more than an indulgent eye. The attitudes to the women's movement among most of my friends were akin to those we adopt when observing the behaviour of a group of naughty but attractive children.

By the early 1970s when the women's movement began to be taken more seriously, despite my affinal feelings, I found the combination of a demanding job, together with the care of three children, time and energy consuming. It was not a problem of coping with both roles. I enjoyed my work most of the time, until it became routine. Working made me a far better parent, improving the quality of the time spent with the family; but I had little time left for joining any organisation or participating in any movement, no matter how compelling.

An avid follower of current affairs, I gleaned as much as I could about women's movement issues through the news media. In the early 1970s more people were interested in vital social issues than in the early 1980s. Television programmes such as *Monday Conference* stimulated debate among my friends. Germaine Greer made an impact on me both on television and at Sydney's Town Hall. Her stance on women's issues spurred me to read more, although ironically I found *The Female Eunuch* flawed. But visits to the Town Hall were a luxury and the basic responsibilities of life seemed to absorb all my time.

However by 1973 my elder daughter entered university and the women's movement had a profound effect on her. She became interested in divorce reform, abortion law reform and human rights. We have always had a particularly close relationship; her interests were always a great part of dinner-table conversation. With her friends she became interested in alternative lifestyles and joined protest groups. I found myself enjoying these activities through her and learning from her 'what's going on'.

When the Whitlam government abolished university fees and some women friends discussed the possibility of doing further studies under the mature-age scheme, I was tempted. Married young, I had had no opportunity to study what I wanted. In my first marriage, no sooner would I start at a local university than we would have to move on due to my husband's career. Here at last was an opportunity; but lacking confidence in my abilities, I mentioned this ambition to no one. My daughter talked me into taking the entrance exam, consisting of an essay. Dozens of times I began writing, as many times deciding this was foolishness. Such cold fear overcame me that were it not for the nagging and being put to shame by my daughter, I would never have finished the essay or sent it off. I was convinced my writing was not university standard; the essay would never be accepted; that I was a fool at my age to harbour such a remote hope as a university education.

On arrival of my letter of acceptance from university, no one was more surprised than I. At first I was afraid someone had made a mistake. Then I was afraid they hadn't and that I could never have the nerve to attend full-time university studies, going to lectures and tutorials with students the age of my own children. I revealed my fears to my family, giving every excuse – we couldn't afford to lose my salary, the two younger ones could not be left alone if I had evening lectures. My husband and all three children stood together as a wall, until wearily I said: 'If I do an Arts degree, by the time I graduate I'll be fifty years old.' A friend of my daughter, another university student, took part in the conversation. He said: 'You'll be fifty whether you graduate or not.' The remark stayed with me and was somehow crazily responsible for shoving me into academia – that, and the support of my family.

In the first weeks at university, in the jumble of finding my way around the concrete maze of the University of New South Wales, I found few mature-age students in my tutorials and lectures. Most were straight out of high school. In the first days, I found the younger students were just as confused as I. Friendships formed with some sustained me through university life and are with me still. The young students were supportive and friendly and full of admiration that a person of my age should undertake such a burden. Like my own children, they were socially aware and idealistic. Many quickly became absorbed into student politics, including feminist groups and Aboriginal land rights organisations. Much as I wished to join them, my priorities included shopping for food, cooking for a family, and some minimal amount of housework. Despite considerable practical help from my family, those obligations and assignments and reading for courses left little time for other interests. Once again my enthusiasms were fired vicariously through my young friends during conversations between lectures and hurried lunches on the library lawn. Every spare second had to be spent in the library where, during the first three years, I found my greatest joy and where, I am convinced, I really received my education.

How did academics react to me? With few exceptions male tutors were patronising, and female tutors – especially one proclaiming herself an ardent feminist in writing and rhetoric – at best were mildly amused at the efforts of mature-aged women students. Somehow, they regarded students like myself and other women who later joined the classes as members of the 'blue-rinse set' trying to prove something to their bridge club; we were not taken seriously.

By 1980 I realised all too late, as did many fellow BA graduates, that our degree would not give us any real leverage in earning a living and I knew I would have to choose further education to give me more choices. I applied for 'everything', not really knowing what I wanted to do. Although attracted to social work, after enquiring about what was actually taught, my life experience told me it was not for me. I wanted to make a contribution to the world around me. Being such a migratory person, I had always felt particularly strongly about the plight of migrant women. I had several languages under my belt, enabling me to acclimatise more easily in a variety of countries. Yet despite this, having raised three children in many new places, without grandparents, family, friends or support systems, I could well understand the predicament of women arriving in Australia with foreign languages, cultures and ways, and I wanted to help. Further, as a member of a minority which had known oppression I could identify with other oppressed groups. I applied to law school thinking that through law it might be possible to make such a contribution. When the letter of acceptance arrived, inviting me to study for a Bachelor of Laws (LLB), I saw it as a good omen and an opportunity to work in ways meaningful to myself and the community.

When I entered the faculty of law, my youngest child was attending university with me. I had pleasant expectations of what lay ahead. My home responsibilities had lessened and I had visions of savouring, analysing and learning the law. With my children needing me less, I thought I could become involved in campus activities. Some women who were dear to me were involved in a practical way in the feminist movement and had urged me to join; but I did not count on the sheer enormity of the work load in the law course.

My only recollection of the first semester is of shock. My fellow students were also graduates, but none of the thirty who started with me (and the numbers quickly dwindled) was prepared for the work. Four subjects each semester meant four assignments together with four exams. As well, each teacher expected students to read numerous cases to prepare for class. If full preparation was done for each class, students would have no time at all to live.

All teachers were men. With minor exceptions, they regarded women students whimsically, and mature women like myself as some sort of special curiosity. If I spoke to my teachers for any reason, almost without exception the question would creep in: 'Why are you studying law?' My answer would always be the same: 'Why does anybody study law?' To this answer came the reply that despite my academic achievements, taking into account my age, there would be nowhere for me to practise law after graduation.

I should perhaps be grateful to these teachers, for it was probably an innate, stubborn reaction to their kindly advice that made me persevere. As it was, I constantly brought home tales of woe; there was no time left to enjoy any leisure with my family; I recall seeing all family events as disruptions to my studies. Considering the vicissitudes of family life and health, I am surprised at having come this far. The biggest single disaster came at the beginning of my third year of law, when my husband had open-heart surgery and hovered for days between life and death. The law school has precious little sympathy for disasters and for students missing classes – some teachers even took roll call! For me, some fellow students were wonderful and caring friends who ensured I had the latest class notes; they were generally very supportive through the crisis. Miraculously my husband pulled through and so did my studies.

After three years at law school I was incapable of enjoying reading a book without feeling guilty about not studying. Although I wanted to take an active part in women's groups on campus, this was not possible. My only interaction with other women was socially or as a fellow student. Male and female students were supportive and friendly. The notion of all being in the same boat no doubt helped keep us together. Younger male students, growing up during the women's movement, seem more aware than were their fathers of problems facing women. I believe this directly results from public discussion of women's issues over the 1970s and into the 1980s.

Looking back, the women's movement, like any significant movement for social change, has brought some disruption, pain and upheaval.

It still has a long way to go in Australia. However these years of the movement have been politically and socially significant. In the early 1970s, backyard abortionists were big business. Divorce was only for the rich and sexual violation of women both in and out of marriage was considered, albeit surreptitiously, each woman's obligation or her fault. Abortion on demand has given women an important right over their bodies and lives; the Family Law Act, with all its faults, has given men and women the right to be divorced without artificial subterfuge and enormous expense; there has been legal and psychological change in attitudes towards rape within and outside of marriage. This is largely due to the women's movement and to the political involvement and lobbying of feminists.

Social change brought about by feminist struggle has been instrumental in providing women with many more alternatives than previously available. I have reaped the benefits of the movement without participating directly in its struggles. This knowledge gives me mixed feelings of guilt and gratitude towards the efforts of my sisters. Guilt, because like a non-participating member of a trade union, I have gained the benefit without being involved; gratitude because feminists opened up opportunities for women and allowed us to think we *did* have choices, we *could* change or combine roles and *could* step out of traditional roles. My only contribution has been the raising of two daughters and a son to be aware and sensitive to the problems of women in particular and to less privileged people in general. My daughters think for themselves and due to the women's movement and, I hope, in some small measure due to my own example, they do not see their futures confined to the traditional roles I had to accept when I was their age.

I graduated in June 1983 at fifty-four years of age. I wanted to work, to use my education and life experience in a useful way. I have that opportunity, despite the jibes of the lecturers back at the law school. I became a solicitor with the Legal Aid Commission. Without exception, my colleagues have been a source of encouragement, support and friendship. Many have extensive experience in family law and unstintingly share their knowledge with me, imparting practical wisdom. And it is a source of amazement to me that my age, rather than being the handicap I was led to believe at university it would be, has turned out to be an advantage inasmuch as my clients often express relief that they are able to tell their problems to a person who obviously has life experience – particularly those who are themselves mature and find it difficult to discuss their family problems.

Even without this, I know the past years have been personally worthwhile, if only because I was provided with a choice to step out of a role I was socialised into believing was a life sentence. Aside from the obvious benefits of education, I have learned a lot about myself. My university experience raised my consciousness about my relations with society as a whole and certainly about women's places in society. Previously I was unaware of the lowly status and limited opportunities for women, but the 1970s put those issues clearly in focus. For the part played by the women's movement in raising that consciousness I will always be grateful.

Part Three

Something's Out
of Kilter

11 | Diana Warnock

Diana Warnock was born in 1940. A radio announcer with her own high-rating talk-back show, she has worked in newspapers, radio and television as journalist, producer, columnist and critic. She helps produce the quarterly newsletter of the Abortion Law Repeal Association in Western Australia and is active in many other organisations.

Diana Warnock is deputy chair of the Western Australian council of the Australian Bicentennial Authority and serves on the national council. She is married and likes spending time with feminists of both sexes.

A Woman's Place Is Every Place

In the early 1970s I was a married, heterosexual journalist with two step-children and a Bachelor of Arts degree. In the early 1980s I was still all of those things – but a wealth of experience and awareness had been wedged between those two dates. For me, the coming of the women's 'liberation' movement – oh, godess, how will we ever solve the problem of semantics? – has meant less a revelation, a flash of blinding light, than the slow fitting together of missing bits of a jigsaw puzzle. ('Of course, that's it: That's why I resented being stared/leered/whistled at; that's why I was angered by the casual contempt for women's intelligence/sexuality/physical ability; that's why I hated double sexual standards, pin-up pictures, and a thousand etcs . . .') Then, I thought little about the position of women in general, only about my own peculiar problems. Now, the two seem interconnected. The question of women's possibilities, women's equal status as human beings, seem as important as any social question. Once I might have judged a civilisation by the quality of its literature, technology or sanitary arrangements. Now, I am uninterested in society's so-called 'advancement' if its treatment of women remains reprehensible. Like Mary Daly, I reject christianity as male-dominated; I see patriarchy as the universal religion of the planet. Daly's research on witch-burning, Chinese foot-binding, female genital mutilation and Indian widow burning is among the most devastating done by any feminist. If only this remarkable work *Gyn/Ecology* sold as well as Barbara Cartland's seductive rubbish.

Like most people working in the wider 'political' arena, I feel the recurring needs for periods of 'R and R' – retreat and refurbishment. Full-on feminism is a wearying activity. Since 1975 my feminist activism (of varying intensity) has been with Women's Electoral Lobby, the Abortion Law Repeal Association, Australian Women Against Rape, the Women's Centre Action Group, Family Planning Association and the Humanist Society of WA. I have worked in two women's refuges – Nardine and Mary Smith – been part of three consciousness-raising groups and belonged to a loose organisation aimed at raising the awareness of prostitutes (our newsletter was called *Pros and Cons*).

In these and smaller groups I've arranged seminars on abortion, domestic violence, rape; written scores of letters to the media and politicians on working women, abortion, rape, sexism in advertising, the family, a women's adviser to government; made submissions to government and opposition on abortion and family planning, new rape laws, family policy; and spoken to numerous women's community/political/ student/professional/school groups on women and the media, sex-role stereotyping, women and psychiatry, depression and powerlessness, women and the church, sexism in the office, women in history, the politics of abortion, the reason for women's liberation. There's been picketing, petitioning, carrying banners and marching in rallies.

In all this I have felt the frustration and anger of any group of people trying to change the way things are. But I have also learned practical skills and come to greatly respect the abilities of other women. Without experience, training or confidence, so many women have become skilful activists and organisers of seminars and public meetings; negotiating with cabinet ministers, addressing conferences and rallies, publishing newsletters and chairing large groups. We *have* come a long way, but we still have far to go!

Throughout these years I was committed to reform (and therefore to the Left in politics), but was frequently disappointed in the ability and even inclination of male politicians of all persuasions to take women seriously. Short of revolution (in this country? Forget it!), we must seek change through the parliamentary system. Thus I believe that women must continue (and in increasing numbers) to gain office in all political parties. Without adequate representation in that male-dominated area, women will never make their voices heard. But the way to the political future is there, if we grasp it: the 1980s elections federally and in Western Australia pointed the way, and voters installed five new Labor women members in state parliament in 1983.

If there have been frustrations in this turbulent period, there have been pleasures too. The development of real and lasting friendships with other women – through common 'awareness', political aims and determination – has been a joy and constant bulwark against the grosser aspects of male chauvinism. What a delight it is to spend a lively evening in animated and amusing discussion over dinner with a group of women whose interests range far beyond the domestic. A major achievement of feminism is that such gatherings – the network dinners, the christmas parties – are seen by women themselves as just as interesting and 'legitimate' as mixed or male-only affairs. Female friendship is much richer when it does not include the shallow sexual rivalry encouraged by male-dominated society.

A personal pleasure has been the support received from both my mother and my husband. My mother, a political conservative, has been unwavering in her support of numerous public stands I have taken on issues such as abortion, rape, and working women. ('Why don't they fine the prostitutes' clients as well? There are two willing parties to these contracts', she once said.) It was she who taught me the value of financial independence, and its importance for female security and self-esteem.

My husband's support for and interest in feminism has been remarkable: he has read widely, and from day to day observation of my activities, he manifests an Alan Alda-like gut reaction to anti-female prejudice in the popular press. The constant support and changes he has made have kept me going. If one man can change and understand, so can many.

For many of us the early excitement, the discovery of ourselves and of the unexpected universality of women's problems, has given way to something else. I sense in many other feminists a quiet determination, a recognition that it is time for new approaches and new techniques. Many are now working in more powerful positions than women could have expected, once. Some have gone into business, academia, politics, or simply higher profile community work. If women in these and other positions can maintain close links with each other, they can operate the influential and supportive networks that men have used for years.

We have yet to reach a multitude of suburban women with traditional views about males and females. Most would have heard of 'the women's movement' and most (according to surveys) support issues like free choice on abortion and women's right to paid work. (That they are also prepared to support women as political candidates has been proved by the success of women in the 1980s elections in Western Australia.) Our efforts to make contact with these women are hampered by the barrage of conservative propaganda regularly served up by television, radio, magazines and newspapers. Many women journalists now support feminists, and the intelligent coverage is vastly different from the sensational nonsense written in, say, International Women's Year 1975. But old attitudes are hard to change. Too many male journalists – no doubt threatened by the thought of so many women who will no longer accept being treated like decorative doormats – still write about the women's movement as if it were entirely composed of boiler-suited, radical lesbians. Just as they write about lesbians as if they all wore boiler suits.

I once taught a pensioners exercise class. I was amazed and delighted at the support that some of my outspoken comments received from these older women. They were outraged at women being blamed by irresponsible judges for rape; they strongly supported the right of women to make their own choice on abortion. More than one thanked me for 'standing up for women'. If we can find some way of reaching the 'silent majority' of women, they will no longer remain silent.

A great pleasure of these years has been to read widely in the vast feminist literature now available. While much can horrify and depress us on the subject of women's oppression throughout human history, much inspires admiration and joy. Women, from the most uneducated to the most scholarly, have shown breathtaking courage in battling astonishing odds. That so few have rated a mention in conventional histories is a reproach to male scholarship. These long-time imbalances of knowledge are being well compensated by feminist research. But the new literature must be read by the widest possible audience. While history books continue to salute only kings and generals, girls will go on believing that boys and men alone are brave and important. And when mothers (and society) stop over-valuing males and under-valuing females, real changes will have been made.

How do I feel after these years of 'liberation'? Much better, thank you, despite being years older and in the so-called dangerous decade of the forties. My life is richer and more satisfying, my friendships closer and more rewarding. I am apprehensive about society and the future like any reasonably intelligent person, but wherever I see women learning to be independent and gaining self-respect, I see some hope. I'm still burning with anger over present (and past) injustices. But if women can learn to act together, we can change the world, fighting off the demons of repression and conservative attitudes.

And what do I want to be when I grow up? A feisty old woman who keeps on fighting until she has no energy left, a role model for younger women who need to know that it's OK to think women are as important as men and it's OK to believe all human beings have equal value and should therefore have equal opportunities.

I know in my heart, in my bones, that the movement for women's advancement can't stop now. That we (and our daughters and grand-daughters) must keep up the momentum. Changes we are seeking are world-shattering. They must be: look at the ferocious backlash from conservative extremists. We must hold the line, for ourselves and for generations of other women.

We women must resist the attacks of male columnists in right-wing newspapers; of women whose own lack of self-esteem makes them fear change; of male 'scholarship' seeking to 'prove' women's inferiority; of religious groups invoking pious words imposing limitations on women's freedom; of male politicians seeking to control our lives through paternalistic legislation.

We must have the guts and energy to keep on fighting. For while there are places in which women are genitally mutilated; sold into prostitution; drowned at birth; burned for dowry money; forced to bear children they don't want; denied the opportunity to work or even walk down a public street simply because they are women, then no feminist can pack up her slogans and go home. I won't.

15 Joan Russell

Born on 22 August 1946 in Brisbane, Joan Russell settled in Adelaide when she was seventeen, after moving around Australia with her army family. A sociologist, she is a graduate of the MA (Women's Studies) programme at the University of Kent, Canterbury, England, and a lecturer in Women's Studies and Family Studies in the South Australian College of Advanced Education.

Joan Russell is member of various boards and tribunals and is a keen cook and dressmaker. Her daughter Christie was born in June 1972.

I Am a Daughter, I Am a Mother, I Am a Woman, I Am a Feminist

I first read about the Women's Electoral Lobby in *Vogue*. It was sent to me on subscription, as a patrol officer's wife on a remote outstation in Papua New Guinea. That was 1972, about twenty-six years into my personal fight against sexism.

Negative aspects of being a girl had occurred to me ever since my father first told the story of our neighbour who, as a girl walking home from school with my father and friends, took off her dress to swim in the creek with the boys, all bare-chested. The boys copped it for being late home from school; she was beaten for walking home 'half-naked'. The injustice was as plain to me, and as confusing, then as now. Later I had a boyfriend who was cheered on in his feats of 'spider walking' up the open doorway, while I was shouted at for trying the same act. It went from bad to worse as I quickly learnt the nearest a girl could hope to come to the top of the class was third or fourth after the headmaster's son and the other clever boys.

It's unproductive dwelling on these experiences of petty sexism, because they were simply contributing factors to a much more important eventuality. All my life I've known my mother as an impressive, strong, competent, infallible and independent person. Her approach to life's minor problems and indignities was to work hard at keeping a sense of individual and personal integrity – do what you think is right always, and prove your case by having the last laugh in the long run. This classic mixture of passive resistence, tolerance and stubbornness was invariably a winner in the end. It gave me my determination to win when I believed I was right. It also convinced me my mother was all-knowing and all-powerful. I have never found her out being wrong. But the sacrifices I saw her make, subduing her strong personality to keep the conventional peace and support her very traditional moral and practical values, convinced me there had to be another way to win.

Mostly, I had a charmed childhood with this 'dragon' standing between me and the sexist world. She returned to work as a trained nurse to get the money for any programme or luxury she wanted for her children or home-life. It never occurred to her that being a worker was a special role; she always saw it as an extension of her role as wife and mother. She worked to perform that role better, so working never altered the way she saw herself in relation to the world outside her home. Her family, and other observers, saw her as a very clever, flexible, resourceful woman while she saw herself as a part of my father's life.

A pet project was getting 'a church school education' for my sister and me. This was intended to turn us out ladies, while providing the necessary prerequisites for some professional training – 'never a load to carry'. My years at Queens CEGGS in Ballarat (where I was a scholarship student) are another invaluable link in the chain leading to my assumption of a feminist activist identity. Just as my mother in her traditional role had provided me with a model of an independent working woman, so the teachers and headmistress at Queens unwittingly taught me pride in my self-confidence, and the acceptance of women's unquestionable right to attempt, and succeed at, anything. Those women were models of 'ladies' in every way, yet they had, almost without exception, made unconventional life choices to survive unmarried or widowed in a society where it was hard for women without men. They were proud, strong, competent and independent women who thought teaching girls important. The absence of boys led, perhaps by default, to the absence of the simpler forms of sexism in the school. There was a single set of standards, so there were no sex-based barriers to high achievement in any field.

For me, as for almost every other young woman then, the next life stage was a short period of work before marriage. The usual plans for entry to acceptable careers (in my mother's terms) were spoiled by my distaste for both nursing and teaching. My own ambitions for tertiary education were foiled by my failure to matriculate on schedule. This was a great relief to my father, who was convinced that universities were where you went to join the Communist Party and wear funny clothes. He need not have worried. I failed matriculation exams three more times before accepting I was just not a scholar.

Work in a research laboratory was the next link. After my dismal exam results, I saw an advertisement in an Adelaide paper for a laboratory assistant in the plant pathology department of the Waite Agricultural Research Institute. I was launched on a career in a nontraditional occupation in a meritocracy, where what you could do was more important than any consideration of class, sex, colour or race, since funds depended on results. Post-graduate students and exchange staff members came from all over the world. I was never happier, or more secure and confident, than in the peaceful 'sheltered workshop' atmosphere of that university backwater.

Then in a fit of reactionary pique I left the Waite, doing nine months' nursing training at Melbourne's Prince Henry's Hospital. I learnt a lot. Apart from the nursing training, which has continued to be most useful, I became aware of women's work conditions as traditional occupations. The contrast with the Waite was infuriatingly obvious. I hated the hierarchical organisation with women ruling other women, abusing power ashamedly borrowed from the male gods they worshipped. I hated being treated like a slave and spoken to like a moron. I hated being deprived of my dignity and openly exploited. No wonder I didn't stay to the end of the first year. The medical superintendent couldn't understand my resignation – I was reported to be such a good nurse. The matron had no trouble understanding. I was overqualified for the job, and she'd known from the start I wouldn't last because education wasn't everything! At Prince Henry's I met more dedicated women-educators and strong-woman models. I also met my first lesbian.

Being lonely in Melbourne had encouraged an increasing closeness with a childhood sweetheart, whom I soon married. Neither of us was happy at home, or living alone. We married because we knew each other well, and to have a home of our own. I knew it would be a disaster. I even feebly attempted to change my mind at the last minute.

The story of the next eight years is a résumé of initial failure to recognise unmatched, and therefore unmet, expectations, followed by the distance between partners resulting from the inability of two people talking different languages to communicate. No violence or serious deprivation: just the steady erosion of caring and respect produced by disappointment and frustration for both. We shared six years of 'colonial experience' with all its isolation and cultural alienation, unwilling members of a powerful minority, the Australian administration in Papua New Guinea. 'Mercenaries, missionaries and misfits' had nothing on it – I met all the overgrown Boy Scouts in the world up there. We were known as 'Peter and the Dragon'. No wonder my friends were the crazies such as field anthropologists, struggling planters and fundamentalist missionaries. The high point of those six miserable years was our daughter's birth in 1972.

My promotion into the 'former generation' (an idea originated by Anne Bergmann) was the closing link in The Chain. Never having paid sufficient attention to becoming a 'real' woman, I was alarmingly inept as a new mother. My natural incompetence and isolation on a small outstation in the Morobe District were the predisposing factors for my final bankruptcy of personal confidence. Sinking further, I needed more from the people around me – primarily from my husband and baby, then from absent family and friends. At the end of 1973 I left New Guinea. I guess I really left my marriage, but didn't have the courage to accept that. I had cooked, sewed, read and written letters to keep myself sane, and it wasn't working any longer. My valedictory salute came from the wonderful Lutheran missionary woman who said she had at first feared I was too 'bright' to last, then came to see that being 'bright' provided me with the resources necessary to survive in adversity, where many others perished.

When I returned to Adelaide with an eighteen-month-old daughter, I had to get a job, and a home. In retrospect I admire myself as job hunter. Despite my recently destructive experiences as wife-in-isolation, I had more confidence, self-respect and assertiveness than I'd have expected. I soon returned to my trade as laboratory technician – this time logging soil for a consulting engineering company. Again I was happy in my technical cul-de-sac with the worst elements of sexism missing, or at least blunted. In the field I never experienced sexual harassment, or condescending accommodation of my 'femaleness'. While I could do my job no one patronised me. In the office it was slightly different. With staff cutbacks I ran the switchboard and made coffee. Those were pretty expensive cups of coffee at my rate of pay, while junior draughtsmen stuck to their draughting.

All the problems of working women at a primary level were there, falling on me in one huge, all-enveloping bundle. I needed day-care, emergency child-care and occasional care . . . what if I was sick . . . and I couldn't even drive a car. My payscale was about 60 per cent of the man writing the soil reports from my bore logs, although we were the same age, and had the same number of years experience in our separate and complementary jobs. I was a worker all day and a mother and housekeeper out of hours; here was the dual-role responsibility problem at first hand. My guardian angels were a motherly Scot (in charge of my daughter Christie's day-care centre) and a shy, sturdy driving instructress. Without knowing it, these two women allowed me to change my life, giving me two essential tools of feminist activism – child-care security and independent mobility. Anti-feminist forces have always recognised the danger to society of adequate and flexible low-cost child-care, and I'm always watching for any sign that they've seen the threat of women drivers. We are all too familiar with disappearing and diminished child-care facilities, but when will they withdraw our driving licences?

I entered the organised women's movement through child-care. It has remained a top priority for me. By the time I heard a WEL speaker address a child-care concern forum, I had just about sorted out the worst of my own problems there, but that made me more fiercely aware of that major problem for working women. Hearing this woman speak on behalf of WEL persuaded me to join. WEL women were obviously effectively organised to do something about what was of paramount importance to me. I remained almost totally unaware of any 'organised women's movement'. I had no idea WEL was part of it, or where WEL stood in relation to other strands of feminism. What was feminism, or a feminist activist? I was pretty long on personal experience, but pretty short on the theory that makes sense out of the various elements and patterns of personal experience.

I teamed up with another new member to re-start the Working Women's Group. We worked together throughout 1975, organising a small-scale survey of Adelaide working women to provide the data for a submission on dual-role responsibility and other work-related problems to the Royal Commission on Human Relationships. The results clearly showed that working women's problems fell squarely onto a small number of categories no matter what the occupational or class basis of their experience, so she and I decided to apply to the Premier's Department for the funds to run a forum for working women. Working Women Speak Out was at once a great success and subtle disaster. Women came, and spoke out. Some spoke out critically against the middle-class assumptions implicit in the organisation and concept of the forum. In retrospect I realise our political and feminist naiveté were outstanding. Now, as a graduate sociologist, I shudder at the arrogance of that survey, and the resultant submissions, but remain unashamed and unrepentant about what we did.

In September of 1975 the Women and Politics Conference in Canberra was my confirmation in feminism, an eye-opener for a working mother from Adelaide. For the first time in three years I had time off from my mothering duties. For the first time in my life I had the luxury of a bedroom and bathroom to myself. Despite the many and varied negative aspects of the conference ideology and organisation, it was a unique opportunity for women from widespread backgrounds and interests to meet and share ideas. There were trade union officials, country women, single mothers, bureaucrats, lesbian separatists and radical feminists, black and migrant activists. Everyone seemed to know what she thought about everything and where she was going.

My husband had returned from New Guinea in late 1974 and we had unthinkingly settled back into married life, but many things had changed between us. Before the Canberra conference I handled the uneasiness at home as painful but insoluble. Lack of co-operation in domestic job-sharing and joint child-care responsibilities, divergence of interests with my rising feminist consciousness and his long-term unemployment and differential rates of growth in adulthood took on a new significance when I faced the question of who I was and what I wanted from the rest of my life. One night following my return from Canberra I silently slipped away from home. That was the start of my gradual leaving of the marriage. I was less prepared to be helpless in my frustration and disappointment. The rows became more angry and frequent. Feminism didn't break up my marriage: I did. I didn't quite know what I wanted, but knew I wanted to change. The conflicts and constraints of a marriage providing me with no support, security, encouragement, attention or affection were part of what I didn't want. On Australia Day in January 1976 I took my daughter and left.

A WEL friend and her husband stood by me. My father came to collect Christie and me from their home. When, after three weeks, my parents thought I had made my point and should return to my marriage, another feminist friend and her husband took us in and cared for us for weeks, until I could finally move back into 'the marital home'. Insofar as it was feminists who provided the mainstay supports for this great change in my life, feminism may be held 'responsible' for what happened. With nowhere to go, I'd probably have thought twice about leaving. Then a feminist lawyer handled the separation, property and custody matters. They were fair, and I remain 'married' because it has never been necessary to divorce formally. My husband and I are bound together as co-parents, and as very old friends, with passing of time.

I lived as a sole supporting parent during 1976. It became increasingly obvious that technician's wages would never be adequate for my new breadwinner role. Through a new relationship with an older and wiser lover came recognition of the need for me to formally join the trade union movement, and go to university. I joined the Association of Architects, Engineers, Supervisors and Draughtsmen of Australia (later ADSTE) mid-1976, immediately seeking union funding to go to the first Women's Trade Union Commission Conference in Sydney. With my Canberra experience, I kept my head in the face of an equally impressive bombardment of ideas that radically altered my consciousness of theory and practice of women's organised labour. Returning to Adelaide I instigated and stood for the position of women's liaison officer for my union. With support of the union, my experience and knowledge of unions and women's problems with them grew. Union membership eventually allowed me the privilege of holding the assistant secretary's position and a position on the United Trades and Labour Council delegation. It gave me entree to the ACTU conferences at the adoption and implementation of the Working Women's Charter and supported my inclusion on UTLC standing committees on women. I was a foundation member of the management committee of the Working Women's Centre in Adelaide.

I went into trade unionism as a feminist, because trade unions influence daily lives of millions of women in Australia. As my commitment to feminism increased, so did my conviction that trade unions should and could serve women at work. Simultaneously with the growing pains of conversion to trade unionism I was fighting the dehumanising effects of being a mature-entry university student. TEAS was insufficient for my child and me, so while studying full-time at Flinders University, I had twenty-hours-a-week work in consulting engineering. For two years I saw little of my fellow students, with minimum exposure to university life. It was lonely and alienating. I learnt to work nine to five, care for my child five to nine, study nine to midnight or one am. I learnt part-time work means part-time pay . . . and without regulation quickly becomes full-time work for half-time pay.

Things brightened when I discovered the sociology of social problems and was introduced to the sociology of deviance, later my speciality. In third year I was appointed consumer representative on the Builders' Licensing Board, on recommendation to the Attorney-General from the UTLC. The small weekly income allowed me to resign my job and attend university full-time. Following a good double major in sociology, I took a place in the 1980 honours class. Outside interests combined with tertiary studies made my BA living experience, keeping my feet on the ground. As publicity officer for WEL I combined university with a running stream of statements and commentaries on topical issues, writing letters to the editor, press releases and submissions, and appearing on radio and television. Practice and theory combined. The effects on Christie were offset by her father's calm rural influence at weekends, but when she heard I'd signed on for a further university year she cried, saying how much she hated seeing me at my typewriter. We talked about the future and my qualifications and she presented me with a typewriter cover decorated with a huge red appliquéd whale. Her classmates saw me on television more often than she, because she simply wasn't interested after accompanying me to studio taped interviews.

In my honours year I launched into a research project on the social control of lesbianism. My conviction that the politics and definition of deviance were crucial was tested. I look at the definition of lesbianism as deviance, the subjective experience of stigmatisation, marginalisation and social control of covert and active lesbians. I stumbled into the essential issue of feminism – the categorisation of women's social position and worth by social control of their sexuality. To cap it off I became infatuated with a vivacious and demanding younger woman. The lesbian experience of social control came true for me in nightmare fashion, while she encouraged and supported me in my work.

The sky fell. The four-year-old stable relationship with my wise older man tore apart, leaving us dazed and bleeding. My parents were shocked into disbelieving Biblical anger. My daughter heard from schoolmates that lesbians were dirty. I was on the medieval rack, pulled apart by increasing demands in opposing directions. I was admitted to a psychiatric ward in a catatonic state. My mother, accompanying me in the ambulance, told doctors I was overworked at university. I lived my thesis. Everyone wanted me to 'get over' this foolishness and turn back into the respectably radical old self. Bolshy politics and crazy feminism they accepted now, but lesbianism was beyond the pale.

No one wanted to know what had happened to me. People were embarrassed that I discussed it so openly. That was my defence – to intellectualise my own pain. My parents, my man and my straight friends didn't want to hear about my difficulties with a lesbian identity and experience. My new lover and lesbian feminists didn't want to hear about withdrawal of love, affection and esteem by the man who had been a mainstay of my social, political and intellectual existence. My supervisor and other university colleagues were uninterested in anything except that my work was erratic, my thesis late and my thinking in disarray.

In a few weeks I returned to my ordinary life as honours student/single mother/feminist activist. 1980 was the worst year of my life. Looking back, I think I lost everything. Crossing the invisible line between friendship-loving and sexual-loving with women did not seem a big step at the time. The closer I came to the line the flimsier it looked, until I knew it did not actually exist. But the impact of crossing the line, to those around me, was as if I'd defected to Moscow. I had not really changed at all, but was treated as though I was a stranger, by people I loved best.

I soldiered on. By the end of the year I pragmatically pulled myself together to finish my academic work. I was proud of my thesis. The examiners' reports ranged from outrageously scathing to courteously constructively critical. I gained a lower second class honours degree. My disappointment, shame and anger were an appropriate end to that saga. Now I can see some of the imputed flaws in my work and accept the low grade, but will never be able to separate that academic disaster from the overall disaster of the year.

Wouldn't you think that would have cured me of academic ambition and the desire for feminist scholarship? Not so. By October 1981 I was enrolled in the MA (Women's Studies) course at the University of Kent at Canterbury, Britain. This was to be the feminist intellectual experience to salve my wounded pride and resolidify my faith. Surely, thought I, there will be two dozen potential Juliet Mitchells and me, the dunce in the corner. If I sit quietly and listen, I'm bound to learn.

It didn't happen like that. My MA year was as difficult a trial, but much less dangerous, as honours. Unreal expectations – the difference in reality and my requirements – led to frustration. Undaunted I set to work to impose my criteria, standards and expectations on the course and my fellow students. Remembering, my overall impression is negative. As the English tend to do, most women listened politely to my colonial ravings, giving in graciously where it cost them least. I may have radicalised the course, but they taught me implacability and civility. Despite individual expressions of care and concern for my welfare, I felt the 'odd one out'. I lived a year in self-imposed isolation. Glad to escape back home at the end of the year, I still longed to return to stand and receive my Master's degree with the women of my course in Canterbury Cathedral.

Returning to Australia with my brand new MA, I was unemployed. Despite my own assessment of my capabilities, knowledge and experience, I was unsuitable for the prevailing job market. Many committees, organisations and consultancy bodies were ready to employ my skills, offering me avenues to contribute to the mountain of work facing feminist activists. I could put in almost a forty-hour-working week in service of my cause, but what I have to offer is at its most acceptable when filtered through respectable agencies. Unemployment, particularly when your time is taken up in urgent but unpaid work, starts out making you angry but ends up making you depressed.

Ti-Grace Atkinson has said 'sisterhood is powerful – it can kill, sisters mostly.' Feminism has caused me pain and made me angry, but not at the hands of sisters. The harm women do to each other is a product of the anti-woman attitudes they have been taught in order to retain support of male power. For women recognising this, ready to weed out those deadly messages, there is an ever-increasing strength in sisterhood. Sisterhood can save, and not only sisters, either.

Feminism has not changed my life – it is my life, but being a feminist has certainly changed me. My feminism means I believe there is nothing we do not want to know about, no change so small it can wait for the revolution, and no prizes for not winning.

16 | Betty McLellan

Betty McLellan, BA, MA, Dip. RE, PhD, was born on 16 May 1938 in Brisbane, and has lived and worked in different parts of Queensland all her life apart from a period of study and work in the United States (1970–7).

A feminist and radical psychotherapist, Betty McLellan was a main organiser of Townsville's first women's conference in 1981. Until recently her full-time job was with Life Line Townsville as co-ordinator of counselling services. She is now in private practice as a psychotherapist in Townsville and has established the Personal Growth Centre where she conducts courses in self-awareness, assertiveness training, and other areas of personal growth.

Towards Self-awareness

It may seem a contradiction to say I am a radical feminist psychotherapist and work as co-ordinator of counselling services at Life Line Townsville. Most of my feminist friends wonder how I cope with the rather conservative philosophy of an organisation like Life Line, while most of my Life Line friends wonder why I never tire of promoting and arguing for a feminist perspective in all things. For me, it's not a contradiction, but a challenge. How did I arrive at this point in my life where, as a radical feminist, I actually feel comfortable working in this kind of conservative environment?

I left high school after my junior year (now grade 10 in the Queensland education system), working in an office as shorthand typist for six or seven years before deciding there had to be more to life than that! During those years, I was also a deeply committed Christian, striving earnestly to discover what God wanted me to do with my life. At about twenty years of age I felt certain God was 'calling' me to be a minister of the gospel. (I'm deliberately using theological or church jargon here, because that's how I thought of it in those days. Today, I prefer to use more realistic, down-to-earth language to explain the decisions I make for my own life.) I talked with the minister of my local church expecting he would be overjoyed at the news that one of his flock was ready to offer herself to the full-time ministry of the church. But he was not. He looked troubled. Then he began to explain to me that the Methodist church did not accept women into the ministry. Strange I hadn't noticed! Women could be lay preachers, but not ordained ministers. Why? I really didn't understand. He told me that if I felt the call to preach, then I ought to offer myself for training as a deaconess, and make it known I was interested in doing general parish work. I accepted that suggestion. I had to, because there was no other avenue open to me as a woman. I accepted it, but puzzled over it for a long time. Did I just imagine God had called me to the ministry of the church? Or did God make a mistake? No, it couldn't be God. It had to be my mistake. So I contented myself with the role of deaconess.

After two years training, I served the church in three different parish appointments for the next eight years, from 1963 to 1970. I enjoyed the work and think I did it well, but there were many times when I felt angry over what seemed to me to be deliberate put-downs of me and my abilities. One incident occurred when I was in a meeting with some ministers I worked with and several laypeople from the church. We had met to make arrangements for three worship services to be held to mark the church's anniversary. I remember feeling really excited when the laypeople suggested strongly that I be the preacher at the evening service. I was excited because the evening service was always the big one. The huge church would be packed to overflowing, and still today I love the feeling I get when I address large crowds of people. But it was not to be. The meeting went on to discuss who would conduct the afternoon service, usually aimed at the children from Sunday School and their parents. All the preacher usually had to do at that service is tell a children's story, which is not very exciting for someone who loves to deliver powerful, inspiring, life-challenging sermons. My dream of conducting the evening service was shattered by just a few 'harmless' words from the senior minister. He said to the meeting, 'Betty is so good with children. What do you say we put her down to conduct the afternoon service and get someone else for the evening service?' Needless to say, I conducted the afternoon service. The minister conducted the evening service.

What did I do with all the bitterness and anger about this and so many other similar incidents? I did what most 'good' Christian women do: I reproached myself for having such thoughts and feelings, then proceeeded to repress them.

In a more personal area of my life, I recall a brief conversation with the man I came closest to marrying. I was twenty-one years old. We had been going together for almost two years. He was a theological student preparing to be a minister; I was a lay preacher just prior to beginning my study to be a deaconess. One Sunday evening, after I had preached what I considered to be quite an inspiring sermon and my friend was in the congregation, he said to me on the way home, 'I don't mind you preaching now, but after we're married you'll be my wife.' I didn't respond. I really didn't understand. I just had a terrible feeling inside me that whatever was happening at the moment just wasn't right. There was no justice in it. I don't know how I resisted the temptation to marry him when the pressure from family and friends was so great, but I didn't marry him even though it would have been the easiest path to take at that time. I didn't marry anyone. I am one of those fortunate women who never married, and now, almost fifty, I can fairly confidently say I will never marry.

In 1970 I applied for study leave and went to the United States. Several of our Queensland Methodist ministers had studied in the United States and most returned with doctorates, but when I spoke with one or two of them about my study plans, I received advice that doctoral study is extremely difficult and it would be better for me if I only went as far as Master's level. I agreed with them, of course, and honestly believed that would be all I could manage anyhow.

I began study in Nashville, Tennessee, at the end of 1970. At first, I was required to complete a BA which, with credits from work done previously in Australia, took me about eighteen months. Then in 1971–2 I began work on a Master's degree at Vanderbilt University in Nashville. A course I chose was 'Woman in the Family of Man', taught by a woman member of one of the religious orders of the Roman Catholic church. Required reading included Simone de Beauvoir's *The Second Sex*. As I read this and other feminist authors, my eyes began to open. I realised I hadn't been wrong to feel as I had all those years. The inequality between the sexes, so blatantly obvious in every sphere of life, was definitely unjust and unacceptable. Other women were feeling it as I had for years. Other women even had the courage to talk about it and write about it. I no longer had to accept it. I no longer had to be silent. My relief and the change that took place in me over the next twelve months – my self-image, self-awareness, self-confidence, self-assertion – defies description.

This transformation came about only because I allowed myself to think through the events of my life up to that point, admit the oppression and injustice surrounding me, and feel the depth of my bitterness and anger. As I looked back, I realised God *had* called me to be a minister all those years ago. I hadn't made a mistake after all. God had called me but the fact was the men of the church thought they knew better than God, and they had said 'No'. (Several years later, the male-dominated hierarchy of the Methodist Church changed the rule to allow women into the ministry, and this continued with the Uniting Church.) Again, the minister who had praised my ability to get through to children ('Betty's good with children . . .') had in fact manipulated the situation to get what he wanted. At last, I could see it so clearly. He worked it so that he had the more important job, and I was confined to a 'woman's place' – looking after and telling stories to children. I realised how right I was to follow my intuition and not marry my friend, who wanted me to be his wife and nothing else.

About half-way through my Master's degree I realised I was doing at least as well as anyone else, so I applied to two universities for entry to a doctoral programme. I remembered with shame a conversation I had had a few months earlier with one of my Vanderbilt professors. He had asked if I was intending to go on to doctoral study. My response had been, 'No, I don't need to go any further than my Masters.' And when he asked why, I said with all the confidence of someone thinking she is offering a supremely logical, rational explanation, 'Well, I'm only a woman.' He seemed stunned. Today I can hardly believe I would ever have said such a thing. But I did.

Both applications for doctoral entry were accepted. In 1974 I moved to southern California to begin research and study leading to a PhD in theology and psychology, which I completed in 1977. As a doctoral candidate I proposed three courses to the faculty committee (one per semester for three consecutive semesters), having each approved. This meant I was able to teach graduate level courses from a feminist perspective, which was exciting, a satisfying experience for a reasonably new feminist. Proposing the courses to faculty was a political act on my part. Teaching them was also political.

My doctoral student years were the time I realised the value of being with, sharing and working with other women. Before I felt competitive with and critical of other women. I became actively involved in the Association for Women's Affairs, an organisation on campus fighting for elimination of discrimination against women and more just and equitable representation of women on committees and other decision making bodies in higher education. We spoke out strongly against sexist language and had all sexist language omitted from official school documents.

The raising of my political consciousness went hand in hand with the raising of my feminist consciousness. Before I studied in the United States, I had no interest in political parties or philosophies. At elections I always voted Liberal/Country Party. I'm not sure why. Perhaps it had something to do with my father, who was a member of the Metal Workers' Union and a fervant ALP supporter. As a professional person it seemed more appropriate to me that I should vote conservative. Or maybe I just wanted to be different from my parents. All I know is I had no interest in being political in any area of my life. I didn't see myself as someone whose opinions mattered or whose words and actions could make a difference in the world, except perhaps in spiritual or religious matters. Therefore I didn't push for change even when I knew of injustices around me. In these pre-feminist days, I seemed simply to accept everything as inevitable, and from my position of perceived powerlessness – I did nothing.

How different it is now. When I became a feminist, it was as though I began looking at everything differently. Not only did I see the oppression of women. I saw for the first time the oppression of Aboriginal Australians, of Islanders, of migrants, the oppression of homosexual women and men, indeed the oppression of all groups in Australia who are different from the mainstream. I had found a whole new way of looking at the world around me, a way far more realistic and enlightened and honest. I no longer saw myself as someone who was powerless. I saw myself as a person with great power, especially through my better-than-average ability to express myself, to speak out for justice and equality. My voting on election day changed too. When I returned to Australia, I began and have continued voting for the ALP, though not making a decision to join the party.

In the few years I spent in southern California I experienced for the first time a real solidarity with other women. Beside the Association for Women's Affairs, I joined a group of women which provided me with an experience never to be duplicated. The kind of intimacy, caring and support group members received from each other is a cherished memory. We were politically aware. Each had some background in theology and some experience in the church. Some were studying to be ministers. One was a retired professor of religious education. One was a psychotherapist in private practice. A few (myself included) were doctoral students doing psychotherapy at a nearby counselling centre. Three had articles or books published on feminist issues. It was a close-knit and interesting group, meeting fortnightly for support and discussion. We called ourselves 'Sister Circle'. With women of strength and energy, caring and love, our meetings were a celebration of womankind. My involvement had a profound effect on my attitude to myself as a woman and a feminist, and my attitude to all women.

A rule I adhere to strongly, which must have formed as a result of 'Sister Circle', is that I refuse to use my energy arguing with or criticising other women, even those groups of women in Australia speaking out so strongly against feminist principles. Women are not the enemy. When women argue with women, we support the male strategy of 'divide and conquer'. I refuse to play into their hands. Instead, I save my energy to do battle with the real oppressor of women, namely man, and the whole patriarchal system on which our society is built.

When I returned to Australia toward the end of 1977, I took a job as director of Life Line Rockhampton in central Queensland. I joined WEL in Rockhampton, but while that was a good experience, I found myself longing for the kind of feminist company left behind in California. Mostly I felt restless, with an unsatisfied emptiness. During that year I met some feminist women from Townsville and decided that, for my own survival, I should move to Townsville. I did so early in 1979.

Over these years in Townsville, I have been associated with a small but supportive group of feminist women. Together we have participated in the opening and closing of the women's information centre, the opening and closing of a women's room at the university, and the re-establishing and going-into-recess-again of WEL. That so many women's ventures in Townsville seem to have a short life-span may be disheartening to some, but my friends and I see it more as our willingness to answer a need when it arises and an unwillingness to hang on to something that has outlived its usefulness. That way, we preserve our energy and enthusiasm for the next time, the next need.

In 1981, some of us decided Townsville was ready for its first women's conference. The theme was Women Taking Control. In the initial stages of planning we spent lots of time talking about the kind of conference we wanted and the kinds of women we should attract. We decided to call it a women's conference rather than a feminist conference, with one of our aims being consciousness-raising. We wanted to attract women from all walks of life and levels of political awareness. We worked hard to ensure everyone attending could feel comfortable being there, whether calling themselves feminist or not. We agreed this was important to achieve our aim of consciousness-raising. We also agreed we would not at any time forsake our integrity by watering down the feminist message. The theme was obviously and deliberately feminist; the guest speaker left no doubt in anyone's mind she spoke from a feminist perspective. All the workshops dealt with women's issues as feminist. More than 130 women from Townsville and surrounding areas registered and attended. All but a few spoke of it as a significant event in their lives. Probably the most exciting part for those of us putting so much time and energy into it was the experience of working together to achieve the goal we had set ourselves. After all these years, now, as a feminist, I still find working together with other feminists a powerful and energising experience. There are some disappointments, of course, but the positives far outweight the negatives. I am committed to women's liberation, seeing no reason for that to change.

Apart from the women's liberation movement teaching me how to work together with women, it changed directly one relationship that was always important to me – that with my mother. We were always good friends with a lot of respect for each other. But when I returned from the United States we seemed to have a different kind of closeness. She was not a feminist and at times was critical of what I said about discrimination and the need for equality. But things were different between us and I think it was due to my changed attitude towards women in general and my mother in particular. She died in 1981, just four years after my return, but I am so thankful my new consciousness enabled us to have the kind of real relationship so few mothers and daughters are able to have in this male-oriented society. It was only four short years, but the effect that changed relationship had on me will remain with me forever.

What does it mean to me to be a radical feminist psychotherapist working within an organisation like Life Line in Townsville? I firmly believe in the work Life Line does in the community. I appreciate that any person can phone or come in for face-to-face counselling for no fee. I enjoy working with large numbers of volunteers who are always looking for ways to enhance their own growth. I appreciate the opportunity through my work to pursue my own journey towards self-awareness and to help others do the same.

Radical therapy began in the United States in the late 1960s and early 1970s, but is still little known in Australia. Radical therapy is concerned to help a person get to the 'root' cause of their psychological and emotional problems, and recognises this often means helping that person understand the particular socio-political situation out of which their problems have arisen. As a radical psychotherapist I have no time for the kind of therapy working to preserve the status quo. That is not therapy at all. Rather it is just another form of social control.

My task as a psychotherapist, as I understand it, is to help people to an understanding of the power-plays existing in their lives and the devastating effects of oppression which always occur when one person assumes power over another, or when society sanctions groups of people having power over other groups of people. As a radical psy-

chotherapist my task is to help people to an awareness of their
oppression rather than allowing them to go on blaming themselves
for problems over which they have no control. If a person is enabled
to see their situation as it really is, we believe they will then be able
to find ways to bring about changes for themselves. Traditional therapy reinforces mystification. Radical therapy emphasises the need for
awareness. Since becoming a feminist, my own particular interest is
in the growth and enhancement of women's self-awareness, and it is
therefore exciting for me to work with women on an individual basis,
or in groups, in their search for a greater awareness of themselves.

Since the early 1970s when my consciousness began its first step
toward feminism and my consciousness began to be raised, mine has
been a journey to greater and greater self-awareness. With the ongoing help and support of my sisters, I will continue that journey into
the future.

17 | Diane Bell

Born in Melbourne in 1943, Diane Bell is an anthropologist with extensive fieldwork experience in northern Australia. In *Daughters of Dreaming*, she wrote of the ritual life of Aboriginal women of Warrabri, where she lived with her children for eighteen months and, in *Law, the Old and the New*, of their role in the maintenance of customary law. Her other publications concern land rights, law reform, biography, oral history and a co-edited volume *Religion in Aboriginal Australia*.

Previously a primary school teacher, Diane Bell has been a research fellow in the Research School of Social Sciences, Australian National University, and is now professor of Australian Studies at Deakin University in Victoria.

Giving In – Or Giving Them Hell!

Walking out of the Exhibition Building in Melbourne that hot December day in 1971, I was greeted by a fresh-faced student of seventeen: 'What are you doing here?' she asked. 'Same as you,' I grinned. 'Sitting for my HSC.' 'But you taught me in 1963 in grade four, remember?'

I boarded the tram to Flinders Street, caught the train to Highett and ran the rest of the way to my parents' home to collect my children. Driving home through peak-hour traffic, I tried to explain my feelings to them. 'I've sat for my last exam,' I told them. 'I didn't think I could do it. It was so easy. I couldn't stop writing.'

Then – doubts. Ten years since I'd left school; I'd done the subjects for matriculation at night school. Sandwiching them between feeds for my infant son and story-time for my toddler daughter, I had little time to study. I spent most days with my children and evenings sewing to earn sufficient to feed us. One day a week I taught at the nearby boys technical school and, more from irrepressible optimism than anything else, I saved money against a possible entrance to university and the $500 first-year fees. We were under a Liberal government, Vietnam could still be justified, a university education cost money and deserting mothers like I was could expect nothing from social security. No TEAS, no supporting mothers' benefit. I was the guilty party, I left and I could pay the price. I was a trained primary school teacher and could have returned to teaching – that was friends' and family advice. I wanted more. Six years teaching in primary schools in Victoria and New South Wales was enjoyable, but I returned home every day feeling I had not given my best. Teaching could never provide the outlet for my boundless energy.

I gave up teaching in 1967, just before Genevieve, my first child, was born. A doting mother, I'm glad I didn't have to face the pressure mothers with careers now face from their peers in deciding whether to take three, six, nine or twelve months' maternity leave. But pressure was there. I couldn't cope with the solitary housewife role. I felt mentally dead. I don't remember having one creative thought for about four years. Probably my mind bubbled along: I wrote short stories and

157

poetry about women who were trapped, then read Betty Friedan's *The Feminine Mystique* and cried out, 'I know the name of that "phenomenon with no name" and I don't want to be there. I want out.' But where to? No money, no real education. When I applied to re-enter teaching, my teaching qualification was no longer adequate for permanency in the education department. To become permanent I should have matriculated before I did teaching. Although I had now matriculated it could not be counted because it post-dated my teacher training. The only way to gain permanency with the department and recognition for the qualification and years of service was to gain further qualifications. However to gain assistance in getting these qualifications I needed permanency. 'Sorry,' said the man interviewing me. 'You're just an anomaly.'

But I had a sense, as did several women friends who shared my vision, that the fault lay not so much in ourselves as in the society in which we lived. We read everything coming out of America and England concerning women's role. We were depressingly certain that they wrote about us. We listened to Germaine Greer. We wondered how we could get out from under. Perhaps education was the way out.

Physics was my passion at school and I scorned 'soft subjects', but I was ten years out of date, with no time to attend practical classes. I chose history and English at matriculation because I could study at home. There began my enchantment with the social sciences. So I grabbed an offer of a place at Monash University in the Arts faculty when it came. My status as an anomaly again worked against me. My computer classification put me at the bottom of the list of those receiving offers. The reason? I already had another qualification! By the time my enrolment date came around, many subjects I hoped to do were no longer available; quotas were full. I wandered up and down the 'Ming Wing' at Monash, asking of various subject advisers, 'What time do you have your lectures?' I had child-minding between 10 am and 12 noon for my son; my daughter was in kindergarten between 9 am and 3 pm. I could take only those subjects fitting that time-table or having taped lectures available. My flirtation with philosophy began in that way – gracious lecturers scheduling classes at convenient times. But the psychology department told me plainly they could fill their quotas without catering to the likes of me. My enrolment in anthropology was almost aborted. There was no place in first year, but I spread out my HSC results, stood my ground while my children dismantled the interviewing officer's office, and after a brief exchange I was in. Then, I intended majoring in history, not anthropology. I wanted to rewrite the early colonial period to reclaim those 'hidden from history'. But the upheaval of 1972, the end of Vietnam, finding women sharing my vision and self-doubts, reading Sheila Robotham's *Woman's Consciousness, Man's World*, propelled me into anthropology. I hoped for the opportunity to develop a critical analysis of woman's place in my own society and in other societies.

Student Parent Association at Monash (SPAM) was my political blood-ing. Growing up in a Labor-oriented household I knew union politics, but had not really been involved in a fight myself. I had sat down in Bourke Street during a moratorium and even marched in Sydney way back in 1967 when already vastly pregnant with my first child, but I had never initiated and carried through a political action. Our first experiment was successful. We got a good press while students at Melbourne University were being charged for storming university offices with similar demands. I agitated, learning a lot about student politics. I found how class analysis could be used against women, can-vassed opinion among staff and students, lobbied and organised. Most women were prepared to do the shit work but not the confrontation. They hated shouting. I didn't like it, but finding a sharp, stinging reply has never been difficult if I was sufficiently challenged. During the campaign the response of certain women holding full-time jobs was amazing: 'Don't make waves,' they told me. 'Accept your lot. Don't you realise we started that fight years ago and all you get are headaches.' From the university administration came a different attack: 'You're a good student and a good politician. You'd better decide which you want to be, because you can't be both,' I was warned. When we presented our carefully worded petition on child-care for school age children, the vice-chancellor told me, 'Universities were not made for people like you.' 'Well, they will just have to change, won't they,' I retorted.

Finally we got our grant setting up the child-minding scheme on a regular basis each school holidays, SPAM grew and ultimately became an establishment organisation. I began to think that a new organisa-tion was needed, but by then was involved in a different battle. With the fall of the Liberal government and abolition of fees came new hope for students with financial commitments outside university. We were able to get some assistance but it was an uphill battle. The student allowances assumed students could work during school holidays, but that meant child-care which cost more than I could earn in most unskilled positions. Anyway it was the only time I had to spend with my children. I continued sewing in the evening to earn. This meant no child-care costs. I was full-time student, full-time mother, part-time seamstress.

During those undergraduate years I never quite managed to join any women's organisation on campus. I attended a WEL meeting, but members spoke of nothing I understood. It was very middle class. I felt awkward and clumsy. The Women's Liberation Group was youthful. I couldn't attend – no child-care. 'I'm too oppressed to attend meetings to discuss the nature of my oppression,' I said. 'Bring the kids,' the younger woman replied. But I was on a tight schedule and a tired or sniffling child would not be welcome at the half-day child-care I had. Neither the women's liberationists nor the WEL ladies were where I was at.

   But those years were important because of the friends I made – women who remain friends, with whom I can talk about the different directions our lives have taken. One of the strongest women I met was in charge of the child-care centre. She was one of my safety valves. With six kids, she loved them all, but had always worked and held firmly that women should pursue careers. Other women became part of my survival. We were all a little crazy I suspect. Anger characterised my style, sustaining me and propelling me into action. Without that anger and sense of injustice, I probably would have given up and accepted 'my lot'.

   By fourth year of my post-graduate career, fascination with social sciences was palling, but I knew what I wanted: to work in Australia and to look at women's place in my own society. Anthropology made me see research with Aboriginal women as intellectually challenging and politically important. I intended to work in northern Australia documenting the ritual lives of Aboriginal women. Writing to scholars for assistance, I received encouragement from some, dismissal and delay from others. Now, I answer such enquiries promptly, with as much encouragement as I can muster. I thought other women in the field would provide role models, but experience showed Miriam Dixson correct: we suffer from a paucity of role models as Australian women. Those at the top are often too busy maintaining their positions to give a friendly word to those on the way up.

   Finally, with assistance of a local community adviser, I was accepted to work in a desert community, Warrabri, 375 km north of Alice Springs. Here 350 Warlbiri speakers lived and I hoped to undertake research with Warlbiri women, grafting this work on to existing work of male anthropologists with Warlbiri men to produce a well-rounded study. I thought I had learnt a lot about women's issues, about the

need for solidarity; I had found enormous warmth and support in
women's friendship, but was desperately disappointed in women who
had made it in a male world by male values and at the expense of other
women. I didn't know what to expect in the field. Contradictory images
of Aboriginal women were recorded in ethnography. Was I to be disillusioned and disenchanted yet again?

All these years after first entering an Aboriginal community, my admiration for the way Aboriginal women organise their lives has not waned.
Our teaching is that for women to gain status they must be 'equal',
infiltrating man's world and demanding equal education, job opportunities, parity; 'different but equal' is a sop. So it is, but putting aside
notions of equality and thinking instead of independence and inter-
dependence, what of the solidarity enjoyed by Aboriginal women? In
Aboriginal society men socialise with men, women with women. By
day women sit in groups, men sit in groups; there is little mixed group
activity. In central Australia, women's groups generally centre around
the 'single woman's camp'. Here, widows choosing not to remarry, girls
too young to marry, women choosing not to enter into second or third
marriages, women visiting from another community, sick women and
women vacating the camp of their husband, are found. The atmosphere
is warm and supportive. Conversation centres on family, health, land
and ceremonies. By day, married women come, sit and enjoy the company of resident women, returning in the evening to the married camp
and their husbands.

In these camps I came to know something of Aboriginal women's
lives. Here I learned of Aboriginal women's perception of white
women's liberation movements. I was accepted because I was an adult
woman with children, but they waited and cross-questioned me before
accepting me further. Where was my husband? How did I support
myself? I said I was divorced with a government pension, and on an
ANU scholarship. They probed my divorce and subsequent relationships with men. I answered honestly. They said they would teach me
something of women's ceremonial life, because I was independent of
men. They explained I was 'just like them': I had my own economic
base. Pensioners are respected in Aboriginal communities because their
income is regular and assured. In the past these women supported themselves by their own hunting and gathering. Today with government
pensions, especially old age pensions, they see some continuity with
the past.

They then asked 'what could I do?' Could I drive? Sure, I replied.
Could I shoot? No, I couldn't. I admitted I dislike guns. Never mind,

we'll teach you to use fighting sticks and digging sticks. They did. They instructed me in self-defence and attack, and in how to treat suggestive comments from men. Some things were 'provocative'. I was warned not to wear tight jeans or short shorts, and given clear instructions on how to sit in mixed company. It was improper to look men directly in the eye; I was taught which men I should avoid completely (say, classificatory sons-in-law) and with whom I could joke openly (classificatory husbands and maternal grandfathers). I was never at risk following this code; I was never considered bold or shameful in my behaviour. Men appreciated the respect I showed their customs and entered into lengthy and introspective discussions with me about Aboriginal culture while avoiding direct eye contact. Thus, rather than this apparently modest behaviour preventing me from establishing relationships with men, it created an atmosphere giving me similar extensive access to men's knowledge as Aboriginal women were given.

The Aboriginal women appreciated my determination to learn to do things properly. Initially they were exasperated with me when I couldn't tell the difference between a snake and goanna hole, but they taught me patiently and in time I hunted beside them. Similarly men appreciated my determination, often approaching me for assistance with repairing broken-down vehicles. There was no shame in asking a woman to assist in repairing a loose fan belt, cleaning and adjusting points or repairing a staked tyre.

Old women were repositories of knowledge of women's ceremonial responsibility. Younger women and women with children of my children's age often stayed with me to keep me company and I learned from them of marriage and motherhood. Some had married men many years their senior, yet did not see themselves as oppressed. Their behaviour indicated no subjugation. They made their own decisions about their lives and considered themselves independent operators. Sometimes they spoke of family life in white society. Some had worked as housegirls to white families, with privileged access to hearth and home. Others had casual relationships with white men and thus some knowledge of our male-female relations. Overall they saw white woman's lot as hard. They considered white women's child-rearing methods selfish, children having one mother only. This contrasted with their society where sisters share child responsibilities. They thought white grandmothers were denied access to their grandchildren, and uncles and fathers had no responsibility for their children's moral conduct, unlike men in their society. They were bewildered by white women with small babies who shut them away when they cried.

Returning to Canberra eighteen months later to write up my

experiences, I had learned that separation of the sexes does not necessarily mean denial of rights. This met with some hostility from
colleagues. 'That may be true, Diane,' I was told, 'but regardless of
what you say women are doing, they are still oppressed.' 'Yes,' I replied,
'But they don't see it that way.' 'False consciousness,' said my marxist
friends. But was it? I contented myself with writing up my ethnography and analysing my data, transcribing my tapes, writing out my
genealogies and discussing results with Aboriginal women in Canberra.

I returned to the field often in the next two years, trying out my
developing ideas with women in other communities. I returned to Warrabri in August 1978 as consultant to Justice Toohey on the Alyawarra
and Kaitatja Land Claim. During the hearing women were asked to
give evidence on their relationship to land. The question-answer for-
mat was difficult; the women's answers lacked clarity. After a frustrating
afternoon several of the senior women approached me, asking if they
could show the judge what they knew of the country. They would
put on a ceremony to provide answers to the questions.

The women spent much time preparing their paintings, their objects,
and the ground on which to dance. When ready, they called in the
judicial party, seating them carefully so they had a clear view. The
women danced, following the tracks of the ancestors pioneering country. After the dancing, a senior woman presented the judge with a board
painted with designs of her dreaming. She was so giving answers to
the questions. The Aboriginal men were delighted that the women
had chosen this way to display their knowledge. It had been the
women's decision, and they had organised and executed the display.

In each of the eleven land claims in the north and centre of the Northern Territory on which I have worked, women have requested they
be able to give evidence in a way appropriate to their cultural style.
Their decision has been respected and supported by their menfolk.
The white man's response has been notable. Sometimes smutty jokes
are passed about white women's involvement in these ceremonies.
Sometimes genuine respect and appreciation are there. In all ceremonies women have brought to the public arena only that information
appropriate for men, women and children to see. Much remains secret.
The predominance of men in the court, from judges through barristers
to advisers, means that with men's secret material there is little need
to compromise or set such limits. However women have had to make
decisions of what they would show. The participation of women anthropologists in the land claim process has enabled Aboriginal women to
bring to the court their knowledge of land and their relationship to

it, in a way acceptable to them. Being able to share the experience and discuss its significance for analyses of Aboriginal society and gender relations in our own society has been a great joy of fieldwork.

During fieldwork on a project for the Australian Law Reform Commission in its enquiry into Aboriginal customary law, I applied to stay in a university-owned house in Alice Springs but was rejected because my children 'might disturb other residents who were "scholars" '. I protested I too was a scholar. Taking my complaint to the director of the Research School at ANU it was agreed I could stay but any damage would be charged to me. When I arrived in Alice Springs, a male academic, his wife and family were in residence. He was not even from ANU. I was out on the streets, with kids. Again I protested. Letters went back and forth. I was characterised as the one who just didn't know when to give in.

On returning to Canberra I found support, interest and stimulation in the company of many strong women friends. In Christmas vacation of 1978–9 I holidayed in the USA, meeting women whose work I had read. They were kind, but firm. It is fascinating ethnography, but what does it mean? they kept asking. What does it mean for other studies of women's status? What does it mean for studies of hunter-gatherer societies in other parts of the world? I could answer their questions only by taking an historical perspective.

In 1980 I participated in the International Conference on the Sex Division of Labour and Women's Status, at Burg Wartenstein. It was the first time the old castle had hosted an all-women conference. How to deal with it? Male academics could be entertained with dancing and music in the evenings, but a bunch of women? We drank less and talked more than the men, one of the staff told me. We formed fewer cliques and seemed to enjoy easier relationships with each other, another said. For me it was a once-in-a-lifetime experience: I met women from Iran, Mexico, Singapore, the Philippines, Egypt, Latin America, England and the USA. Eleanor Leacock, who had helped me with my work, was an organiser.

I set my Australian material of a hunter-gatherer population into the wider framework of peasant studies and studies in urbanising and urban communities. For ten days seventeen women sat around a green baize table mulling over issues confronting us in our respective fields. The majority were warm, encouraging, giving me enormous intellectual and personal support. One or two saw the conference as an opportunity to further their careers, in a way I associate with male power play.

Returning to Canberra, in six weeks I rewrote and submitted my PhD thesis Daughters of Dreaming. After ten years of being a student, it was time I entered the paid workforce. I went to Darwin with the newly formed Aboriginal Sacred Sites Protection Authority, choosing working with women on matters affecting sacred sites rather than lecturing in sociology at the University of New South Wales. In the Roper River region, the Victoria River Downs and Daly River area (joining Jane Goodall and seeing through her eyes), I was continually struck by the way women expressed their right to hold views and behave as independent operators. Still I had to confront the male bias of bureaucracies ultimately handling my material. Federal government funding was cut; the Northern Territory government chose not to fund the authority for some time. 'Prune the fat', we were advised. Although deemed important, the Women's Advisory Council, which I was in the process of establishing, was seen to be 'fat' – it could wait. The important work was where the men were. Finally, I resigned.

Once again I was 'stranded'. I had moved children, household, books – everything I owned – to Darwin. I had intended making a commitment to the work. Now I had to seek re-employment and possibly relocate. I had no funds. I bought an old three-ton truck, and am now licensed to drive up to 45m of articulated vehicle. With children and belongings, I drove from Darwin to Canberra. Conversations with truck drivers began with a ritual greeting – leaning on the window of the cabin and kicking a front tyre with one foot and asking, 'How's she going?' After exchanging pleasantries about our relative machines, I would be asked what I was trucking. Furniture, I would reply. Not much money in that, I was generally told. Still, someone's got to do it. See you down the track, they'd say.

One day, I'll write the ethnography of trucking.

Wanting to expand into comparative research I applied for post-doctoral fellowships. The Society of Fellows at Ann Arbor, Michigan, invited me to work, from mid-1983, on a project comparing the changing role and status of American Indian women and Australian Aboriginal women. My children, now in their high school years, were reluctant to move; my daughter was hostile to the idea. Complicating matters, the scholarship did not provide fares for the children. I requested some assistance, but was given a one-way fare only. Then late in 1982 came the ANU offer to participate in a workshop on Gender, Ideology and Politics in the South Pacific. I readily accepted the opportunity to stay in Australia to allow my children some continuity in their education; to extend into another field; to work with women who had worked in communities with similarities to those where I had worked, but also with marked differences. And most of all it was an opportunity to sit and reflect on the past decade.

I have said little about men's involvement in my work or personal life. When I returned to school I was in the process of getting out of a marriage. I have chosen to remain unmarried. However I have found certain men are able to provide support, friendship and intellectual stimulation in my work. Other men, indeed the majority, have been threatened by my work, my style and have made it extremely difficult for me, at times, to undertake the work I have set myself. Even those professing affection have called my forthright manner 'unbecoming'. Once I asked a colleague (not a lover), 'Why do they (that is, men) behave so peevishly? What shall I do?' 'Keep going,' he said. 'Give them hell.'

Women have been important to me in my professional career and in sorting out my personal life. But I have remained unaffiliated with any of the women's movements. Why? I am not sure. Partly the answer is that I have never had time to join. Another answer may be that I am never in one place long enough to attend meetings. A more honest answer may be that I am a loner: if there is something to be done I will probably do it myself. This is not to suggest I work alone. Some of my best field trips have been with other women.

The 1970s till now have been hectic years of working on three books and writing some twenty articles, producing submissions – some twenty to thirty – radio programmes, interviews, writing reports, and generally being available. I have learnt new skills with cameras and sound equipment, to survive in the bush, another language, another where. I set myself aims back in those early undergraduate days, but I now have other goals. In these years I have found it necessary to work on short-term goals, though having a longer-term goal in mind. My first goal was to matriculate. My next to complete my BA. Next, a PhD. Those goals were governed by external constraints. I also had personal goals. These involved the things I wished to learn and those I wished to understand, and to pass on to others. So now I'm concentrating on my writing, on finding ways of making available to those outside my specialist field the experience and knowledge of the last decade. In the process I continue to learn about myself, from other women, and about our society.

18 | Myfanwy Gollan

Born in 1933, Myfanwy Gollan has been a journalist and freelance editor since graduating from the University of Sydney in 1956. Among publications to which she has contributed are the *Observer* (Sydney), the *Australian Book Review*, the *Bulletin*, the *Sydney Morning Herald* and the *Australian*.

She was an editorial consultant to the *Australian Encyclopedia* (Grolier, 1977). Her editing includes *Kerr and the Consequences: Record of a Public Meeting* (Widescope, 1977), and *The Struggle for Political Rights in Australia, 1788 to the Present*, a pictorial exhibition which was on show in 1977 at Sydney Town Hall and later in other states on a tour arranged by the Visual Arts Board of the Australia Council.

Myfanwy Gollan is married to the author Donald Horne, and they have two children.

Conversations with My Memory

Outside the entrance to a cave temple near Ubud girls picked lice out of their hair, looking as if they were posing for a post-impressionist painting, giggling and talking but still with that centuries-old grace and dignity that is characteristically Balinese. Inside, the caretaker lit candles and explained haltingly the gods and the stone statues we stood before. Brahma the Creator, Siva the Destroyer, Vishnu the Preserver, the three great Hindu deities. Later we sat, a nuclear family, in the compound at Sanur, watching the terrible beauty of a cockfight. My mind played with classifying people I knew, or knew of, as destroyers, creators and preservers. Willy-nilly I was a preserver, I decided; the nine-year-old and the six-year-old beside us, watching the blood and feathers with awed intensity had, if unintentionally, seen to that. Not for my generation of mothers approbation for willingly choosing destruction and its potential for renewing and cleansing (children need a stable environment) nor the fulfilment of creativity, except in the intellectually undemanding terms of home and family or in those few other pursuits time and energy allowed.

I had been classifying people as long as I could remember: believers and sceptics (and cynics, their darker cousins); haters and lovers; givers and takers; performers, audience; bosses, workers; dominant and submissive; rulers, ruled; leaders, followers. People by their natures seemed inclined to particular roles, even if their natures were frequently thwarted. Since I had had children I had added another classification: parents and non-parents, although the latter could include people who had sired or given birth, and I had known childless people with parental qualities.

It was 1971. The liberating 1960s had caught with their aprons on mothers of children born at the beginning of the decade. We knew about Simone de Beauvoir and Betty Friedan and Mary McCarthy's *The Group*, and who would be unaware of 'women's lib', a term as catchy as suffragettes or flappers or the New Woman? But all of it had been like the grumblings of a distant storm that would never break. Now Germaine Greer had published *The Female Eunuch*. And now, as we got the ingredients together for our Elizabeth David recipes,

or played our chatty tennis (while children practising the new mobility wandered onto the court), or blew up the balloons for a birthday
party, or bought wool for knitting or crochet or weaving, worried about
the side-effects of the pill or whether we were pregnant with a child
we couldn't afford, read Penelope Mortimer, Edna O'Brien and Muriel
Spark, pushed atavistic anxieties about husband and children to the
backs of our minds, washed the socks, we had Germaine Greer telling
us to examine ourselves as prisoners, even if she was only defining
with a new urgency attitudes that had been around for a long time.

'What a woman needs is a wife,' someone calls across the tennis court.
'What a man wants is a mother,' is the reply.

Six of us made the nucleus of a tennis-luncheon group; all born to
families believing in female education, we had been encouraged, and
were naturally inclined, to value things of the mind and spirit. Becoming mothers, although that was what we had intended, had come as
a shock. Most of our lives had been spent as students. We had been
used to periods of solitude and privacy, thinking time, and not used
to physically demanding work. Non-labouring sections of society are
no oddity in history, but earlier they depended on slave societies or,
if women were involved, on a large amount of domestic help to keep
house and family running. Now there was a generation of educated
women not trained to see running a house as sufficient in itself, lacking the physical stamina to meet acceptable standards and belonging
to a community which was suspicious of paid domestic help. We were,
in the new phrase, intellectually underemployed, and in an age in which
fear for the future of the race was not directed towards extermination
by a declining birth rate and which was beginning to see working wives
as the model (although there was a suspicion of them, too), we lacked
role approval on an almost unprecedented scale. This lack was a major
factor, in spite of the joys and delights many women continued to find
in their children and family life, in the suburban neurosis beginning
to be accepted as a clinical diagnosis and a subject for sociological study.
    It was the age of material affluence and, given the self-confidence
and security affluence can produce, it was not surprising that the
post-1940 vitamin generation (superficially at least lacking some of the
self-doubts of their more plagued forbears) would start some cleansing destruction, and that the women among them at least would have
the downgrading of women as one of their targets.
    Among the explosion of 'movements', permissiveness, hippies, anti-
Vietnam, pro-conservation, the women's movement was given the

opportunity earlier convulsions in history had denied it. It had been waiting in the wings for centuries. Now the hour had come.

I had never been a joiner, not at any rate since leaving university, partly because of a sense of detachment my training as a journalist had encouraged and partly from a paralysing tendency to see the other person's point-of-view. In the late 1960s I had engaged in the odd bit of activism. I'd organised residents' approval for council tree plantings; I'd gone to a Save Centennial Park public picnic, and I had rather enjoyed what was described as 'joining the zoo' on a friend's urging in one of the pioneering 'friends of . . .' organisations aimed at getting public involvement in traditional scientific and cultural institutions.

But not until 1975 did I experience the anger that takes people into the streets. I became a real activist, because a governor-general sacked an elected government. There were newsletters on the sitting-room floor, ideas exchanged around the dining-room table, worry about getting the numbers at public meetings. Most involved were as blazingly angry, and as inexperienced in the new activism, as I. Most were good but a handful was horrid, with a pettiness and suspiciousness I had never before encountered, at least not so undisguisedly.

As long as I could remember I had been on the side of people victimised for what they had been born. But I had never felt particularly discriminated against as a woman, except for a brief early period at co-educational schools when I had not fully absorbed that might was not right and that the sort of male ego that thrived on female subjection was not very interesting, even if explicable as a sort of uterus envy. At school and university I was encouraged to develop *my* potential, but also to develop skills to help me get a job if 'ever you have to go back to earning your own living'.

I had no sense of sexual cringe (indeed it seemed to me that I knew as many men subjected to female exploitation as the reverse). If I had to make a generalisation I would have said that we were all victims. The people I admired, leaving aside qualities like gentleness, compassion, good humour, I admired for their wisdom and clarity of thought. There seemed no sex barriers in those.

Where there did seem barriers was in roles. Women's role was to marry, have children, run houses, and within those boundaries to make their lives satisfying and fulfilling. Men's role was to support their wives and children and within those boundaries to make their lives satisfying and fulfilling. You make your bed and you lie on it, and apart from exceptionable circumstances it was to be a double bed.

The abandonment of the universal principle – the rebellion of so many women against the ordained role – seems the most significant development of the last twenty-five years, and, along with the dramatic drop in the size of families in the western countries at the beginning of this century, one of the most significant social developments in history. This coincided with the development of the modern women's movement, and got and gave strength to and from it. But the main cause was the post-war affluence providing hitherto undreamed of educational opportunities, and demanding that women join the workforce both to help produce and earn the means of acquiring the new necessities of civilisation.

I knew no one in my parents' generation who had been divorced, although in the generation before, a great-aunt, after an arranged marriage and two children and with sentimental memories of a maidenly attachment to a handsome church organist, was divorced with the support and approval of her family. Another great-aunt, a golden girl according to those who remembered her then, skated over thin social ice but her well-to-do and well-connected family stood implacably by while her rich future husband organised his divorce. My grandmother on the other side left her husband, taking her three young children because of her stern standards about even social drinking – or that's what some were to say later, in one of those attempts people make to simplify the complex reasons for the collapse of any marriage.

In the last fifteen years two of my close friends (perhaps significantly those with substantial private incomes) have been divorced, and the suburbs seem to be splattered with broken marriages.

But my parents' generation was not necessarily the norm, as is sometimes suggested, and its apparent marital stability may not have been so much a result of emotional maturity and a belief in binding contracts as a consequence of Great Depression economics, as 1970s marriage break-ups were a consequence of the Age of Affluence and its adoption of behavioural patterns that had earlier belonged to the smart set or the strong-minded.

Democratised affluence and higher education, the decline of parental authority and status, the encouragement of self-expression and experimentation, medical miracles and their promise of better health and increased longevity, all have forced more women to become independent, which along with its many pluses also has minuses. Independence of both men and women has possibly led to increased wariness: trust and loyalty do not seem the strong social currency they did once. Death, usually in childbirth, was the great divorcer, allow-

ing men to be unexceptionally multi-marital (war left women single).
Now many more women have more than one marriage, if they decide
to get married at all. But in the search for personal identity and self-
fulfilment the question no one seems to answer satisfactorily is what
to do with the children. Here the women's movement has made an
enormous contribution. It has made it uneventful for men and women
to decide they don't want to have children; by hammering the right
to contraception and abortion, it has decreased the number of unwanted
children by reducing the number of unwilling parents. The plaintive
adolescent cry, 'I didn't ask to be born', must strike a nerve in the prac-
titioners of planned parenthood.

My mother usually drove her own car. To her generation of women
born in the first decade of the twentieth century the motor car had
not only been a status symbol, but to the drivers among them it had
also given a unique independence: protected in their metal and glass
they had a previously unimaginable safe mobility. On this occasion
I was driving her through Sydney's Kings Cross. She was enjoying
being chauffeured, looking at new buildings and new shop signs.
    'Good heavens,' she said. 'What's that?'
    I glanced sideways. 'That's a sex aids shop.'
    'A sex aids shop! Do people really need aid?'
    It was one of the few conversations about sex I had with my mother.
She and my step-father, used to films with straightforward plots, clear
enunciation and characters obviously upwardly mobile, had registered
shock a few years earlier, in the 1960s, when they had gone to see
one of the new movies, and I don't know what my father who had
died in 1961 would have made of the new permissiveness – he, lover
of sixteenth- and seventeenth-century verse that he was, hater of the
bowdlerisers of Shakespeare, tolerant and good humoured, but at the
same time enormously fastidious, punctilious about courtesy, especially
to women, and with a great sense of personal privacy.
    But there is no doubt that the changing sexual climate, even if some
of its representations on stage or screen or in print are at best vulgar
and at worst boring, has been a factor in women's independence.
    In the early 1970s I was writing an article about the bestselling book,
*Everything You Always Wanted to Know About Sex but Were Afraid
to Ask*. I mentioned it to my family doctor, a few years younger than
my mother, expecting him to turn up his nose. His reaction was unal-
loyed approval, his argument that doctors' surgeries would be much
less busy were more information generally available about sex. More
bestselling books, vulgar or not, not fewer, he announced.

The women's movement appears to have removed a lot of panic out of sex, not only in providing information but also in the side effect that women's greater sense of self-confidence has meant a wider understanding of women's needs. But the fact that this understanding is not *universal* is surely pitifully demonstrated in the continuing need for rape crisis centres and emergency shelters. The women's movement's initiatives on such long-needed shelters deserves a gold star.

I'd had to get a daily housekeeper because I'd pulled a nerve in my shoulder and I was more or less immobile for a month. She was a nice widow whose first job it was, and necessary, she explained, not so much for the money she earned as for that she didn't spend. Loneliness had driven her to the local leagues club where she spent more than she could afford each week on the poker machines.

While working for me she decided she didn't want full-time work, but did I know anyone wanting light housekeeping one day a week? I'd been looking for someone for just that, to give me a clear day to concentrate on some work I was doing. The evening before she was due to start, her son rang to cancel the arrangement. He would not have his mother doing someone else's housework.

In a society tending to value things only if a price can be put on them, unpaid labour is seen as second-rate. The contribution of wives and mothers is ignored in any sense of assessment of the national product. Australia has no examples, for instance as the Flemish and Dutch do, of famous paintings of cosy domestic life. In Australia housework is downgraded as merely tedious. (A favourite cartoon is the *Bulletin*'s when William Lane was mustering his dreamers to start a New Australia in Paraguay: a working man leans on his spade and asks, 'But who's going to do the washing up?') Gardening, cooking (on a fairly high level) and certain do-it-yourself projects receive varying degrees of community applause, but not a well-run, well-cleaned house, although its opposite is criticised.

I have not been badly off with household help. Thank you, Miss Pitts, for all those hours of babysitting and devotion and looking after me when I had mumps, and thank you, Margharita and Jenny and Rosaria and Pilar who succeeded each other as homesickness for Spain got too demanding or the call of well-paid office cleaning too seductive, but did not leave until finding someone else to do my weekly cleaning. But there remains a certain distrust of the woman employing someone else to look after her house, as well as the feeling that it is demeaning to do domestic chores in another woman's house, although this seems to be changing as new working women demand

their nannies, and university students happily take to house cleaning
to earn money, and also because a generation is dying off that can
remember the arrogance and condescension of the 'mistress' when jobs
were hard to come by and most girls were 'in service'.

The 1970s saw many benevolent effects of the women's movement:
with less deference paid to the male simply because he was male, there
was a greater ease of women with each other, women were more self-
confident in restaurants and theatres, alone or with other women,
neither objects of pity nor of community mockery that they were
without male escorts; more men took more women seriously, because
society's programming had changed.

There have been other positive gains, or at least the adoption of positions against sexual exploitation and against discrimination in gaining
jobs or in borrowing money. In some, not all, of these areas it has
suited male interests to have a semblance of female equality. In others
I suspect equality has produced another sort of exploitation: you can
take out the rubbish tins, but I can't sew on that button.

Aspirations of men as well as women have been dramatically altered
in the last twenty-five years, not only by social but also by economic
forces. And when I think about this I wonder if women have not again
been conned. The women's movement has been humanely concerned
with exploited women. It has helped women generally to have a much
greater sense of their worth and potential, but certain sections of it
seem more concerned with accommodating women to the male world
than the reverse. A book can be called *The Female Eunuch*, but *Male
with the Barren Womb* as a title would be more puzzling than intriguing.

Although the experts can point to figures like 95 per cent of known
criminals being male (for as long as records have been kept), the traditional masculine and feminine qualities have nothing much to do with
being male or female. But civilisation as we know it has been dominated by qualities perceived as masculine: aggressiveness, ambition,
competitiveness and arrogance, while the feminine ideal virtues of
patience, compassion, concern and gentleness are acceptable only when
it suits those who are in power.

And this is where I wonder about the directions of the women's movement. Is it mainly concerned with the politics of the pay-packet? Just
as the machine created the job as we know it, so it is destroying it,
along with much of the drudgery and boredom going with it. I do
not see why this should be cause for despair, unless we cannot create
other ways than a pay-packet to give people dignity. Trying to preserve
a worn-out system would be a measure of our inadequacy.

But with the passing of the 1970s, and into the 1980s, I have increasingly firmed in my view that economic dependence is at the bottom of the lot of women. ('A Wage for Housewives?' asked the newspaper clipping pinned to the notice board of the rented house in Sydney's Neutral Bay while the mother of four made the bunk beds.) It is unfortunate that now that the women's movement has helped bring the truth of this home to most of us, economic independence in its traditional form is becoming increasingly less certain for all, and alternatives do not seem to be vigorously canvassed.

Part Four

To the Barricades

19 | Di Graham

Born on 2 December 1909, Di Graham joined the Women's Electoral Lobby in 1973. Prior to becoming involved in the women's liberation movement, in the 1950s she joined the Aboriginal-Australian Fellowship and later became a member of the federal council for the Advancement of Aborigines and Torres Strait Islanders, and a foundation member of the Aboriginal Education Council of New South Wales, of which she is currently a vice-president.

In 1978 Di Graham was awarded the Queen's Jubilee Medal and in 1980 the Order of Australia Medal (OAM). She is co-author with Jocelynne A. Scutt of *For Richer, For Poorer—Money, Marriage and Property Rights*, published in 1984, and is currently lobbying for matrimonial property reform in Australia by means of a system of equal rights to marital assets.

Through Life in Pursuit of Equality

Before the early 1970s my life, outwardly, was that of a middle-class woman. Inwardly I was 'burning up', aware of being out-of-step with acquaintances and friends about the lack of women's rights contrasted with men's. In my pre-marriage business career I was reasonably successful (for those times), quickly rising to secretary to the managing director, then to assuming responsibility for the running of the company – office, stores and repairs sections – during frequent absences of the managing director overseas and interstate. Of course I received lower wages than the men whose work I oversaw. In response to my protests I was told it was inevitable, as the government made the rules on wages. The firm took this attitude despite often publicising my capabilities in trade journals.

In 1935 I took six months' leave of absence to marry. Yet I did not return to business. My husband, increasingly successful in his own career, thought my return to paid employment would signify his inability to provide for me. This outlook was prevalent then, and I understood it. Instead, I joined several women's organisations. I found that none constructively challenged sex-discriminatory practices. Then an older friend suggested joining her in working to improve conditions for women prisoners in Long Bay Jail. The prison matron asked me to become the special visitor of a young woman serving a life sentence, who had no visitors. A friendship developed between the young woman and myself. Hers was a crime of passion. She shot her young husband in a fit of jealousy when he continually went out at night without telling her where he was going, while she stayed home with three young children. Long conversations with her, and shorter discussions with other more experienced women at the prison, introduced me to lives I had not known of. I became aware that some women felt they had to lie and cheat to survive, yet fundamentally they were rather noble people.

At this time the overseas political situation occupied public attention. The Spanish civil war and new regimes in Italy and Germany featured prominently. Wanting to see how lifestyles differ outside Australia, I persuaded my husband to take a year off for travel. We set out in late 1938 – by ship in those days. We went by cargo vessel, stopping at many cities and towns along the coasts of countries on the route to Europe. We left an Australia where the majority opinion expressed repugnance toward Nazi Germany, but a sizeable minority thought perhaps Hitler was only trying to right the wrongs inflicted on the German people at the Treaty of Versailles, and reports of atrocities against Jews may have been anti-Nazi propaganda. In England, there was the same division of opinion about Hitler's Nazi regime among the people we met. However after Hitler's troops marched into Prague in March 1939, defiant of the Munich agreement with England and France, we heard no open support again for Hitler, except in Germany.

English newspapers contained similar evidence of male arrogance and insensitivity to women's rights as in Australia. One morning newspaper reported findings of a medical committee enquiring into whether or not women should be permitted some form of pain relief at childbirth. By a majority decision the male members of the committee decided women should not have relief, as pain may be necessary to establish a mother's love for her child. The two women on the committee recorded a minority finding in favour of pain relief during childbirth.

Leaving England, we drove through Europe. In Berlin I visited the Foreigners' Service Office where I received information on the Nazi system and Nazi women's organisations. We grew wary of the claimed advantages of the procedures. When visiting the British Consul in Frankfurt, the reception room was crowded. As the consul opened his office door to admit us, everyone in the room waved papers in an effort to attract his attention. They were German Jews wanting British visas to escape. We left Germany in June. World War II erupted in September when we were two days out of Colombo en route to Fremantle.

Back home, when I voiced concern about discrimination against women in many areas of everyday life, I was usually greeted with laughter, condescending smiles or anger. An evening spent with other than close friends, during which I expressed views on current affairs, invariably ended with a departing male guest patting me on the shoulder and patronisingly advising me not to worry my head about such matters – I had two wonderful children and a devoted husband so should content myself with home affairs. That was in the late 1940s and early 1950s.

Toward the end of 1946, our younger child had an undiagnosed, serious illness; we were told he was dying. In an agony of guilt at having sent the child to pre-school at three years old, I dropped all outside interests including women's organisations, visiting him daily in hospital for nearly twelve months. On recovery he needed attentive home care for many more months.

Then in 1949 some friends and I decided to sit in at English lectures and drama lectures at Sydney University. We asked no one for permission – but sat enthralled through the classes, daring but eager to learn. Following this experiment, we later applied and received official permission to pay fees and continue attending lectures through 1950. During the lectures I was frequently appalled by the unconscious sexism of the statements of some male lecturers, such as, 'Jane Austen's novels, like those of most women novelists, contain grammar of low quality.' Probably this was because Jane Austen used non-sexist language which was perfectly acceptable at the time of her writing – like 'Everyone has their own books', rather than 'Everyone has his own book', the latter being foisted upon the English language by Fowler.

During the first half of the 1960s, 'confrontation' and increasing misunderstanding between Indonesia and Australia motivated me to attend Bahasa Indonesia language classes. Over three years of study of the Indonesian language, history and customs, including study camps and seminars attended with Indonesian university students in Australia, I became aware that some of the misunderstandings between the two countries were exaggerated through not only different background and customs, but also through the ambiguities stemming from lack of understanding of the nuances in the respective languages. Such divisions and misunderstandings seemed to me analogous to the lack of understanding often arising between men and women owing to sex roles imposed from birth onwards, together with our literature and language using male gender for persons of both sexes; this relegates females, in the eyes of girls and boys and women and men, to a secondary and less important status.

By the 1960s I was strongly interested in ancient history and archeology. Visiting archeological sites, I looked in vain for significant signs of recognition of women's contribution to achievements and well-being of ancient civilisations. In Greece, Athena, like Eve, was born out of man! In ancient Egypt, although the Karnak temple in Thebes and other buildings from the reign of Queen Hatshepsut – seen as the first great woman in history – were left, all mention and all depictions of her were destroyed by her successor, Thutmose III, to cover up the hated rule of a woman. In Mexico, a newly excavated site in the Yucatan (said to be thousands of years old), revealed small clay figures remarkably like earth-mothers. But excavating males called the site the 'Temple of the Dolls'. In Peru, evidence of ancient women's existence lay in small clay figures, depicted pornographically in the Museum of Pornography. The strengths of women and women's achievements were trivialised by this 'evidence' of women as sex-objects only.

Throughout marriage, despite my close relationship with husband and children, I was ever-conscious that society expected I should spend the most productive part of my life in housework and cooking. To society, it was irrelevant that I found no satisfaction there. I wrote off steadily to churchmen whenever I heard radio church services blaming Eve for sin's beginnings in the world; to the grandmaster of the masonic lodge for saying on air that all adults irrespective of race or creed were welcome to join masonic lodges, but of course no women; to an airline company for their sex-discriminatory advertisements showing their special care in the air to protect men from garrulous women passengers. And on and on. It was a lonely crusade over the years.

The injustice and futility of the Vietnam war struck me heavily. I attended seminars, meetings and marches in Sydney opposing Australia's involvement. Earlier I joined the Aboriginal-Australian Fellowship, conscious of unfair attitudes and practices inflicted on black Australians. I supported the environmental lobby, particularly about the reduction of the lead level in petrol and the need for proven guarantees on safe disposal of nuclear waste *before* building nuclear power plants. However, history taught me that women's issues are taken generally to be of minor importance, and unless women concerned themselves, they would continue to be so. Thus, in the late 1960s and early 1970s the reactivation of the women's liberation movement came as a beam of light through a fog.

I welcomed the knowledge that other women were sensitive to discriminatory and patronising attitudes. The media was unsympathetic, ridiculing and denigrating, but I hurried to join the first meetings of the women's liberationists, held in Glebe Point Road, Sydney. The women were sincere, speaking openly of matters I had felt compelled to keep to myself. Much younger than I, they yet had the perspicacity to start a new brand of feminism in Australia, which I had not thought to do. At the meetings, listening to young women protesting against discrimination, I knew I had heard the same vehemence, distress and four-letter words in previous protests. And so I had – at Aboriginal meetings when young Aborigines protested against race discrimination. Here was evidence that race discrimination and sex discrimination made similar wounds, arousing in victims very similar reactions.

During the 1972 federal election, the publicity of the Women's Electoral Lobby on the campaign to assess prospective parliamentary candidates' awareness of feminist issues coincided with my conviction that only positive action would overcome male dominance and female subservience. I read the published results of the survey of candidates with a growing conviction that this was what was needed to expose the biases of those ruling the country. I joined WEL in July 1973. My first meeting was in the Sydney Bradfield electorate. One topic was death duty laws. In those days, since most family assets, if there were any, were held in the husband's name, when her husband died a widow often had to sell the family home to pay heavy death duties. If the wife predeceased her husband, because few assets were in a wife's name, a widower usually paid a negligible amount of death duty, or none at all. The meeting asked me to convene a probate action group to research the problem and present lobbying tactics for WEL to follow.

My life took on new meaning. The need to change unjust laws that had no negative effect on men, just women, fired me. I sent out letters to numerous consulates for information on death duty laws operating overseas, and followed up the letters with as numerous phone calls. The group and I researched the position in Australia and drew up documentation for WEL. In Western Australia Senator Negus had earlier been elected on the sole issue of abolition of death duties; his New South Wales' representative accepted an invitation to speak at the inaugural meeting of the WEL probate action group. At a later meeting we decided not to support Senator Negus' proposal to abolish all death duties; instead, we lobbied for abolition of death duties on estates passing between spouses only, because the law was discriminatory against women. This decision became WEL policy throughout Australia as a result of resolutions passed at the 1974 WEL National Conference in Melbourne.

Throughout 1974 all members of federal and state parliaments were lobbied and responses and queries individually answered. Toward the end of that year, a federal parliamentarian asked for a WEL submission on probate reform, offering to circulate it throughout federal parliament. The submission was drafted in January 1975 and a followup was produced in March 1976. Most of the work of the probate campaign (except in Queensland, where Gold Coast WEL took on the load) fell to me, but would have been impossible without the total support of WEL during the three to four years it ran. For a woman who had felt she was alone in a fight against put-downs of women and inequality, it was like 'coming home' for me to find in WEL so many women who understood the nature of the problem I had railed against for years.

Early in 1977 the campaign succeeded. Governments around Australia had abolished or promised to abolish in the near future, death duties levied on estates passing between wives and husbands. Soon after, state and federal governments abolished *all* death duties. (The Premier of Queensland, Joh Bjelke Petersen, led the way.) This had never been WEL's policy, which was aimed directly at sex-based discrimination.

As the probate campaign neared its end, the research that had been done on the law showed up other areas of injustice. As a result, the group drafted submissions to the New South Wales Law Reform Commission's enquiry into the legal profession. Complaints were received by WEL about inadequate and inaccurate legal advice to widows by solicitors regarding probate.

Because WEL took this up, other injustices were reported to WEL. One was the reluctance of victims of rape to report the crime, due to the trauma of police and court procedures. At a WEL general meeting, a drafting party was established to produce the WEL draft bill on sexual offences. I was in the group, taking the reins as convenor when the permanent convenor was absent overseas looking at the law in Michigan. In May 1980 WEL was represented by Kerry Heubel, another member of the group, and myself as delegates to the National Conference on Rape Law Reform, held in Hobart by the Australian Institute of Criminology, the Tasmanian Law Reform Commission and the University of Tasmania law school. The conference endorsed the principles of the WEL draft bill, and later they formed the basis of law reforms in New South Wales, the Northern Territory, Western Australia and South Australia, and proposed in Tasmania.

Throughout 1977 and 1978 the WEL (Sydney) office had been receiving an increasing number of complaints about family law and Family Court practices. The WEL family law action group was formed to investigate these complaints, to research problems arising and if necessary to propose reforms and lobby government. The vast majority of complaints were about property division on divorce. The broad discretion vested in judges under the Family Law Act and the flow-on effect of their decisions, affecting settlements before registrars and out of court, was causing problems, particularly for women.

The group set down to looking at the sexism inherent in judicial decisions and registrars' and lawyers' advice. Our work showed that despite marriage being called an 'equal partnership', economic equality for women and men does not exist under present marriage and divorce laws and arrangements. Each marital partner can legally claim ownership of assets each financially contributed during the marriage. Because pregnancy, childbirth and child-care responsibilities usually fall to women and interrupt women's career and income prospects, the value of a wife's financial contribution is ordinarily much less than her husband's. On divorce, assets are divided according to the judge's individual opinion about respective contributions. Women are frequently disadvantaged in the process. That a few men may sometimes be financially disadvantaged on divorce is often used in debate as evidence of the court's 'even-handed' approach.

WEL sent submissions to various committees and commissions, attorneys-general, members of parliament, and individuals and organisations outlining the problems and putting forward constructive suggestions for administrative change and law reform. The group simply ignored the slowness of response of the federal Liberal government of the day, and in 1981 produced a discussion paper on equal rights to marital assets. The aim was to propose a system to operate fairly, eliminating court delays, unjust property settlements and traumatic adversary tactics employed in the court process. Later, in October 1981, the federal Attorney-General stated that as a result of the findings of the parliamentary Joint Select Committee on Family Law: 'A specialist committee of enquiry will investigate whether there should be new laws to clearly define the property rights of husbands and wives.' No action was taken until the Labor government was elected and referred the matter to the Australian Law Reform Commission. Meanwhile, I collaborated in the writing of *For Richer, For Poorer – Money, Marriage and Property Rights,* canvassing the arguments for the introduction of equal rights to marital assets as a sensible and just law, and later on a submission to the Law Reform Commission arguing that proposition persuasively.

I was irresistibly drawn to the new feminist movement. In 1975 the week-long Women and Politics Conference in Canberra, sponsored by the Labor government in celebration of International Women's Year, inspired me. The International Women's Day marches each year through the streets of Sydney were heady affairs. We all felt proud to be women, our self-esteem no longer low; we marvelled that any Sydney women could refrain from joining in.

The 'new' movement occurred late in my life. In 1970 I was sixty years of age. The movement's effect on my personal lifestyle has not been as great as it no doubt has for many younger women. My husband was fully supportive of feminist causes. Following his retirement from a very active business and professional life and until his death in 1984 my husband carried out household responsibilities. I was able to spend as much time as possible at my desk. My two sons are in agreement with feminist principles, and have always been supportive. Certainly my life has changed inasmuch as most of my days are devoted to the women's movement. I have regrets that it is only so late in life for me that the movement came along to match the knowledge of women's oppression which I have always had.

But my perspective has been widened through my involvement. Being with women prepared to discuss and debate sex discrimination has reinforced my awareness of the need for a feminist response to patriarchal institutions. Without it, women's liberation is impossible. Social structures detrimental to women and ultimately to children and to men will change only if women get involved and develop a feminist philosophy, and take action around it. At the same time, my involvement and campaigns have brought the knowledge that changing entrenched attitudes, procedures and laws – even where they are blatently unjust or redundant – is difficult.

Apart from discriminatory attitudes encountered by women throughout our adult lives, a small incident recently related to me illustrates the unconscious sex discrimination still encountered by girls. At an inner-suburban state primary school, a girl of nine years was told by a teacher to stop running in the playground. When the girl politely answered that the boys were still running around, she was told not to be cheeky and to stop running.

Why such invidious distinctions? My observations during the past years of the feminist movement reinforce my previously held view that such distinctions are wrong. There is very little difference, if any, in the capabilities and brain power of women and men. The contrived male dominance of women existing in and accepted by society at large is analogous to the situation which would exist if physically smaller men were dominated through laws and customs by physically stronger men – irrespective of capability. I remember an Aboriginal woman saying years ago that white people have always expected Aborigines to adjust to the white man's values and his way of life. She thought it time for white people to learn about Aboriginal values so that black and white people could together choose the better aspects from both cultures. This racial attitude of white people (often the men in power) is analogous to the sexist attitudes of men. Men's values have been considered the normal way of life, to which women are expected to adjust. Otherwise women are regarded as inferior and not eligible for promotion in the business and professional areas or acceptance in the arts world, or in other 'masculine' areas. It is time for males to learn about female values so that women and men together may choose the better aspects from both sets of values to be the norm in our society.

Yet there is a long way to go. Although women make up 51 per cent of the population, Australia still considers women as a minority group, together with Aborigines, migrants and homosexuals. It is hardly recognised that within those minorities there are women, too.

But feminist activism has increased public and individual awareness of the injustices suffered by women. The feminist movement of the 1970s and onward has influenced some governments to introduce laws specifically designed to provide ammunition for attempts to eradicate biases in laws and practice against women's rights. Far from the feminist movement waning, as some wishful thinkers on the other side protest, it is consolidating. I mean to remain fighting with it.

20 | Sue Bellamy

Sue Bellamy was born on 22 September 1948, and has been involved in women's liberation since its beginnings in Sydney. Over the years of the movement, she has been a teacher, organiser, artist, writer, historian, speaker; worked on *Mejane, Mabel,* The Awful Truth Show, The First Ten Years; organised the first Women and Labour Conference, held at Macquarie University, New South Wales in 1978; worked on magic, memory, the exploration of women's psychic potential.

Since writing her contribution, she has moved to an 80-hectare farm in southern New South Wales. This rural project is now on the way to becoming a centre for women's creative work projects, national and international, an archival and education centre, and the eventual home of her monumental ritual sculpture circle, to be completed by 1999.

Sue Bellamy's sculpture is in collections of women's art in all states of Australia as well as New Zealand and the United States of America.

Freedom from Unreal Loyalties

There were two voices ringing in my ears, as my twenties began: my grandmother: 'Never marry, be independent'; and my mother: 'Get an education, don't ever have to rely on anyone'. They were my tradition. The shape of my mother's life had touched me since childhood. We were in unspoken conspiracy together against a world which sat her at a sewing machine, on low pay, from the age of thirteen, for all her working life. It gave me a kind of political passion by 1970 far outweighing any books and theories. All it needed was a place to be heard and explored.

I found it at 67 Glebe Point Road, in Sydney's inner city. It was the meeting place of Australia's first ongoing women's liberation group, the Glebe group. Walking up from the bus-stop towards the front lawn of Sydney University, I heard Barbara Levy, through a microphone, say 'women's liberation', and I felt its meaning in my bones, right then. Even before my first meeting in March 1970, I had passed the point of no return.

It fitted like a glove, even though I could never have imagined the wild thrills of this new experience. Among the group, formed in December 1969, were Sandra Hawker, Julie Gibson, Deidre Ferguson, Lyndall Ryan, Martha Kay (now Ansara) and Barbara. We talked and read and listened all at once, hungry for everything from the new American women's movement, yet inspired by our original selves. The methods and structures of men's organisations, so long used to silence, divide and depersonalise women and ideas, were thrown out the door. There was never great unity, and often bitter argument, but then this was the birth of a new politics – no books, no teachers. Women came from everywhere, a great mixture of ages and life experiences, mostly white, some confident and many speaking for the first time about themselves. Early meeting impressions – what stands out still was the effusiveness, originality, humour and honesty of Gale Kelly, who taught us all more than I can yet assess. Scenes from a movie . . . full of smoke, dirty coffee cups, passionate talk into the night, weeping, deep laughs I had never heard from women before, a new body language. The Glebe group had a definite 'house style'. I see it as an embryonic separatism, the first glimmerings of radical feminism – anti-centralist, anti-male, anti-press, unaligned with any male left groups, tactically imaginative, stressing consciousness-raising, defining sexual oppression as basic.

On the surface, I fit well the presumed stereotype of the women forming those first groups in 1970 – twenty-one, involved in radical student politics, working on *The Old Mole* (a left newspaper), just left home, a history honours graduate just beginning post-graduate work. Two major differences stand out. I was a 'scholarship girl', awkward and self-conscious around the confident children of the bourgeoisie. I had been doing female factory work all through my undergraduate years, and was strongly class conscious, although my education had effectively made me alien in both worlds. I rejected the dry theoreticism of most middle-class intellectual socialists, and I liked it no better when I struck it in the women's movement.

My other difference was not being heterosexual. I know now I was lesbian, but at the time it felt more like confused resistance. I didn't know to whom or how to talk about my sexuality, though my passions were all about women, and always had been. But I had lived among people who were cruelly anti-lesbian, mocking and ridiculing those many women I remember from my childhood who must have been lesbian, although the word was never spoken. I waited my time, holding safe that key to my energy until the coast was clear.

Those early years weren't easy to live through. My life suddenly had different levels of experience, impossible to harmonise. There was the living pulsing reality of the meetings, the other women, the visions and inky leaflets – my real new life. Outside those times, I was in tatters. I was writing a history thesis on a scholarship, yet I really wanted to be an artist and writer. From twelve years, I had been streamed into academic subjects and I knew it was the only realistic economic route. But, also at twelve, I had first vowed to sculpt and write. The bitter irony was that one path had made a kind of escape possible but seemed to bar entry to the other. Mistaking youth for health, I decided to juggle all the parts – apprentice historian, full-time women's liberationist, and artist. I kept us all on the road, including doing four years training in ceramics and sculpture. This was the one really quiet and private part of my life, never troublesome, just long in its gestation.

The tensions of this overfull life finally burst. I remember screaming out one night at a meeting: 'How can I write history when we're so busy making it!?' It was a pivotal moment in life: a sudden consciousness of being a woman of my time, not on the periphery. We had all decided. We were actors, seizing our chance before the moment passed. This touch of consequence marked my first period as a feminist up to 1975, during which women's liberation and I were like symbiotic partners. We went along together.

The historian in me didn't die at that point, but was revitalised. My research on women eventually made the university a place of confinement, but there were to be more performances before I solved my ambivalence about learning and universities, recurring battles sharpened by the gradual discovery that we had to control our own history, be our own teachers, in our own spaces.

The first half of the 1970s, then, was my New Education, learning on the job. Inventing and absorbing new ideas had a spiralling effect, gathering in everything we focussed upon. It felt like a new world view. Inequality, prejudice, injustice – these words gradually gave way to sexism, patriarchy, misogyny. We saw an all-pervasive culture reflecting maleness and imposed femininity – films, jobs, education, government, music, art, sexual politics, treatment of children, rape, homelessness, violence, body language, landscape, historical erasure, invisibility, crude humour, phallic architecture, animal abuse ('husbandry'), sanity and madness, theology and 'sin', language itself, the power to name what we see – 'the personal is political'. This new kaleidoscopic reality was like waking from a coma into a nightmare. The state of collective mind was impossible to catch in flight. Our feeling and belief in sisterhood and support for one another was a tactical necessity, rather than a practical reality. We were none of us in such good shape to offer the kind of caring you need in such times. We did what we could, found our priorities, acted out our differences from one another.

I continued to thrive on my transition from Glebe to *Mejane*, Australia's first women's liberation paper (first issue, March 1971, last in April 1974). I devoured new books – Valerie Solanas' *The Scum Manifesto*, Kate Millet's *Sexual Politics*, Robin Morgan's *Monster*, 'The Clit Papers' in *Off Our Backs*, Monique Wittig's *The Guerilleres*, Elizabeth Gould Davis' *The First Sex*, and *Notes From the First Year*. I recall great battles on the collective around pornography and censorship, academic style, printing lesbian material, should we print men's articles, how 'heroic' were the Vietnamese (an argument over the style of reporting on women and the war), how responsible were we to the rest of the growing movement, the autonomy of small groups, the nature of collectives. I really believed in the intrinsic power of ideas themselves rather than seeing change come only through the block power of masses of people. Counting heads, building 'the mass movement', making blueprints and tight lists of demands were not my first priority, though I wanted the movement to grow. I fought hard against the style and implications of single-issue politics and the dilution of our precious new thoughts before we had pushed to see how far they could take us.

I remember reading a paper by Jane Alpert, an American fugitive, about 1973. She said we were not so much building a revolution for power as creating a reformation in the consciousness of the world about power and life itself. It really mattered to me to be uncompromising about our ideas. They were so powerful and manifest, they would spread without watering down. Without underestimating our enemy's multiple power to deceive, I have come to hate the patronising idea that 'women in the suburbs' were ever any different from us. When I began running suburban classes I found I was right.

Our 'public image' was much discussed. We received many letters at Glebe and on *Mejane* about our style and 'language'. There was a great deal of hilarious 'bad language' at Glebe. We loved it. Kate Jennings was one of the women who created the definitive Glebe style. But there were more serious questions about images – the notion that *in being ourselves* we could hurt the movement. I feel this underlay the stormy growth of the debate about lesbianism, naming and claiming it as part of our politics and experience. True, there was a lot of heterosexual fear and prejudice within women's liberation groups during the first years, proving the slogan: 'Lesbian is the word that keeps every woman in line.' I remember my thrill and identification one night opening overseas mail at Glebe (we wrote and received thousands of letters) and finding an American pamphlet from a group calling themselves *Radicalesbians*. Even so, it was a long process to be able to speak openly in groups, and even after I had begun my first serious relationship with a woman in 1971, there was an unofficial reticence operating. The story of the growth of lesbian feminism is too complex to capture in a few lines here. For myself, I knew that my political heart was always in the women's movement itself, and I never wanted to join gay liberation or any of the other mixed homosexual groups. I didn't feel lesbians and male homosexuals had much if anything in common, whereas I knew all women were affected by violence, war, rape, poor jobs, rearing children. I decided quite early that being a lesbian was a blessed state, and obviously heterosexual women (if such a fixed state existed) had a much worse time, given what we thought about maleness! I knew enough early to see that the lesbian in me made me a dangerous woman in a man's world. A lot more living showed me how deep that ran.

My mistrust of men's politics meant I hadn't felt too much elation about the election of the Whitlam government in December 1972. I had already read too much women's history. When the money began to trickle and the carrots dangle, particularly around International Women's Year, my cynicism rose.

There was always the sense of containment, of energy pouring down bureaucratic drains, weakening our own autonomous initiatives. I realised then that my politics had really taken shape: I had become what I called radical feminist. The endless arguments about paid government work versus voluntarism both seemed locked into the same system to me. I wanted to use my energy to create a new political culture, on our own terms. I could never grasp the idea of being paid directly by governments to be a radical feminist. I had a strong gut reaction against funding, and suspicion of the concept of women's advisers. Since 1972 I've been fascinated by this battle between feminists and government, but never chosen to be directly in it myself. I saw funding as the process by which we would have our teeth pulled; the oldest trick in the book.

In a time of general optimism among women, the *Mejane* collective (me, in particular) opposed the establishment of the job of prime minister's adviser. Liz Reid got the job in 1973. Elizabeth herself was an admirable woman, but I thought our uncritical acceptance of the position was wrong. The women's movement seemed to allow itself to be seduced and flattered, without critical discussion of what might happen. Ironically, after Elizabeth resigned on 2 October 1975, following years of frustration, ill health and a sense that women had deserted her, she invited me to her farewell lunch at the Women's Club in Sydney, given by Ruby Rich of the League of Women Voters. I asked her why. (It was a very small gathering indeed.) 'Because you have an appropriate sense of history,' she said. It had many meanings.

How quickly we dismember our own history, continuing to make men's politics our landmarks. Some women still say women's liberation started in 1972, coinciding with the Whitlam years. By then I had lived three intense years in a growing national movement not solely or centrally dedicated to electoral change. As a date, December 1972 is no more important to me than December 1969, beginnings of Women's Liberation or March 1971, the first *Mejane*.

The most complex emotional experience of my years to 1975 centres on a plan to leave the city. I was sick (mainly from stress) by 1973, became a vegetarian, gave up orthodox medicine, and longed for a cleaner way to live, in community with other women. We tried to extend the meaning of 'control of our bodies' to the air, water, food, environment and emotional psychic spiritual energies around us as women in connection with a deeply rich tradition of healing and magic.

My new lover and I, with a small group of other women, had found a place in the country where we began to plant, build and imagine an economically feasible life – at last a place to write and sculpt, but feel in touch with the city and the movement. Mid-1974 I made a difficult decision, taking what I thought would be a short-term job as a tutor in politics at Macquarie University. It would help get the equipment necessary to move to the land. I held my uneasiness about being back inside an institution. Other political work went on – working with Bessie Guthrie on organising her years of research and experience on the child welfare system since the 1950s, and through *Mejane*, building a campaign which led to the closure of Hay Children's Prison and the end of compulsory virginity testing. I was working on organising the Women's Commissions of 1973, 1974 and 1975; founding with Gale Kelly the Art Workers' Group and the Radical Therapy group; teaching WEA classes and going to the land as often as possible.

In the middle of IWY, after three years work and hope, my vision of the new life in the bush fell in a heap – a combination of differing ideals and the traumatic break-up of a relationship. It was the end of my innocence. While others went off to the Women and Politics Conference in Canberra in August 1975, I went to the land for the last time to see if there was some way to salvage the dream. It was a damaging time, sorting out myths from reality, facing the knowledge that we women can be very cruel to one another. In the end I just left it all.

I was in shock for a long time. But by then so was the whole country. I was back in the city in good time for the turmoil leading up to 11 November 1975, and to a vision of patriarchy more transparent than usual. There were women's emergency meetings, marches, fundraising and finally eight memorable days without sleep on a collective which produced the first *Mabel*: 30 000 copies sold and distributed before the elections, reasserting our autonomy.

In the following three years I made a real shift in my relationship with the women's movement. The movement itself changed greatly with the times, with a size and diversity straining at the limits of its old structure. Artificially inserted funding under Labor had weakened some of the original independent structure around Women's Liberation House, and this in turn put an extra burden on the funded centres themselves. It was a time to move out into new territories and try a few experiments.

Ironically, the immediate context for this new enterprise was Macquarie University. I took on women's studies teaching in my department, but something more was pushing me. All those resources, all that space. There had to be something to do with it. My chance came at the beginning of 1977 when I decided to become national convenor of a conference, which became the Women and Labour Conference held in May 1978. If the growing chasm between movement feminists and academic women's studies was ever to be bridged, this was the time, slowly building a network of enthusiasm and involvement, untapped before in any of our projects. The key was time and personal contact. I wrote a thousand letters. It was a new challenge because I had to make it acceptable to a wide spectrum of women and organisations. The university had to agree to provide free venues, the National Library to tape everything, academic women not to try to stop me, movement women to catch on that this was really ours, older women activists of the labour movement to know that this could be trusted.

Mine was eighteen months of unpaid work, knowing that no matter how many women became involved, it was my responsibility to bring it all together. Among the hundreds who worked and the 3000 women finally coming over the four days there was a spirit of openness I will never forget. It may not have lasted, but at least we couldn't say it was never possible. I had wanted to prove we could go that big without government money and control – in fact it was not only self-supporting, but made a profit! As well I wanted to demonstrate organisational integrity despite the venue, and make visible to the wide range of women who came the changing forms of women's long political resistance. Then I could let it go.

The women's movement has given me unique opportunities to work creatively with women of very different ideas from my own. In 1977–8 Joyce Stevens and I began both *The Awful Truth Show* (a women's theatre project) and The First Ten Years (an archival collection), celebrating our long and fiery friendship. A socialist feminist in the Communist Party, Joyce Stevens is the most complex skilled and committed political woman I have met, who taught me the practice of never settling for narrow sectarianism however passionate I might feel about an issue.

In the middle of many new and old projects, my dear friend Bessie Guthrie died at the age of seventy-two on 17 December 1977. She was the first of the friends from my real world to die. Close since the old Glebe group, we had become working partners on the child welfare campaign. The last two years had been about caring for one another, when she was going blind and I was going crackers, with loss and over-zealous organising. I found her body. We arranged a feminist funeral she would have loved (the police stopped the procession and hearse on its way – illegal to the end!). I have her ashes in my garden. She had no blood family – she belonged to us.

An owl flew into my garden the day before Bessie died, ancient omen of death, healing and a new life. Within three months I had begun a new relationship and, in the years since, found a new way to live my life. (My new lover had two children, now young women. We have been through much together – battles over custody, space, and learning to understand each other.) There were tough old patterns to break, and I held my breath through a time of dramatic shedding. I remember a surreal time in June 1979. I was writing two ABC radio programmes (beautifully produced by Jill Lennon) on Virginia Woolf's feminism, particularly in *Three Guineas*; reading Mary Daly's *Gyn/Ecology*; and teaching a WEA class with forty women and one man. The entire class of women had collectively resolved to ask the man to leave after weeks of tolerating his childish and voyeuristic behaviour. As a result, I was dismissed instantly on the man's charge that I was 'a lesbian extremist who prevented free speech', and the forty women's opinions discounted. We had to waste our precious time fighting a three-month battle after being given an ultimatum – take the man back or I was sacked. We refused both options, and I 'kidnapped' the class (their charge) by moving to a new venue. I decided it was harder to hit a moving target! I continued to teach, sent in roll sheets, demanded my pay – and the women (mostly inexperienced) gave the WEA heaps! They were inspiring, and I was deeply moved by their fierce loyalty to me.

It was exhausting, and I knew it had a deeper meaning for me. We completed our class. Finally I was paid, though shabbily (with an *ex gratia* payment, presumably to prevent me from suing for damages). Within a few months of this, inspired by Woolf and Daly, I made my decisions – no more easy set-ups, no more being forced to teach in the presence of men, no more working in men's institutions. It was time for this artist, writer, historian to merge as a free woman out on the road. I resigned from Macquarie and went to America and Europe with Janet Ramsay for five intense months of learning and renewal.

The world of women's diversity began to look bigger. It was a pilgrimage – Abiquiu and Georgia O'Keefe's erotic desert landscapes; Maria Matinez, great potter of San Ildefonso; Natalie Barney's old house at 20 Rue Jacob; the Standing Stones of Cornwall, Scotland,

Britanny; Crete; back and back in time stretched the evidence of women's lives. I sat in the New York Public Library's Berg Collection, holding the manuscript of Virginia's Woolf's *Three Guineas* in my hands, vowing not to let our work be captured like this.

We visited many feminist archives and libraries (especially the inspiring and completely independent Lesbian Herstory Archive in New York), women writers and artists, new scientists and old campaigners. It broke the hedged-in feeling of all the years before. Whatever this thing was, it was big.

I could end there on a point of resolution, but it would be unreal. I'm still learning, have my best work ahead of me, and am part of a women's movement moving into new battles for the future. I had another important illusion to lose; one of the hardest yet. I still had a lingering desire for some observable unity among women. It was an ideal preventing me from seeing that our next battles would come in unimaginable ways, and not without facing our differences from each other. Women are spread across a fractured planet and we carry the scars of all those experiences.

My moment to face this came unexpectedly during the huge meeting in Sydney on 24 August 1981 addressed by American radical feminist writer Mary Daly. Janet Ramsay and I had invited her to visit us, following our time with her in America. The big meeting was one of those complicated decisions where you know the risks but are pushed by a kind of historical inevitability. All the drama of nuclear fission had nothing over that night – rage, insult, cruelty and paralysis. When I walked into the hall, overcrowded with a thousand women in every available space, it was like a Hollywood movie set of the French Revolution, a scene from the Assembly, . . . an eerie surreal moment. What followed was something in the spirit of the trail of Danton. Was this our revolution's Thermidor? – when tearing each other to pieces filled the gap of lost directions. Mary Daly is a great scholar, not a cheap-thrills performer, but what were we? I watched the turmoil with detachment as though I had seen it before, with words of Virginia Woolf ringing in my ear. 'Freedom from unreal loyalties', she said. I felt a deep release, a surge of new energy, seeing women with their eyes and words of hate and passion far beyond the specifics of that one night. We had moved from a kind of respect and informal unity to what? Were we following the patterns of patriarchal revolutionary movements, from early days of passion and experiment, through consolidation, and on to revision and purge – or was there another model of change? There is no reason to think this was any more critical a point of choice than any of the others over these women's movement years. The paradoxes have always been there. For me it was a moment in the great ugliness that is part of the beauty of the movement. There are two great imperatives – find each her own way, and see the mix. All the forms are there – revolution, reformation, renaissance, and some maverick wild new unnamed unknowable. That's what keeps it all going.

Whenever I go on an International Women's Day march, as I did in the middle of writing this, I feel the ever-present spirit of women's connections, old friends, new women, deep loyalties, old wounds. As I develop my own new work, like our Lesbian History Research Project, my sculpture, new writing, our archive, a new School for Women, the daily crises of response to this culture, I know I've never been more intensely engaged on the rough edge of the future, than now.

Sue Bellamy's work on these and other issues has been recorded in the following sources:

How Can We Get What We Want – The Neurosis of Having a Programme, printed discussion paper for general meeting, Sydney Women's Liberation, undated (mid 1970), copy in First Ten Years Collection; *Women in Factories*, paper presented to Women's Liberation Conference, Sydney, January 1971, later published in Words for Women booklet, *Women at Work* (Glebe 1971) under the title 'Factory Work' (in First Ten Years Collection). The following appeared in *Mejane*: 'The Dawn and Woman Suffrage – Louisa Lawson', no. 1, March 1971; 'Children and Liberation' (based on taped interviews), no. 3, July 1971; 'Women Cannot Paint . . .', no. 4, September 1971; 'The Music Lovers' (review), no. 4, September 1971; 'Tarzan and the Big Virility Myth', no. 5, November 1971; 'Intrigues and Censures of 1894 – Our Feminist Past', no. 6, 1972; 'Minnie Not Mickie – Must Men March?', no. 7, April 1972; 'Nuclear Family Perspectives', and, with Bessie Guthrie, 'The Child Protection Racket – Child Rape' no. 10, March 1973; Response to letters: 'Nuclear Family Perspectives', vol. 2, no. 1, July 1973; 'Robin Morgan's *Monster*' (review), vol. 2, no. 1, July 1973; 'Through the Maze' (autobiographical), vol. 2, no. 2, April 1974. The following appeared in *Refractory Girl*: 'The Heroine as Myth, or male cultural baggage we've been forced to carry', no. 1, Summer 1972–3; ' "Fucking Men is for Saints" – A Review of Elizabeth Riley: *All That False Instruction*', no. 11, June 1976. 'Opening Address', Sydney Women's Commission, October 1975, printed in *Macquarie University Women in History Documents, 1980, 1981, 1982* (Social Sciences Resources Centre, Macquarie University); ' "I Used to Quote Saint Paul". The Life of

Mary Andrews' in *Women, Faith and Fetes*, Sabine Willis (now Erika) (ed., Dove Publications, Sydney, 1977) with G. Kelly, D. Caine, 'A Reply to "The Great Wave Cometh" ', Digger, no. 44, May–June 1975; 'Power' (anon.) and 'The Moral CIA' (anon.) *Mabel*, no. 1, December 1975; 'In Memoriam Florence Valeria Freeman – My Maternal Grandmother' (poem) in *Women and Labour Conference Papers* (May 1978); 'Form – "We Are the Thing Itself" ' in *All Her Labours – Embroidering the Framework* (Hale and Iremonger, Sydney, 1984, p. 69); ABC Television, *Chequerboard Programme*: 'Sisterhood is Powerful', three interviews: Sue Bellamy, Lesley Lynch, Tricia Egan, July 1971; Tape interview, 2XX Canberra, with Biff Ward, Sue Bellamy and Sara Dowse, December 1977 (tape distributed by Sydney WEL and held by the National Library); 'Virginia Woolf – A Profile' (two programmes), *Coming Out Show*, ABC Radio, July 1979; with Janet Ramsey and Sarah Gibson, 'The Psychic Research and Gossip Show – Lesbian Artists in History', a visual and verbal performance/presentation, Alpha House, 22 November 1982, in the Lesbian Arts Festival, Sydney, 1982.

21 | Suzanne Dixon

Suzanne Dixon was born in 1947. She graduated from Sydney University in 1967 with a first class honours degree in Latin, sub-major Greek. She taught for a year at an Anglican girls' school before departing for Scandinavia and London, with some time in Uppsala.

Suzanne Dixon's work in the Classics Department at the Australian National University and in the United States on a scholarship resulted in the publication of *Wealth and the Roman Woman*. She is currently lecturer in classics and ancient history at the University of Queensland and in that role organised the conference on Domineering Dowagers and Scheming Concubines – Historiographic and Media Representations of Political Women, held in Brisbane in August 1986.

Confessions of a Sisterhoodlum

In 1972 I came to Canberra with a six-month-old baby boy, a scholarship to begin an MA thesis in classics, and a husband who was beginning a job in Foreign Affairs. It was a big change. We'd left Australia as suspect young radicals in 1969 with no intention of returning, living on the fringes of the counter-culture in Scandinavia and London. Now, though we felt we were the same people, with the same suspect radical views, we were catapulted into respectability and relative prosperity by parenthood and a regular income. I was very high on the idea of the women's movement: I had joined a women's liberation group in South London, but the involvement offered by the Canberra group was more intense and demanding. I felt I had come home.

I was very smug: I have been a feminist for as long as I can remember, and had been arguing the subject for years with people who showed not one whit of interest. I couldn't understand either the earlier indifference or the reason for the sudden upsurge of awareness of things I'd always taken for granted. I think I saw myself as a veteran condescending to the fresh recruits, and it never occurred to me to think *I* had anything to learn from the 'new wave'.

Nonetheless, I was glad to have a bit of company at last and threw myself into consciousness-raising groups (I would help raise *their* consciousness) and a task force gathering material for a parliamentary submission on divorce law reform. What I would not admit to myself was just how traumatic I found my newly changed status. I had looked forward for several years to having a baby and was thrilled to be a mother, but unprepared for this making other people view me differently, especially around a university. In 1972, it was still a haven for institutionalised youth, where children were seen as oddities and motherhood an embarrassment. Within a week of my arrival in Canberra, while still learning about the great bogey CHILD-CARE, I attended the first session with my MA supervisor, baby in tow. Baby became restive. After obtaining consent to my apparently ambiguous request whether it was all right to 'feed' him, I popped a breast into his mouth, to the visible consternation of my (female) supervisor. Thus was a new ANU legend born.

Life was exciting, what with the MA, which I greatly enjoyed, making new friends and beginning to organise for child-care around the campus – when one night at the chaotic Women's House, my eye fell on a long quotation from Susan Brownmiller. I later copied it from the poster, which has since disappeared, but never discovered its source. I'm paraphrasing it: the substance was that women have been taught to see friendship with each other as a temporary measure, a stop-gap to tide them over until the 'real thing' presents itself, and that we are taught to compete and hold back from each other; that only when women respond to each other *as* women, with an immediate sympathy, will we have cast off all the shackles.

Yes, the message was all about sisterhood, and it hit me like a thunderbolt. I *had* always thought I was different from other women; that I was, in effect, an honorary man because I was clever and articulate. I was also dismayed to find that this sense of uniqueness was shared by all other women; that we had all decided we were better than our fellows because we had swallowed what men told us women were like rather than looking at them for ourselves. When we had made friends with other women, it had been a matter of mutual congratulation that *we* were different. What simpletons, to fall for such a transparent con! How had I failed to see it, when I had prided myself on rejecting so many myths about women? And when I had always upheld the rights of women like a screaming banner?

I didn't catch much of the talk that night. I went home reeling. As time passed, the effect of the shock was translated into euphoria, into a glowing awareness that there were all these women around that I could get really close to. For there were. It was a heady time, the early 1970s. You would find yourself in a group of strangers at a party, where a man would make some offensive sexist remark, and you and other women (whom you had never met before, either) would flash a look of supreme understanding at each other before moving in to point out the error of his ways – or carve his balls off, according to your stand.

This began to affect my private life. One reason I had not made friends on a one-to-one basis with other women was that my husband Rob and I had been best friends since we met and fell in love at age sixteen. It was always a fetish with us to do things together. It was unthinkable for one to read a book without passing it on to the other immediately, let alone go off separately to make friends. Our friendships were strongest with other couples. The women's movement made a big difference in this, even before my epoch-making discovery of sisterhood, simply because I had taken to attending meetings and sticking up posters without him. This discovery seemed to give me a licence to go further.

It put a strain on our relations, although not as much as other factors. While I was off getting high on my friendships with other women, he was having trouble making friends with a group of people – chiefly men – he would have to work with over the next few years, and getting used to a new job. I was under pressure at work, where a visiting American professor who had fallen in hate with me at first sight was giving me a hard time. I hit a crisis of confidence where I needed support. For once Rob wasn't giving it.

Everything was happening at once. In July I found some people interested in forming a co-operative crèche on campus. Looking back, when the co-operative crèche is now relatively established with a beautifully equipped university house and grounds (albeit erratically funded), it is hard to believe the hassles, just getting people to listen. The students' association was only marginally more receptive than the university administration, which was already worried about the existing centre, expecting them to pay the electricity bill forever if they set a precedent by doing it this once. I found it hard to put up with the pointless 'policy' discussions over cups of tepid tea – apparently a necessary precursor to any administrative step – and was in favour of a sit-in with children to let the administration know they existed. I was into direct action. I suggested I form a breakaway group, Parents on Campus (marxist-leninist), and take the task of storming into offices, pounding the table and swearing, to be followed by the milder co-worker, who would politely agree that, yes, Sue *did* get very excited, and certainly they could manage with a little less than she was demanding. Without resorting to these tactics (a pity, perhaps), we eventually managed to gain ground and get a foot in, with woefully inadequate facilities which slowly grew (see, they were right: give us an inch . . .).

This took time. I was also tearing out my hair with the usual thesis traumas and hassles with baby illnesses and housework exacerbated by the fact that our son never took much to sleeping, so a solid eight-hour stretch was not something we achieved for some years. Neither Rob nor I had ever gone much on housework, always sharing the little we did. Now, the fact that the work was greater and parenthood imposed some need for order, became another source of friction. Not to mention our commitment to A.S. Neill-type free child-rearing, meaning neither of us (esp. guess who) was able to let up on the constant stimulation, patience, etc. required: free child-rearing, it emerged, was defined solely in terms of the freedom accorded the child, emphatically not the mother. For the first time, I had serious doubts about my marriage and retreated into a kind of hard shell where I invested everything in my son, my work and the movement.

By 1973 I had joined the newly formed Women's Electoral Lobby, which I saw as the pragmatic arm of the women's movement, with a wider base of appeal, and the Australian Labor Party. I had joined the ALP at fifteen but drifted out in my disorganised student years. I believed in reformist action, as well as theoretical overhaul. The new year of 1973 swept in on a wave of optimism: Aborigines, women trade unionists and all brands of social reformers believed we would see a new, just society achieved by a Labor government committed to a different vision. More heady stuff.

Somehow, marriage problems and work hassles got sorted out and I worked like mad to get my thesis written before we had to leave for Ghana in June. In May I helped convene a national delegation which met cabinet to submit a list of proposals about the government's childcare programme. That represented a lot of hard work between Canberra WEL, women's groups around the country, and Liz Reid, who persuaded the Prime Minister to receive us.

Just before leaving for Africa, I went to Sydney to check on some books unavailable in Canberra and to meet another historian who had written on a subject related to my thesis. I was planning to spend my first months in Ghana compiling my work on treason laws in the early Roman empire into a book or articles. When I learned the other historian had already written such a book, expecting it to appear the following year, finishing my thesis became a chore to be got out of the way. I handed it in just before I left the country. I had finished, as intended, and knew it was good. But the zeal I had brought to the subject in 1972 had gone.

Diplomatic life in Accra was something of a change from the hectic political rush of Canberra. I applied for a job at the Classics Department of the University of Ghana. I was told a position had been offered to a Ghanaian studying abroad, but I would be considered if he decided to spend another year in the United States. After a few more weeks isolated in an air-conditioned mansion with disapproving servants, a freaked-out two-year-old and nothing to read, I despaired of getting the academic job. I took one with the international school teaching sixth grade. Although I had no teaching qualification, I had taught school children in Sydney and London and enjoyed it, particularly young children. My original plan had been to write – both creatively and academically – but I felt in need of a regular job. I was also trying to get pregnant. Some months later I learned that the Classics Department had in fact wanted to give me the job but for some reason did not choose to pick up a telephone to tell me. My exasperation with academe reached its peak. I felt disgusted and could see no point in attempting to pursue a career in an area I had always felt ambivalent about, torn between the joys of pure scholarship and distaste for the realities of university politics and wilful navel-gazing in the ivory tower.

We were depressed about the place we were living in, which did not suit our free and easy lifestyle, and dismayed at being stuck with servants. We had always insisted we would never have servants. On arriving we found that getting rid of servants would not only put people out of a job they could not replace, but would also deprive them of their home. Reluctantly we agreed to retain the existing staff of maid, steward, gardener and night-watchman, resolving to go on living as we always had. Not possible.

After the fourth night of being released from work at 5 pm, the steward (who had already suffered at our lack of a tablecloth and habit of going barefooted) appealed: 'Madame, I can cook very well. Not only Ghanaian food, but English and German food.' It emerged that he was humiliated at having us cook our own meals, for everyone saw him return to his hut. Similarly the maid's professional pride was hurt when I tried to help her make the bed and only got her to look after our son when we went out. It was partly fear of losing a job, but more I think the fact that we made them look superfluous – as they were, to our way of thinking.

As time passed we became good friends with our servants – in two years we all went through different problems, especially children's illnesses, which drew us together. They came to understand and accept the ways we differed from their idea of an employer. For the children, it was a wonderful life, very communal. They always had other children living with them and other adults to appeal to when they were displeased with us. Yet throughout it all, I resented that so many initiatives were taken from us and even in our home so many alien standards were imposed on us.

Outside was, not surprisingly, worse. We had instant admission to the world of the whingeing expatriate, as we possessed the necessary requirements of white skin and hard-currency income. It was akin to the world of nineteenth-century novels, with a leisured class ensconced in huge homes, attended by servants and able to indulge whims such as cheese on toast at midnight and golf every afternoon, without any personal effort. On the whole, such people were *not* very nice.

I discovered how hard it was to maintain my own standards in such isolating surroundings, where everyone we met had such different ideas from us. By the end of the first year we were demoralised. I had given up work after the birth of my daughter. I had resumed wearing make-up – a sign of sinking self-confidence – and was finding it hard to get any writing done with a new baby, an equally demanding three-year-old and a society where you did *not* refuse invitations to coffee mornings because you were doing something so eccentric as writing.

The second year we decided we had had enough of this kind of thing and stopped seeing the really worthless expatriates – persistent refusal of invitations brought them to a halt. We concentrated only on those we really wanted to see, which generally meant Ghanaians. I took a job teaching at a Ghanaian school. Within certain limits, we tried to lead our own lives. This worked pretty well, but it was now 1975 and I could not help feeling I had missed out, for back in Australia things had been happening during International Women's Year. In Ghana, I had met some very energetic women organisers, generally interested in feminist ideas, but the racial set-up made it impossible for me to push my own barrow if it could be seen as cultural imperialism. I was looking forward to getting home, where I could involve myself directly again.

What a shock. I came back to a completely different women's movement. While I was away, I had noted regretfully the jobs advertised for the newly formed women's secretariat, feeling I had rather missed the bus. But I had missed lots of buses. The Women's House had moved. Nobody seemed to spend any time raising consciousness or talking theory. Lots of things we had pushed for had gained central funding: there was a women's refuge and an abortion counselling centre, there was an employment re-training scheme. It was action, action. Great. But where was the sisterhood? Out in a new suburb, I languished with the children, trying to get used to wearing so many clothes (Canberra in August was colder and muddier than Ghana) and to having a house of our very own. The old self-esteem plummeted even lower, and was not raised by occasional visits to the secretariat, where my erstwhile sisters shamelessly patronised me. I joined in WEL and Women's House activities, but felt lost, and half-awake except for a brief burst during the Women and Politics Conference, when I first resolved that Canberra should have a rape crisis centre. At twenty-nine, I felt life had passed me by.

My plan was to arrange part-time child-care for 1976 so I could write at home, and perhaps gain an early childhood teaching qualification in the following year. Then two things happened. Kerr sacked the elected Whitlam government and I heard there was a tutor's job going in the Classics Department at ANU. Both galvanised me into action. I was awake. In November 1975 I rushed around like my old frenetic self, organising a women's march for Labor, heckling Liberal candidates about their child-care non-policy, shouting at demonstrations and selling non-sexist calendars to fund some of these activities.

The next two years – of cut-backs and gradual realisation that unemployment and inflation were here to stay – I spent working hard with my students and helping start the Canberra rape crisis centre, as well as the usual lobbying for WEL, ALP meetings and bringing up two still young children. I also began giving puppet shows at schools and arts council functions, and began a women's history group. I think I must have been crazy.

I had some health problems during those years. The rape crisis centre was colossally demanding – everyone agreed we needed it, but somehow melted away. I collaborated on law reform submissions, addressed community groups, filled in on the roster and did all the typing. I was ill-tempered and distrustful of the reliability of others. More disillusioned than ever with the disappearance of sisterhood (though from the second I landed an academic job I was not patronised) and crapped off with our phoney 'structurelessness' – which I had always advocated and which was supposed to be so egalitarian but ended up leaving one or two with all the work and responsibility – I began to envy the unquestioning, hierarchical approach of the Festival of Lighters who at least turned up when they said they would – and if they didn't, you were allowed to bawl them out.

So, at the end of 1977 I took stock. If I didn't want to get stuck with so much, how did it happen? The answer came back: duty. I felt I *ought* to be available to my children and my students, and never set any limits on the work I did for them, while still keeping up ridiculous commitments to the women's movement out of a similar sense of duty. This was as dumb as trying to look like a fashion model. I had locked myself into a situation where I was frustrated and tired and terribly resentful of the people I was doing all this uninvited sacrificing for. I concluded it was a bummer, and determined on a saner, more selfish plan. Instead of continuing as an underpaid, exploited academic (forgot to mention: I also organised meetings on campus of women employees – a remarkable number were in the same position), with no future in prospect, a frustrated writer and half-qualified school teacher, I would work at each of those aspects until I was in a position to choose, instead of always saying, 'Oh, if only I had done x . . .'

So I did. I got my graduate Diploma of Education in primary teaching, and extra units in early childhood education and teaching English as a second language. After much consultation, we decided Rob should stay in Foreign Affairs if he could get a European posting, so I could get on with my great *opus* on Roman women and property which I never seemed to get time for in Canberra. He scored Denmark, and I did most of my work in Copenhagen and Rome. I wrote a lot – both scholarly articles and 'real literature' – and began to be published. In spite of times of terrific isolation and despair, I resisted the temptation to get a job because I knew that teaching would again swallow up all my energies and I would be left with yet another half-finished project to regret. I later wrote my PhD in Australia, in the course of it reviving the women's history group and networking with others around the country trying to write the history of women, to give us our past.

I learned to say 'no' to some things, and consider more carefully the things I was prepared to take on. Before, I would feel obliged to agree to give a puppet show, help a rape victim, join a lobbying group or take on office just because someone appealed to me – in addition to self-imposed trials like reading groups in the local school.

Apart from avoiding frustration, I was influenced in my 'move to selfishness' by the thought of my children, especially my daughter. I did not want them to have a martyr model, frustrated and hard working with so little to show for it. It seems to me that when we look around, we see women expending a hell of a lot of energy for a hell of a slight return in terms of status, appreciation or money. Look at all the voluntary work, so scrupulously and thanklessly carried out – whether for charity, rape crisis centres, or the public school system. Look at the way hard-working women are concentrated at the bottom of each professional hierarchy – especially 'caring' ones like nursing, teaching, social work. Do we really want our daughters to go on seeing us on the lowest rungs of the ladder, because we work for the work's sake, for noble ideals, and don't like to demand more (or any) money?

Masculine ambition is repellent in its single-minded, inhuman selfishness, but the other extreme is also bad. I made a personal decision that my 1960s-type rejection of status was a mistake: another con, leaving women behind, always with the best of motives. None of us is immune to the effect of predominant social values, no matter how strongly we repudiate them. This is where sisterhood comes into its own. I have always seen myself as a strong woman, with a high opinion of her own abilities. Yet my strength waned in Ghana, a setting where I got little reinforcement. Home with children and where everyone treats you as a mindless nothing, it takes a lot of willpower to see yourself any other way; if others think it weird of you to write, or to study in middle age, you need extra fuel to push you through it; if others type you as the shit-worker, it's poor consolation to think you'll get your reward in heaven. We need each other – to reassure ourselves, to cry on each other's shoulders and laugh together at the things that get us down, then go back in there sparking on all fours. The changes in my life over the 1970s and into the 1980s are not as dramatic as some – I feel almost embarrassed I didn't suddenly tumble on feminism, or join a lesbian commune – but I think I would have slipped by the wayside without the movement, and the friendships and support that are part of it, the reminder that you're not a nut, that we all know we're right and it's the others out there who are wrong, that together we have changed things so much and will go on doing it.

22 | Carol Ambrus

Born 20 February 1938 in Kyogle, New South Wales, Carol Ambrus worked from 1965–9 as a librarian in the Commonwealth Public Service and completed the registration certificate of the Library Association of Australia. She graduated from Canberra College of Advanced Education with a Bachelor of Education in 1975.

Carol Ambrus has exhibited her art in Barry Stern's Gallery, Sydney and Profile Gallery in Melbourne, as well as in Canberra. Her book, *The Ladies' Picture Show – Sources on a Century of Australian Women Artists*, was published by Hale and Iremonger in 1984. She is working on a history of Australian women artists and is lecturing at the Centre for Continuing Education at Australian National University in Canberra.

A Closet Artist

When I was a teenager I was a devout Christian. At least I thought I was. I read the holy scriptures, prayed and wondered why the holy ghost had not seen fit to illuminate the dimness of my adolescent meanderings. In accordance with the initiation rites into the feminine gender practised in the fabulous 1950s, I shaved my legs, stuffed my bra (sized 32) with cotton wool, and discovered that a wallflower had more embarrassing and ominous connotations than any horticulturist ever envisaged. Every Sunday I tarted myself up and attended church and entertained myself during the long service by casting pious sidelong glances at the boys in the pew across the aisle, with the sonorous rhythm of 'Rock of ages cleft for me let me hide myself in thee' punctuating the action. Then after the service and after the obligatory handshake with the parson at the church portal and after dodging the ministrations of frothy frocked, wrinkled, elderly female relatives, the boys and girls walked home together with at least one hundred yards separating them.

Every summer the boys and the girls attended church youth camps, which were basically hot-beds of sex, sin and evangelical hysteria. The camps were an event anticipated with hardly religious fervour; furthermore they were blessed with the innocence of parental sanction, obviously the result of shortened memories or more pressing concerns. The pinnacle of each camp was a public 'witnessing' of the holy faith by some distraught teenager who was condemned to eternal damnation for the sin of 'self-abuse' and who was hoping and praying for some sort of trade-off from the almighty. I must have been pretty cunning, for I managed to attend a string of camps without witnessing anything more than the fleeting sweaty encounters of boys and girls who managed to give the beady-eyed chaperons the miss. Apart from that I kept my virginity intact and played a lot of cricket after prayers.

So – I never received the holy ghost, but got pregnant instead by a bloke who should have been a one-night stand but who hung around for a few years making sure he cast his long miserable shadow everywhere and with his reverse Midas touch made sure everything he touched turned to sackcloth and ashes. I got rid of him eventually but not before I did time in a government hostel and my children did time in a church home for waifs and strays because he had misappropriated the matrimonial home: it was in his name, because in those days de facto wives had no legal or moral clout. I was the only unmarried mother I knew in the latter days of the 1950s, which was a hell of a social handicap because I was either too stupid or too honest to lie and to sport a Woollies wedding ring like a few others whom I suspected were also careless in leaving the matrimonial knot untied and their legs uncrossed. So I toughed it out and 'came out' by declaring to all and sundry my lack of matrimonial status.

I finally gathered the scattered fragments of my life, set up house and home, this time in my own name, having married and divorced the aforesaid male because the (then) Department of Interior would not give me a house unless I produced a marriage certificate and I was sick of living in a pokey, second-floor, cold-water flat with a perennially unemployed spouse, three children and a very remote downstairs laundry. So my (by now) exhausted ex-husband left town and joined the nameless, faceless ranks of absconding husbands who deranged their lives by keeping one step ahead of the maintenance collector or alternatively doing time in jail, which he did because he got some girl pregnant and became traceable. I raised our children on 5/8 of the male wage on the basest of base grades in the third division of the Commonwealth public service because my parents had the foresight to insist I get my leaving certificate. It was marginally better than being a waitress.

After my ex-husband left town and after I paid the last of the hire purchase on the vinyl nite-and-day lounge, I discovered I had more talent than that which I habitually sat upon, so embarked on a lengthy career as student, with the benevolent support of the government of the day which regarded divorced mothers as being a cut above unmarried mothers and deserving of support and retraining, even. I had quite a nice time for the next few years dashing to and from classes in between being a mother and running a stormy love affair. I qualified as a librarian, then went to do art for a while in the Canberra School of Art and East Sydney Tech., completing 3/5 of a diploma of painting. I rounded it off with a Bachelor of Education at the Canberra College of Advanced Education, specialising in art and librarianship. In the middle of all this education, in the early 1970s, I discovered feminism and having completed my service to the species, abortions notwithstanding, I figured that I had served my apprenticeship to feminism.

Those early days of the feminist movement turned my head around 365°. It came as a shock to my resident but barely house-broken male. Being of ethnic origin he had a few fixed ideas of what comprised a woman's place, which was only a slight variation of the home-grown variety. After more fights than feeds I managed to knock some of the ideas sideways, which had the effect of raising the tone of our conversations somewhat, but did little to alter the action. I still cleaned, cooked and washed and because I had a god-given duty to provide these domestic services for my children, he stood there and said 'me too', which absolutely confounded me because I could not think of anything to say. So I cleaned, cooked and washed with an observably higher degree of resentment than I did before feminism.

Meanwhile I enjoyed being a feminist. I became a politically motivated animal for the first time in my life, rather than one who reacted to the action. I painted slogans, screen-painted T-shirts, wrote submissions, screamed obscenities at demonstrations and wept with my sisters at orgies of consciousness-raising. Sisterhood was indeed powerful and the enemy was identified and made manifest in our homes and our hearts. We worshipped the holy trinity of Greer, Firestone and Millet and pored over their pronouncements, chapter and verse, deep into the break of a new day. Feminism made the world tangible, rational and accessible and sisterhood was a more heady beverage than any communal blood of the lamb.

Carried along on the surge of a tide, I was beached along with the majority when International Women's Year corrupted the incorruptible, debauched the sisterhood and made a hollow mockery of ideology. That was the year I recognised dogma and derided the dogmatic who had traded their brains for fat salaries or for a status screw. I recognised the chasm between ideology and real life and gave up trying to bridge it, so when it came to a conflict I threw out ideology and followed my instincts. I felt an adolescent sense of outrage at the muddy feet my idols hid beneath their trendy long skirts, and it took many years for me to forgive them their shortcomings, and myself for compromising my individuality. But I lost something wonderful in the feeling of unity between women and the unquestioning acceptance of blind faith which allowed me to be one of 'us' against 'them'. My emergence from feminism was to be the most painful passage of my life. The year 1975 ended my innocence and at the ripe old age of thirty-seven I became an adult.

I housewifed with less rancour, tried to empathise with my son's adolescent traumas (exacerbated by my feminism) and planned a white wedding for my daughter. I tried teaching, clutching in my hot nervous hands my recently acquired credentials which assured the world that I was qualified to drive a class of hapless teenagers into the same rut I had spent most of my life trying to climb out of. But I found that I did not like kids, or schools or other teachers, so as a career for me it was a dead loss. I lost 2 stone (13 kg) in weight between 1975 and 1978, and by February 1978 I was down to an emaciated 7 stone (44.5 kg). This was also the month of my fortieth birthday, the birth of my first grandchild and the end of it all, otherwise euphemistically known as a nervous breakdown. Up to this point I had tried christianity, drinking, mothering, drinking, feminism, studying, popping pills, teaching and finally the nervous breakdown, because there was no place left to go except into the mind labyrinths I had accumulated during the course of a chaotic life.

I wrote an autobiography because it was a good idea at the time, but it magnified and aggravated my nervous breakdown which was the result of having excavated so many depressing tragedies to celebrate well into the endless, sleepless nights. Then I wrote another book which had its genesis in 1975, because it seemed to be a good idea at the time, being about women and artists, but in my post-feminist, post-art student frame of mind it amounted to an exercise in agonising irrelevancy. However I applied myself and finished the project – I regard the unfinishment of anything an obscenity and a personal reproach to my protestant ethic and also because women tend to litter their lives with unfinished projects, being constantly reminded by their spouses and children that their priorities are off-centre. I then turned to and found a publisher for the book, a traumatic experience which made me feel like a very small school child trapped in an endless parents and citizens meeting and all I wanted to do was burst into tears and run for cover under my mouldy Linus security blanket. After I finished the book about women artists I became one myself, which was what I wanted to do all along and writing about women artists was a convoluted way of avoiding the issue.

I became a closet artist and made so-called feminist art, and after a couple of years I found enough cheek to confront the gallery system with a modest degree of success. In 1980 I exhibited drawings and paintings at the Canberra Theatre Centre; exhibited in the *Canberra Times* Art Award; exhibited in the women's art show at the Niagra Lane Galleries; exhibited drawings at the Australian National University Arts Centre; exhibited in *Animals on Canvas* at Barry Stern's Gallery in Sydney. Through 1981 and 1982 I continued in the gallery system. This all impressed me but hardly fazed the male-dominated avant-garde.

When I consulted a psychiatrist during the course of my nervous breakdown, he tried to turn me into a Divine Lighter which made me laugh, because that was where it all began in my protestant youth. I told him that the Lord was not my refuge, neither was the Maharaji Ji, nor was sisterhood powerful; that Marx was a male chauvinist wog, that bureaucracies are people-eaters and that drink and drugs are the sojourn in a fool's paradise.

So here I am, me, at age fifty or thereabouts, with a permanent case of nervous dyspepsia and with no refuge but the frail edifice of the material I write and paint, which is eventually an incestuous hall of mirrors. I have written another book on woman artists because it seemed to be a good idea at this time. During the writing, I exhibited some of the paintings I had made in the three preceding years, feminist in content, so they say. I just don't know because I don't know what feminism is anymore. I am a cat that walks alone, both from choice and necessity, but I hunger after my own kind if such kindness exists. I have packed a lot of life into a little living. I have confronted myself and survived.

23 | Jocelynne A. Scutt

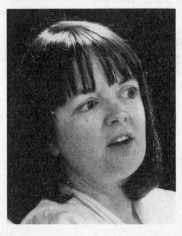

Born on 8 June 1947 at Subiaco in Western Australia, Jocelynne A. Scutt is a feminist, lawyer and political activist, long having been involved in the women's movement in Sydney and Canberra, and more recently in Melbourne. She appeared as advocate for the Women's Electoral Lobby in the 1983 National Wage Case before the Australian Conciliation and Arbitration Commission in Melbourne, and has been heavily involved in WEL's campaign for rape law reform and equal rights to marital assets.

Jocelynne Scutt is currently writing and researching in the areas of rape and sexual exploitation by professional men, and the new reproductive technologies.

Good for Women

We regard our personal experience as the basis for an analysis of our common situation . . . We will not ask what is 'revolutionary' or 'reformist', only what is good for women.

Redstockings Manifesto

Just as the revitalisation or re-recognition of the feminist movement and its development under new names, like women's liberation, met with differing responses in the general community and among women in particular, so evaluations of its effects in the past fifteen or so years vary. Anne Summers, involved in the establishing of the feminist women's refuge Elsie in Glebe, Sydney, in 1974, as well as the setting up of *Refractory Girl*, the women's movement journal, and author of *Damned Whores and God's Police— The Colonization of Women in Australia*, is reported by the media as saying that the media no longer pays any attention to 'women's issues': in the late 1960s and early 1970s, she says, the media approach was one of sensationalism; today, to the media the women's movement is a non-event. Germaine Greer, who for many women began it all in 1971 with *The Female Eunuch*, is interviewed by ABC radio on the *Coming Out Show* in 1979 only to say: 'My life since *The Female Eunuch* has been a disaster area, and it's getting worse . . . I seem to have gone through a goodly wedge of the world's population, leaving it virtually unchanged.' Betty Friedan, who for many women changed their lives with the publication in 1963 of *The Feminine Mystique*, is touted by the press as 'changing her mind' about the women's movement, and professing to believe 'it's all gone wrong'.

Yet should we just believe the reports, down tools, renounce our past, forget the feminist future we planned, and return to what went before, in the belief that the women's liberation movement is a flop, a fearsome failure? In the women's movement, if there is one thing we have learned, or should have learned, it is to recognise clearly and precisely our gains, and those of our sisters, and not be overwhelmed by the impossible standards women too often set for themselves: the standards of perfection, of winning every trick, of gaining a feminist world overnight. Simultaneously another feminist lesson should be firmly fixed in our brains: not to accept that, because it is widely said so, those whom we think of as the stalwarts in the movement, or who prompted us to rethink our own lives, have somehow become turncoats, no longer worthy of our appreciation. Did we agree with every word of Germaine Greer in the 1970s? In *The Female Eunuch*? Was every word of Betty Friedan a pearl? *The Feminine Mystique* utterly unflawed? The differences within the movement, between women, among women from the beginning were there. But that does not lessen the importance of what women were saying, nor of what we heard and learnt. The differences could be used (and sometimes were used by forces outside the movement) to 'show' that women cannot work together, and that sisterhood is a lie. But the reality is that the differences can be worked through in some instances, and have; they can be accepted as real in others – but made to work for women positively rather than to open the women's movement to attack from outside. And even attacks and distortion can have differing results for different women, just as the media coverage of the Women and Politics Conference in Canberra in 1975 led Elizabeth Reid to resign as Women's Adviser to the Prime Minister, when she assessed her efforts at changing government for women would no longer have an effect; yet for the hundreds of women attending, the event was cataclysmic in other ways. For Pat Eatock, despite the trauma surrounding her participation, the conference was a positive event; for Di Graham it was a highlight of her involvement in the newly active women's movement.

In 1965 when I enrolled in law at the University of Western Australia and on-campus agitation against the war in Vietnam was gradually being voiced, at the law school endless arguments raged about law students' dress – or rather male law students' dress: 'All students should wear dark suit, white shirt, tie and academic gown'. One student, Higgins, persisted in coming tieless, in shorts, without academic gown – and thonged, ignoring regular censure motions against him and his dress. Women's dress was never mentioned. Women weren't 'seen', or simply didn't count. In 1982, things had changed a little, in that men students' eyes had been forced to open, although their teachers' might not. Alicia Lee reported on the *Coming Out Show* the story of the law lecturer who 'insisted on referring to the entire class as "gentlemen"' although one-third were women:

Halfway through the semester his students got a bit fed up with this, particularly the females, of course, and they persuaded the male students to stay away from one of his lectures. When the lecturer walked into the lecture hall and looked around and noted that there were no males present, only females, he said, 'Well, seeing there's nobody here we'll finish early', and in fact lectured for only fifteen minutes before leaving.

Sitting through criminal law classes in 1966 I fumed inwardly at rape 'jokes'. I had personal protests to make about legal and law school sexism, but no defined ideology or channels through which my anger might be made known. In the 1980s, the sexism continues but there are channels for protest and recognised ideology for understanding and denouncing. Thus students write assessments of their (named) lecturers in published reports:

No doubt . . . will be teaching Crime in 1984, and no doubt many of you have already enrolled in his stream. BAD LUCK! Especially if you happen to be female . . . If you like smutty jokes, 'daddy and the maid' style, explicit descriptions of all the sexual offences, repeated hundreds of times, bit by bit accounts of the rape cases – 'he was only wearing his socks, don't ask me why' – you'll love . . .

   If you don't like sexist language, jokes, degrading women, and lots of nervous giggling in the class then you won't like . . .

   Believe me, hissing and booing and even walking out will not suffice to remedy this man's approach. If you're likely to be offended, enrol in one of the many other streams.

Yet I went to law school shows where the only conversational stimulus came from male students, apart from one woman in my year (there were only four women, among about one hundred men, and two of the women were required by the Dean to enrol first in Arts, not Law) – and (somewhat like Suzanne Dixon in Canberra) we both thought we were 'different' from other women. Other women at these law school parties came from the Arts faculty, seeming interested in little apart from smiling and chirruping in an inane manner. I decided then there were two sorts of women: those simpering gigglers who thought of little apart from marriage – a lawyer was such a good catch; and those like myself, interested in career, doing things, changing the world.

I didn't realise the truth until 1973 when I went to the United States after graduating from Western Australia and the University of Sydney. At Southern Methodist University, Texas, I attended a foreign students' course, then remained working on campus organising conferences until moving to Ann Arbor, Michigan, to do post-graduate work. I was friendly with women students, joining their sorority functions. They were mostly tall, honey-blonde Venus de Milo types. Good health bloomed from their shiny pink cheeks. Gracefully, they strode the campus, their long limbs glowing, golden tanned. They contrasted remarkably with the older women I met at social functions: in their mid-thirties, layered in make-up, caking their cheeks like smooth china, mascara dripping from false eyelashes, painted doll-like, the only point of commonality they had with their younger sisters was their demeanour in the presence of men. Vapidly, they hung on each man's every word. Yet I knew those women were intelligent, well read. At first I could not understand why, with me, they were able to discuss politics, black–white issues, even women's rights – then suddenly revert to worshipful obeisance whenever a man hove in sight. Then – click! That was it: the demeanour was like that of all the women I had known from the Arts faculty, who had partnered the law school men to parties back home. Just like the southern belles, the women at the University of Western Australia put on the act they thought was required of them. I was duped into believing there were two types of women in the world – those with a desire to learn, to use their brains; and those without a brain in their heads. In America I learned the truth: that if there are differences in women, the major difference is that some have learnt to play the game on male terms; others have somehow escaped that part of female socialisation.

My US learning did not stop there. In Ann Arbor I learned the value of collective action. Like Myfanwy Gollan I had not been a 'joiner', but there I joined the Women Law Student's Association. I joined in discussions and demands about sexist language. I saw collective action could work, when the association lobbied against the use of sexist language during lectures, and won.

My anger at the disparagement of women grew – but so did my sense of being able to control, to some extent, the means of gaining ascendancy over everyday put-downs and oppressions. At the University of Sydney I had researched penology and women's crime. In Michigan I developed this work in new directions, taking up sexual exploitation of women and simultaneously dealing with 'straight' constitutional and criminal law. In 1974 Virginia Blomer Nordby, teaching a course on women and the law, was drafting the Michigan sexual assault law. I researched marital rape law, analysing the English cases to show the dictum that a man cannot rape his wife was wrong in law as well as fact. My concern about the duplicity of the law increased.

Then, as I was leaving the US for the University of Cambridge in late 1974, my plane was delayed and passengers were taken to the John

F. Kennedy airport inn for the night. Travelling alone, I lounged luxuriously in my room, turning on the television set. There was being played out a drama that should shock anyone. A documentary on rape and its consequences, victims were interviewed about their reaction to the legal system, police interrogation, and outcome of the prosecution case. Every woman was adamant that she suffered dual trauma: first from the rapist, then from the criminal justice system. I flew out of America next day, those scenes strong in my mind, determined I would – we would – end the horror for women victimised by men hell bent on abusing their power.

International Women's Year 1975. In Australia Elizabeth Reid was organising conferences, discussions, consultations with women around Australia. Pat Eatock went to Mexico for the non-government forum. Some women – like Sue Bellamy – had doubts about the injection of funding into the women's movement; Carol Ambrus had direct experience of the monetary aspects of IWY: she received a grant to research the history of Australian women artists. Joan Russell and Di Graham went to the Women and Politics Conference. Sue Bellamy went to the country instead. Suzanne Dixon found her sisters at the IWY secretariat, controlling the funds, shamelessly patronising.

And I was holed up at Girton College in Cambridge, beginning to think my United States' experiences were a dream: perhaps it was untrue that women are oppressed – although I had known it all my life; perhaps rather than 'soul sisters', I had been confirmed by my American friends into a false consciousness; perhaps it was *true* that I was different, as I had thought all those years before. At Cambridge, 15 per cent of students were women. They seemed to believe that they were there because they were far more intelligent than those women who had not made it. They seemed not to recognise 35 per cent (or more!) of the male students were more stupid than the women outside and sexism operated to keep women out. In the very act of 'allowing' some women in, the authorities confirmed they were acting to discriminatory standards.

I looked vainly for signs that women's liberation was alive. Now, from Beatrix Campbell and Anna Coote's book *Sweet Freedom*, I know it was there. Back in 1971, reading Fay Weldon's *Down Among the Women*, I knew women in England experienced what Australian women experienced – lonely years of single parenthood while men who are, according to census figures, full-time fathers, play the absentee role of 9 to 5, or 8 to 6 (or worse) office or factory worker.

Cambridge was beautiful. Daffodils and crocuses pushed their noses up through rich brown earth. At a Sussex University conference I had to hold my own in criticising Home Office pronouncements on the criminality of women, debating the sexist bias of Eysenck's personality tests. The leaves turned gold in Cambridge. Once, I found a women's liberation meeting in a large Queen's College room. (One of the few colleges that had gone co-ed.) Discussion raged for an hour about whether men should be allowed to stay: three sat stolidly through the meeting, one talking more than any woman there. I left before they did. I had reached the point some time before that such a debate had no time in the women's movement: if one woman objected to having a man present at a meeting of women, then my solidarity was with her. It still is. Men have many forums. They can keep women out. They can ride rough-shod over women. They can refuse to hear when women speak. They have no problem asserting their authority in meetings, whether women are there or not. Women's presence makes no difference to a male-dominated meeting, unless men choose it should. For women, and women's meetings, the rules are necessarily different, because society has rendered many women speechless in the presence of men, or made women's voices go unnoticed, unheard. Society has forced women to take a stand against the presence of men which, even if they say nothing, is disruptive in a meeting of women.

In 1975 Liza Newby was in England too, studying criminology from a marxist orientation. This was not Cambridge style. For me involvement with criminology in England meant the destruction of some illusions about academic breadth and encouragement of ideas. I had admired the writing of one of the major lecturers at the Cambridge Institute of Criminology. His book on crime and insanity was to me, reading it in 1970, written by someone with a great scope for innovative thought and academic enquiry. The peremptory way he dealt with any ideas of students shattered this assessment. The class comprised scholars from many countries, coming from a wide range of disciplines. Their expertise and experience were ignored. Another lecturer talked about women and crime, uncritically. I transferred to legal studies and was free to research under the guidance of a wiser supervisor. Later, in Freiburg, West Germany, I discovered feminism again, read Alice Schwazer's *Der Kleine Unterscheid (The Small Difference)*, and found intellectual stimulation. Equilibrium returned.

Late in 1976 I returned to an Australia that in a little more than three years had surpassed anything I had known back in May 1973. Then, Australia was a country where it was irrelevant to the dominant culture that recent immigrants spoke other languages: in that year Patricia

Boero, fluent in five languages, was sent by Hobart CES to a service job in a casino; Franca Arena had completed three years working with *La Fiamma* as a journalist and was continuing her fight for recognition of ethnic minorities as equal. In 1973, Elisabeth Kirkby was playing Lucy Sutcliffe in *Number 96*; in 1976 she had considered embracing the alternative lifestyle but was preparing to get party political, joining the Australian Democrats in 1977. In 1973 women like Marjorie Luck and Vera Levin had taken strong stands against prevailing middle-class ideals and returned to the paid workforce, polishing their secretarial or teaching skills, braving a world they found was hostile to the idea of married women working – for money! In 1976, the right of women to paid employment was more openly spoken of – outbursts against that right were sometimes blatant, and became more pronounced as the economic recession grew into depression in the 1980s. But women protested strongly against the outbursts, holding their own with research as well as rhetoric.

In 1976 the women's movement had weathered – just – International Women's Year and by 1977, the resignation of Sarah Dowse (who followed Elizabeth Reid) from office as advisor to the Prime Minister, when the Liberal government demoted women's affairs to the Department of Home Affairs, presided over by the minister lowest on the hierarchy. The country was smarting still from the turmoil of a recalcitrant Senate refusing Supply and an unelected Governor-General summarily dismissing the elected head of government. For most women involved in the women's movement, and those politically aware in other ways, 11 November 1975 was a date to be remembered. Myfanwy Gollan first met Franca Arena at a meeting called to deplore the action of an appointed, expatriate monarch's representative. They later organised conferences and meetings debating the dismissal. Suzanne Dixon and others organised rallies around Australia demanding that the Liberal government publish reports drawn up by the IWY secretariat. Women who had fought for funding for women's refuges, securing grants through the Whitlam Labor government, were now confronted by the 'new federalism' which threatened to stop payments to women's services – not only refuges, but also women's health centres, rape crisis centres and children's services, particularly child-care. Women – like Di Bell, who had fought for child-care at Monash University, Suzanne Dixon, who had done the same at Australian National University, Joan Russell in Adelaide and Elsa Atkin in Sydney – saw their hard work, and their successes, threatened.

Yet by 1976 the women's liberation movement had fought for and won many important victories. The demands of Women's Liberation

and the Women's Electoral Lobby, and the many women's organisations existing over the years before, were firmly on the political
agenda – the right to abortion; the right to define our own sexuality;
equal opportunity in education and in employment; child-care; the right
to contraception. Women had learned to write submissions for child-
care, community health centre and rape crisis funding. Each state had
its women's house: in Canberra, Women's House moved from Brem-
mer Street to Lobelia Street, O'Connor – but was still there as a meeting
place for WEL, the Rape Crisis Centre, Abortion Counselling Service and, later, Lesbian Line; in Sydney, Women's House had had an
up-and-down history, but the collective was holding on – a grant had
secured an old terrace shop in Regent Street, Chippendale. Women's
movement newspapers, magazines and journals had flared, died, hung
on – *Mejane, Mabel, Womanspeak, Refractory Girl, Scarlet Woman,
Hecate*; in later years more – *Common Knowledge, Girls' Own* – were
to come . . . and go. In local government elections, women worked
to get women up – succeeding in emulating the efforts of women of
the 1950s and earlier: Elsa Atkin and others in North Sydney/Mosman
WEL canvassed, roneoed newsletters and handouts, licked stamps and
stuck envelopes – and Carole Baker was elected to the council, later
becoming mayor. WEL – particularly lawyer Helen Coonan – had lobbied hard for the passage of the Family Law Act in 1975; it passed
against strong outside opposition, and a free vote in parliament. In
1974 WEL member Susan Ryan was elected Senator for Canberra,
acknowledging the importance of WEL support. Germaine Greer had
been back to Australia several times stirring movement and media to
more action; Anne Summers' book, *Damned Whores and God's Police*,
was fast becoming a classic. Miriam Dixson's *The Real Matilda*, Bever-
ley Kingston's *My Wife, My Daughter and Poor Mary Ann*, and Ruth
Teale's *Colonial Eve* were to be published, becoming important sources,
as were the collections produced by Kay Daniels, Mary Murnane and
Anne Picot, and Janet Reed and Kathleen Oakes. There had been join-
ings and agreements, splits in collectives, schisms in the women's
movement, eddies and flows of information and exchanges between
women and women's movement groups and organisations around Australia. Women moved back and forth between the states, paying the
expensive airfares where they could, travelling miles in cars and loaded
in buses, attending conferences, bringing new ideas, new ways of working together, replicating old ways of past women's movement activity.
Australia was different from what it had seemed. I was different.

No longer a non-joiner, I signed up at my first WEL meeting at
Humanist House in Chippendale shortly before WEL's move into the

city, to Grosvenor Street. One member, Anne Elysee, presented a submission to go to the ABC on non-sexist language and non-discriminatory employment and promotion of women workers at clerical, back-up and on-air levels. The process was impressive: women getting on with it. Later, at Grosvenor Street, Di Graham protested against the anti-woman rape laws. We set a time for a working party. This was the genesis of the WEL Draft Bill on Sexual Offences. It was the beginning of a strong friendship and working relationship between Di Graham and myself.

Rape law reform in New South Wales was a new political experience for me – five years of intense lobbying, debate and at times acrimonious discussion and sexist criticism (mostly from men). After drafting the WEL bill I departed for the US, leaving the project with Di Graham for WEL. Carmel Niland and Kerry Heubel, then at the Women's Co-ordination Unit in the Department of the Premier, succeeded in having the WEL bill incorporated into a report of the NSW Department of the Attorney-General on rape law reform, an unprecedented achievement, for the women's movement, which has never been repeated.

Following the National Conference on Rape Law Reform held in Hobart in May 1980, the government put promotion of rape law reform into the hands of the Women's Advisory Council. (Astonishingly, two women lawyer members of the New Suth Wales delegation to the conference had voted, with no other support, not even from the men delegates, against a recommendation that the law should state clearly that no husband could be immune from prosecution for raping his wife! One was a member of the Women's Advisory Council. It was a bad omen.) A 'position paper' incorporating the WEL and conference proposals was distributed throughout the state. Council members were funded to travel through country areas talking with women's groups' representatives, local lawyers, police, health workers and others about the proposals. As a member of the council, I visited Albury, Wagga, Lismore, Grafton, Tamworth and Armidale accompanied variously by council members Margaret Doyle, Lorna Bartlett and Betty Crofts. Discussions with bureaucrats were less productive. Sadly, personnel changed: Carmel Niland and Kerry Heubel moved to other positions. Political dealing and bureaucratic commitment gained priority in the council and women's unit operations. The government was firmly in support of rape law reform. It had become a popular measure, due in good part to the issue itself, Sydney Rape Crisis Centre's changing collectives but continuing highlighting of rape injustices, WEL's persistence and the later strong involvement of Labor Women. The women's movement was in a prime position to influence markedly the terms. Not all involved understood this, or they had other concerns. At the end, when the law finally passed (a great improvement on the Crimes Act 1900, and a win for the movement, but not as good as it should and would have been if solidarity had prevailed) I emerged feeling as if someone had gouged me, head to foot, with a sharply tined fork. Deep. I had not anticipated women being such bitter opponents. My blood, I felt, had run.

Like Sue Bellamy, I had longed for – and believed there could be – 'some observable unity among women' at all times. The deep wounds of the Women's Advisory Council experience taught me there are significant differences among women that must be recognised and reckoned with. The very nature of patriarchy promotes conflicts in loyalties. Rather than ignore the conflicts, it is better to face up to them, planning for the contingency rather than being ambushed in innocence. (With time, we should be able to prevent the switch of loyalties from us to them, if we get a handle on the process.) Whatever the reasons for conflict – even if engendered by the strength of patriarchal forces facing the women's movement – feminists have to be aware that our ultimate goals can be subverted unless we are aware and design strategies with the possibility of (internal) subversion in mind.

At first, I did not see this so clearly. I had continued hoping for absolute commitment from all movement women. After three similar experiences in areas of my greatest caring – criminal assault at home, and the hopelessness it creates, which will not be met by needless changes to laws; positive demands for changes to laws governing marriage and divorce, recognising women's right to economic equality; and decision-making within WEL and honesty between women's movement women – the truth has at last sunk in. In discussion with women I am close to, I have come to recognise 'sisterhood' does not mean dedication to process, nor blindness to ideological differences. These differences can be just as real between women and women as between men and men.

Even then, working on the Women's Advisory Council was rewarding. Together with Pat Eatock, Carol Ambrus, Suzanne Dixon, Patricia Boero, Elizabeth Williams and others, I have irrepressible doubts about the ultimate value of the women's movement becoming involved in government action through committees, councils and boards; dangers of co-optation are always present. But does the learning process out-weigh the danger? Like Elsa Atkin, I learned lots about political manoeuvring – not to use it in the same way, but to know it. Learn-ing to recognise game-playing is important. Perhaps if I had never been appointed, it would have taken me years. Now, I know it.

As well, there were those country trips, meetings with women all over the state, and city meetings. We learned of women's problems and strengths, finding women everywhere committed to feminist ideals. Comradeship built up on these trips with council members can lift the pain of less happy memories – warm remembrances of driving along dirt roads outback with Franca Arena, talking, talking. An early appreci-ation of Dorothy Isaksen, now MLC in the New South Wales' parliament, after my first few months' membership. Kate Butler's support. Jeanette McHugh's spirit and openness. Joyce Clague's warm friend-ship. A supportive note from Faye Lopo when I drew my three-year term to a close.

And resources, sometimes, to get things done. Memories of the almost endless expansion of an idea for a women and arts conference I had thrown around and bounced off Kerry Heubel, and she off me, then with Cultural Affairs in Premier's. That idea was attributable to the success of the Women and Sport Conference, an initiative taken through the WAC in 1979 by Barbara Wertheim. To get women's movement women together with women who might never have thought about sexism and feminism, but were interested in a particular issue – like sport, or the arts – was vital. Some months later Chris West-wood, then at the Nimrod Theatre on the Women and Theatre Project (funded by government when Kerry Heubel steered a submission through Cultural Affairs) wrote to me about her becoming involved. A WAC committee co-opted others. The event became a festival. Elsa Atkin, Kate Butler and I gained WAC approval. Chris Westwood then joined WAC. Jo Caust became director. The success of the Women and Arts Festival was months long and its effects continue.

There was the memorial for Anne Conlon, too. I regretted, along with so many others, her death at the too early age of forty-one. Deter-mined her contribution to the women's movement should be appreciated, my resolution went through WAC, with Margaret Doyle as seconder, for an annual Anne Conlon Memorial Lecture. Topics would be women and work, women and prisons, women's history, Anne's concerns. Then, negotiating with Susan Magarey of *Labour History* to secure annual publication. The first Anne Conlon Memorial Lecture was presented by Edna Ryan, friend and colleague of Anne, co-author with her of *Gentle Invaders*, on the first anniversary of her death, in 1979, and published in *Labour History*, which has now become an impressive series.

The women's movement has grown up around discussions, consciousness-raising, conferences. Some stand out. 1977. Houston, Texas, the US Women's International Decade Conference, 10 000 women strong. Bella Abzug there; Kate Millet in a small group, earnestly talking; T-shirts and buttons declaring: 'It WAS a Man's World'. Being at the first vote, on women's equal access to credit – and the vote nearly unanimous, with women from radical delegations embracing those from conservative states, amazed that near unity could show on any issue at that conference. (Scare stories abounded of Eagle Forum and Stop Era women being bussed in by domineering men's organisations. Anti-abortion fanatics swamped the streets with their ugly literature and placards.) Then, procedural tactics designed to stave off debate on more controversial recommendations – ERA, violence against women, sexual preference. Hearing Betty Friedan speak, with deep emotion, of the desperate need to support and pass the Equal Rights Amendment plank. Later, during the sexuality debate, Betty Friedan acknowledging her mistake in not supporting lesbian rights as intrinsic to women's liberation; acknowledging her part in divisions in the movement. At the vote – cheers as the resolutions went through, the blue and pink balloons streaming towards the high stadium ceiling, bearing the words 'We're Everywhere'. Later, travelling back to Detroit with a wonderful planeload of women. Flight attendants unable to handle an almost exclusively female passenger list: crying out at the few women who stood talking in the aisle to 'Sit down at once!' though Michigan and touchdown were miles away; then, much later, frantically shoving trays, half-eaten food, cups and napkins into the servery as the wheels met the runway. (Lesson: airway management, read the signs – introduce non-sexist training courses for staff; they can't expect to serve men passengers or mainly men passengers forever.)

Back to Australia and Sue Bellamy's Women and Labour Conference in May 1978. I didn't know, then, that Marjorie Luck was as thrilled as I at the sense of purpose, the fun, the scholarship, the history of this gathering of 3000 women. The women's movement dead? Women came out of their factories and offices, their carrels and CR groups, out of their homes to share experience and research. The usual distress was voiced about the middle-classness of the movement. One woman halted the breast-beating. A factory worker, she said middle-class women working during war years had radically affected all women workers. The middle-class women had refused to follow the rules – like going to the toilet in scheduled breaks only. 'We'll go when we want to,' they said, and did. She said: 'We suddenly realised the foreman was not god. He could be defied. We had a right to go to the loo. We learned he couldn't stop us, in other things too. Your 'middle-class women' taught us that. Defiance. Action.'

Other conferences – the 1979 National WEL Conference in Adelaide: Joan Russell's generosity as publicity person. The 1979 Women's Liberation conferences, starting with Getting It All Together, then Working It Out. One young woman reporting back from a workshop that the group felt older women used their long experience in the movement to hold younger, newer women down. Kerry Heubel turning to me and saying: 'I don't feel they do that to us, Joce.' Me replying: 'Kerry, we *are* the older women in the movement!' Then, 1980 and the Second Women and Labour Conference, Melbourne this time – remembering the appreciation welling-up in me when, during my paper on sexism and violence, the women identified with what I said. (All-women audiences are far more critical, far more satisfying, than mixed or male audiences. When you say something right, by godess! they let you know it. I was humbled and hyped up for days.) Again 1980, the National Rape Law Reform Conference – losing my voice through wintry weather, exhausted (almost) from the psychological warfare, ecstatic at the coup for the women's movement. 1981, Women Taking Control – Townsville Women's Conference and 300 women from Rockhampton, Cairns, Weipa, Townsville and surrounds; invited by Betty McLellan to speak on violence against women, and women and work. Again, the feeling of connection, warmth, support. A wonderful conference in Perth in 1983, where Irene Greenwood, long-time feminist and one of the most generous women I know, led a standing ovation, and me hyped but humbled once more.

What of the meetings and the press releases, and the persuasion in non-feminist circles? Spending four years living simultaneously in Canberra and Sydney, flying and bussing between the two capitals in the late 1970s and early 1980s, I developed welcome supports in each, combining political activism with friendship. (Without such friends, the battle would be hopeless.) Back home to Canberra I would race from family law action group meetings with Di Graham, Jennifer Aldred and others, to meetings in Queanbeyan with Lesley Norris and Yvonne Carnahan. At the Sydney group it was raging debates and press releases about equal rights to marital assets. In Canberra we concentrated on rape law reform for the Australian Capital Territory,

and federal equal opportunity laws. We wrote and distributed hundreds
of petitions for federal sex discrimination legislation, and later Robin
Joyce organised and delivered up the many signatures to parliament.
Our press releases were iconoclastic, penned on the lounge-room floor
and earning a figurative rap over the knuckles on at least one occasion
from the (then) office of Women's Affairs, which called our demands
for women's rights 'too strong'! Neither the demands, nor the press
releases, ceased. And after the Rape Law Reform Conference in Hobart,
Lesley Norris and Yvonne Carnahan rang through a 'phonogram' to
the man-in-charge of rape law drafting in the Attorney-General's
Department: 'roses are red, violets are blue; when is our rape law
reform coming through?'

In Sydney, being director (then deputy chairperson) of the Australian
Institute of Political Science meant joining Jennifer Aldred, executive
officer of AIPS, in organising conferences on topics the institute had
never before addressed: directions for equal opportunity; affirmative
action; women and party politics; women and the bureaucracy. The
boards' support may have begun reluctantly – but attendance figures
won the day; later the Melbourne AIPS group covered the same
territory. As well, women speakers began to figure prominently in AIPS
Australia Day weekend summer schools in Canberra.

And there are the marches, and the demonstrations. Trips to Brisbane
with Yvonne Carnahan, National WEL Communications Officer then,
and Sandra Ellims, feminist and trade unionist. The Pregnancy Termination Bill debate. We met with Brisbane women in the Queensland
Council of Social Service offices, above a funeral parlour on Mother's
Day, caucusing on strategies against the National-Party-supported bill.
The situation called for a dramatic response. Taking reems of black
cloth from the boot of Julia Freebury's car, we picked white crysanthemums from someone's front garden, put out a press release headed
'Death on Mother's Day' – the other side of Mother's Day, women
dying in the backyards of butcher abortionists. We called the local
newspapers, radio and television stations. The ABC and commercials
came to film a row of twelve women, heads and upper bodies draped
in black, white crysanthemums clutched beneath the bosom, walking
slowly, single file, before the wreathed window of the funeral parlour.
There, we solemnly knelt, lay down the flowers, bowed our silent heads.
The demonstration was first item on commercial and ABC news that
night. A point was made.

International Women's Day, 8 March. In 1979 Sydney women spray-painted a bridal store window with the slogan: 'Marriage is Slavery'. The owners hurriedly drew a counter sign, prominently displayed: 'Buy Your Slave Dresses Here'. In 1980 the march stretched its thousands along Broadway, on its way to Sydney University, past pubs and shops which had never seen so many women en masse before. 'Dead Men Don't Rape', read the T-shirts of the Sydney Rape Crisis Collective. 1983, and the march set out from Sydney Town Hall, along George Street and its old resting place in Hyde Park. Di Graham was there, and Sue Bellamy, and Patricia Boero marching sometimes with the Third World Women group, sometimes with Anglo-Australian contingents. And 4000 other women. In Perth, Melbourne, Adelaide, the women were marching.

After the 1970s, what? Patricia Boero and Franca Arena fight on, with their sisters, for the rights of women of ethnic origin. Pat Eatock, Lila Watson, Elizabeth Williams and company continue fighting for Aboriginal and Islander women. Liza Newby and Di Bell use their professional expertise in learning of indigenous people's oppression and changing laws inimical to black Australian women's interests, and their own. Di Graham's work with the Aboriginal movement predates her women's movement activism, and goes on through the Aboriginal Education Council. But Elizabeth Williams still feels the racial barbs, as do the others, even within our movement against women's oppression.

The fight has not ceased in universities. In the early 1940s Pat Eatock looked from afar at the white buildings of St Lucia. Today, Lilla Watson teaches social work at the University of Queensland, struggling with courage from within, as Pat Eatock strove from without. In the mid-1970s Vera Levin found a few lecturers in Arts who understood the oppressed position of women, then was shocked by overt and covert sexism operating in the law school. I tutored in criminal law at ANU in 1981, discovering the old rape 'joke' routine remained standard. So, in 1983 Patricia Boero took on the fight at law school in New South Wales; Liza Newby continued it back at the University of Western Australia.

Relationships? I have constantly repeated back to me a comment I made on Sydney radio in 1980, that were I to wed or have a long-term relationship, I would live in my house and he in his! Said in jest, the sentiment is sincere. Why should that design for living make life any less fun. But where's the time for marriage? Life's too busy, too full. Today is my own. I am solitary when I choose, with someone when it suits me – and them! No one else's life is mine. My work, action is life. And yes, women's movement anger at men is inevitable – just as black Australians' anger at white Australians is inevitable. Now, I cannot see a film on the consequences of rape, the violence of pornography, or the horror of women being abused and exploited in everyday ways – and go off calmly to sup with a male friend. It's too real, the rage against their brutality, pain for my sisters and myself too great. But I care about male persons, despite constant media impressions that women's movement women 'hate men'. Our problem is we care too much. I care about creating a world where women and men live amicably. This world will come, as Andrea Dworkin says in *Our Blood*, when men concentrate not on learning how to cry, but how to *stop* raping, exploiting, bashing, beating, using, despising women, and how to take responsibility for their brothers' actions.

For most women there have been divorces, fallings out, remarriages, living together, living apart, break-ups, breakdowns. Through it all, some men seem capable of learning, or are born able to sympathise, empathise, support women. Vera Levin, Di Bell, Marjorie Luck appreciated the support of sometimes sympathetic men in work, study or organisational situations. Diana Warnock, Elsa Atkin, Di Graham, Vera Levin, Elizabeth Williams, Suzanne Dixon found male sympathies important in their personal lives. Lilla Watson's father, like Franca Arena's husband, was supportive and admirable. For me there is a handful of good men to appreciate as mentors and role models, men trying to overcome sexist conditioning in a male supremacist world.

Other women? Each of us, through the 1970s, has learned to appreciate other women. As children we had the message of the male world, that women are not much; some escaped some of it, others unlearned a lot of it, learning of the world of women. Patricia Boero had her Cuban aunts; Diana Warnock, Suzanne Dixon, Myfanwy Gollan, their mothers. I had my grandmothers and mother Marjorie, my aunt Nita Needham Sewell. Today I have my sisters. Maude Helen Needham, my maternal grandmother, was an independent woman, staunch John Curtin supporter, early member of the Australian Labor Party and delegate to the 1912 Labor Women's Conference in Western Australia. Seeing as crucial the independence that comes with mobility (like Myfanwy Gollan's mother in a later era), my grandmother drove her own car in the early days of this century – no mean feat. She used it, as a neighbourly gesture, to drive local young women to their weddings. Ideologically sound, I wonder today? Perhaps she wanted to give them a picture of woman as independent that would remain in their minds should they need the vision of 'It can be done' if the need to escape became strong. Her spirit had a profound effect on me: verbal sparring was a daily intoxicant. There were no refusals to debate. So the women's movement built on that past experience. It taught us women how to love each other, and thus to love ourselves. It made it possible for women like Sue Bellamy and Joan Russell to acknowledge a love for other women, ribboning their fortunes and hearts with them.

The late 1960s. The Vietnam war. The 1980s. The Peace Movement. Biff Ward, together with other women, is working at changing the meaning of Anzac Day from a glorification of war to a mourning for all women, of all countries, raped in all wars. Elisabeth Kirkby has gone from the temptation of 'opting out' to pleading vigorously from a parliamentary platform for less defence spending, more on the real concern – peace. Di Graham was outspoken in the early 1930s against the rise of fascism in Hitler's Germany. She, like Biff Ward and the other women in the Anzac Day marches, sees war as the traditional enemy of women.

So we have come full circle. Here in the 1980s, back to the 1960s – and women marching and striving for what is important. Now, we do not need the backing of men to do it – if ever we did. Today, women are involved in the political process at many levels – Elisabeth Kirkby joined the Australian Democrats, worked hard against sexist odds, and won a Council seat; Franca Arena joined the ALP, worked hard, and became the first woman of non-English-speaking background to be elected to an Australian parliament. Suzanne Dixon joined the ALP, then became involved in the women's movement. I joined the women's movement, then became involved in party politics and the labour movement through ALP and union membership.

Now, Liza Newby sees her role as using her expertise for the women's movement, putting back some of what it has given her. Betty McLellan looks forward to a continuing process of growth – her own, and other women's. Pat Eatock, Biff Ward, Joan Russell, Lilla Watson look toward more work – with support from their sisters. Elizabeth Williams sees racism, not sexism as the main concern, but does not discount its ravages. And I? I am years older, tens of years wiser, and still determined that the world I want, that the women's movement demands, is achievable. The women's movement has disappointed Carol Ambrus and others. We must deliver them up the goods.

I am resolved to find new ways of working, new ways to achieve the goal. Or renewed ways. Never do I, nor would I, repudiate the work of the 1970s – work each of us has put in through energy, time, commitment, sheer muscle and brain. Yet in recognising we are now in a new era – with the horror well behind us of seven years of a federal Liberal government true to every patriarchal ideal in the destruction, or attempts at destruction, of our programmes – there is a need for a reformation. As Sue Bellamy says, the women's movement should not measure itself by patriarchal dates, ceremonials and watersheds. But there is a need in the 1980s and 1990s to discover renewed ways that come directly out of the women's movement itself. Charlotte Bunch, sometime separatist, said in 1981 that to work in new ways is not to say that the old ways were wrong or misplaced. There is no hierarchy in the women's movement. Each method of working can be equal to another, earlier method. The process is as important as the outcome. Maybe the process is the outcome.

On 8 March, International Women's Day one year in the early 1980s, I attended an official Women's Day government celebration in New South Wales, high on the 31st floor of the State Office Block. The room was crowded with 'successful women'. Probably a large proportion of the small number of women all over Australia earning more than $35 000 annually were there. In the Premier's absence a government minister delivered a speech telling us how 'successful' we are – we sit on boards and commitees, he said.

Is this what we want to hear? Indeed, should we be there to hear it? Where are those women from the outer suburbs, from the country towns, the shacks and shanties of Moree and Nowra? The women on small incomes, or no incomes at all – the representatives of the majority of Australian women? International Women's Day is named *for all of us*. As Diana Warnock and Sue Bellamy found when they taught women in the suburbs, pensioners, WEA students: women out there want what we want; they are wanting a new world, not just some of us striving a bit further up the ladder in the old one. In that room on the 31st floor, I felt the women's movement had stopped. Right there. Jogging on the spot and going nowhere, each of us gazing in a mirror, preening. We have forgotten about *women*. Have we forgotten we are women? We sit on boards and committees. Some hold middle-ranking public service positions – much lower than all those men at the top, but much higher than all those many more women at the bottom. What are we doing to change it?

Right now, I'm stopping listening to the man who tells us we're 'so successful'. (We sit on boards and committees.) I'm aiming at making those boards and committees irrelevant in the long run (if the men don't beat me – haven't beaten me – to it in the short run). Let's take the battle back out into the streets again, and fight anew. We're stifling in those board rooms. And who's listening? Out on the streets, they can't help but hear. Our voices are pitched to carry well in open spaces.

Index